SOURCE READINGS IN *M*USIC
HISTORY

D0083771

Source Readings in Music History, Revised Edition:

Also available in a one-volume composite edition.

SOURCE READINGS IN
OLIVER STRUNK

EDITOR

Revised Edition
LEO TREITLER GENERAL EDITOR

VOLUME 6

The Nineteenth Century

Edited by RUTH A. SOLIE

 W·W·NORTON & COMPANY
New York · London

Copyright © 1998, 1950 by W. W. Norton & Company, Inc. Copyright renewed 1978 by Oliver Strunk.

All rights reserved
Printed in the United States of America

The text of this book is composed in Caledonia
with the display set in Bauer Bodoni and Optima.
Composition by the Maple-Vail Book Manufacturing Group
Manufacturing by Maple-Vail Book Manufacturing Group
Book design by Jack Meserole
Cover illustration by Mary Frank

The Library of Congress has cataloged the one-volume edition as follows:

Source readings in music history / Oliver Strunk, editor. — Rev. ed.
    / Leo Treitler, general editor.
        p.   cm.
    Also published in a 7 v. ed.
    Includes bibliographical references and index.
    ISBN 0-393-03752-5
    1. Music—History and criticism—Sources.   I. Strunk, W. Oliver
(William Oliver), 1901–   .   II. Treitler, Leo, 1931–   .
ML160.S89   1998
780′.9—dc20   94-34569
                                                          MN

ISBN 0-393-96699-2 (pbk.)

W. W. Norton & Company, Inc., 500 Fifth Avenue, New York, N.Y. 10110
http://www.wwnorton.com

W. W. Norton & Company Ltd., 10 Coptic Street, London WC1A 1PU

1 2 3 4 5 6 7 8 9 0

FROM THE FOREWORD TO THE FIRST EDITION OF *SOURCE READINGS IN MUSIC HISTORY*

*T*his book began as an attempt to carry out a suggestion made in 1929 by Carl Engel in his "Views and Reviews"—to fulfil his wish for "a living record of musical personalities, events, conditions, tastes . . . a history of music faithfully and entirely carved from contemporary accounts."[1] It owes something, too, to the well-known compilations of Kinsky[2] and Schering[3] and rather more, perhaps, to Andrea della Corte's *Antologia della storia della musica*[4] and to an evaluation of this, its first model, by Alfred Einstein.

In its present form, however, it is neither the book that Engel asked for nor a literary anthology precisely comparable to the pictorial and musical ones of Kinsky and Schering, still less an English version of its Italian predecessor, with which it no longer has much in common. It departs from Engel's ideal scheme in that it has, at bottom, a practical purpose—to make conveniently accessible to the teacher or student of the history of music those things which he must eventually read. Historical documents being what they are, it inevitably lacks the seemingly unbroken continuity of Kinsky and Schering; at the same time, and for the same reason, it contains far more that is unique and irreplaceable than either of these. Unlike della Corte's book it restricts itself to historical documents as such, excluding the writing of present-day historians; aside from this, it naturally includes more translations, fewer original documents, and while recognizing that the somewhat limited scope of the *Antologia* was wholly appropriate in a book on music addressed to Italian readers, it seeks to take a broader view.

That, at certain moments in its development, music has been a subject of widespread and lively contemporary interest, calling forth a flood of documentation, while at other moments, perhaps not less critical, the records are either silent or unrevealing—this is in no way remarkable, for it is inherent in the very nature of music, of letters, and of history. The beginnings of the Classical

1. *The Musical Quarterly* 15, no. 2 (April 1929): 301.
2. *Geschichte der Musik in Bildern* (Leipzig, 1929; English edition by E. Blom, London, 1930).
3. *Geschichte der Musik in Beispielen* (Leipzig, 1931; English edition New York, 1950).
4. Two volumes (Torino, 1929). Under the title *Antologia della storia della musica della Grecia antica al' ottocento*, one volume (Torino, 1945).

symphony and string quartet passed virtually unnoticed as developments without interest for the literary man; the beginnings of the opera and cantata, developments which concerned him immediately and deeply, were heralded and
reviewed in documents so numerous that, even in a book of this size, it has
been possible to include only the most significant. Thus, as already suggested,
a documentary history of music cannot properly exhibit even the degree of
continuity that is possible for an iconographic one or a collection of musical
monuments, still less the degree expected of an interpretation. For this reason,
too, I have rejected the simple chronological arrangement as inappropriate and
misleading and have preferred to allow the documents to arrange themselves
naturally under the various topics chronologically ordered in the table of contents and the book itself, some of these admirably precise, others perhaps
rather too inclusive. As Engel shrewdly anticipated, the frieze has turned out
to be incomplete, and I have left the gaps unfilled, as he wished.

For much the same reason, I have not sought to give the book a spurious
unity by imposing upon it a particular point of view. At one time it is the
musician himself who has the most revealing thing to say; at another time he
lets someone else do the talking for him. And even when the musician speaks
it is not always the composer who speaks most clearly; sometimes it is the
theorist, at other times the performer. If this means that few readers will find
the book uniformly interesting, it ought also to mean that "the changing patterns of life," as Engel called them, will be the more fully and the more faithfully reflected. . . . In general, the aim has been to do justice to every age
without giving to any a disproportionate share of the space.

It was never my intention to compile a musical Bartlett, and I have accordingly sought, wherever possible, to include the complete text of the selection
chosen, or—failing this—the complete text of a continuous, self-contained, and
independently intelligible passage or series of passages, with or without regard
for the chapter divisions of the original. But in a few cases I have made cuts to
eliminate digressions or to avoid needless repetitions of things equally well said
by earlier writers; in other cases the excessive length and involved construction
of the original has forced me to abridge, reducing the scale of the whole while
retaining the essential continuity of the argument. All cuts are clearly indicated,
either by a row of dots or in annotations.

Often, in the course of my reading, I have run across memorable things said
by writers on music which, for one reason or another, were not suited for
inclusion in the body of this book. One of these, however, is eminently suited
for inclusion here. It is by Thomas Morley, and it reads as follows:

> But as concerning the book itself, if I had, before I began it, imagined half the pains
> and labor which it cost me, I would sooner have been persuaded to anything than to
> have taken in hand such a tedious piece of work, like unto a great sea, which the
> further I entered into, the more I saw before me unpassed; so that at length, despair-
> ing ever to make an end (seeing that grow so big in mine hands which I thought
> to have shut up in two or three sheets of paper), I laid it aside, in full determination

This principle of exclusion worked for Strunk because he stopped his gathering short of the twentieth century, which has been characterized—as Robert Morgan observes in his introduction to the twentieth-century readings in this series—by "a deep-seated self-consciousness about what music is, to whom it should be addressed, and its proper role within the contemporary world." It is hardly possible to segregate historian from historical actor in our century.

For the collection in each of the seven volumes in this series the conversation begins explicitly with an introductory essay by its editor and continues with the readings themselves. The essays provide occasions for the authors to describe the considerations that guide their choices and to reflect on the character of the age in each instance, on the regard in which that age has been held in music-historical tradition, on its place in the panorama of music history as we construct and continually reconstruct it, and on the significance of the readings themselves. These essays constitute in each case the only substantial explicit interventions by the editors. We have otherwise sought to follow Strunk's own essentially conservative guidelines for annotations.

The essays present new perspectives on music history that have much in common, whatever their differences, and they present new perspectives on the music that is associated with the readings. They have implications, therefore, for those concerned with the analysis and theory of music as well as for students of music history. It is recommended that even readers whose interest is focused on one particular age acquaint themselves with all of these essays.

The opportunity presented by this revision to enlarge the book has, of course, made it possible to extend the reach of its contents. Its broader scope reflects achievement since 1950 in research and publication. But it reflects, as well, shifts in the interests and attitudes that guide music scholarship, even changes in intellectual mood in general. That is most immediately evident in the revised taxonomy of musical periods manifest in the new titles for some of the volumes, and it becomes still more evident in the introductory essays. The collections for "Antiquity and the Middle Ages" have been separated and enlarged. What was "The Greek View of Music" has become *Greek Views of Music* (eight of them, writes Thomas J. Mathiesen), and "The Middle Ages" is now, as James McKinnon articulates it, *The Early Christian Period and the Latin Middle Ages*. There is no longer a collection for "The Classical Era" but one for *The Late Eighteenth Century*, and in place of the epithet "The Romantic Era" Ruth Solie has chosen *The Nineteenth Century*. The replacements in the latter two cases represent a questioning of the labels "Classic" and "Romantic," long familiar as tokens for the phases of an era of "common practice" that has been held to constitute the musical present. The historiographic issues that are entailed here are clarified in Solie's and Wye Jamison Allanbrook's introductory essays. And the habit of thought that is in question is, of course, directly challenged as well by the very addition of a collection of readings from the twentieth century, which makes its own claims to speak for the present. Only the labels "Renaissance" and "Baroque" have been retained as period to have proceeded no further but to have left it off as shamefully as it was foolishly begun. But then being admonished by some of my friends that it were pity to lose the fruits of the employment of so many good hours, and how justly I should be condemned of ignorant presumption—in taking that in hand which I could not perform—if I did not go forward, I resolved to endure whatsoever pain, labor, loss of time and expense, and what not, rather than to leave that unbrought to an end in the which I was so far engulfed.[5]

OLIVER STRUNK
The American Academy in Rome

5. Thomas Morley, *A Plain and Easy Introduction to Practical Music,* ed. R. Alec Harman (New York: Norton, 1966), p. 5.

FOREWORD TO THE REVISED EDITION

> *Hiding in the peace of these deserts*
> *with few but wise books bound together*
> *I live in conversation with the departed,*
> *and listen with my eyes to the dead.*
> *—Francisco Gómez de Quevedo*
> *(1580–1645)*

The inclusion here of portions of Oliver Strunk's foreword to the original edition of this classic work (to which he habitually referred ironically as his *opus unicum*) is already a kind of exception to his own stricture to collect in it only "historical documents as such, excluding the writing of present-day historians." For his foreword itself, together with the book whose purpose and principles it enunciates and the readings it introduces, comes down to us as a historical document with which this revision is in a conversation—one that ranges over many subjects, even the very nature of music history.

designations. But the former is represented by Gary Tomlinson as an age in fragmentation, for which "Renaissance" is retained only *faute de mieux*, and as to the latter, Margaret Murata places new emphasis on the indeterminate state of its music.

These new vantage points honor—perhaps more sharply than he would have expected—Strunk's own wish "to do justice to every age," to eschew the "spurious unity" of a "particular point of view" and the representation of history as a succession of uniform periods, allowing the music and music-directed thought of *each* age to appear as an "independent phenomenon," as Allanbrook would have us regard the late eighteenth century.

The possibility of including a larger number of readings in this revision might have been thought to hold out the promise of our achieving greater familiarity with each age. But several of the editors have made clear—explicitly or implicitly through their selections—that as we learn more about a culture it seems "more, not less distant and estranged from ours," as Tomlinson writes of the Renaissance. That is hardly surprising. If the appearance of familiarity has arisen out of a tendency to represent the past in our own image, we should hardly wonder that the past sounds foreign to us—at least initially—as we allow it to speak to us more directly in its own voice.

But these words are written as though we would have a clear vision of our image in the late twentieth century, something that hardly takes account of the link, to which Tomlinson draws attention, between the decline of our confidence about historical certainties and the loss of certainty about our own identities. Standing neck-deep in the twentieth century, surrounded by uncountable numbers of voices all speaking at once, the editor of this newest selection of source readings may, ironically, have the most difficult time of any in arriving at a selection that will make a recognizable portrait of the age, as Morgan confesses.

Confronted with a present and past more strange and uncertain than what we have been pleased to think, the editors have not been able to carry on quite in the spirit of Strunk's assuredness about making accessible "those things which [the student] must eventually read." Accordingly, this revision is put forward with no claim for the canonical status of its contents. That aim has necessarily yielded some ground to a wish to bring into the conversation what has heretofore been marginal or altogether silent in accounts of music history.

The sceptical tract *Against the Professors* by Sextus Empiricus, among the readings from ancient Greece, is the first of numerous readings that run against a "mainstream," with the readings gathered under the heading "Music, Magic, Gnosis" in the Renaissance section being perhaps the most striking. The passage from Hildegard's *Epistle* to the prelates of Mainz in the medieval collection is the first of many selections written by women. The readings grouped under the reading "European Awareness of Other Musical Worlds" in the Renaissance collection evince the earliest attention paid to that subject. A new prominence is given to performance and to the reactions of listeners in the collection from the Baroque. And the voices of North American writers and writers of color begin to be heard in the collection from the nineteenth century.

There is need to develop further these once-marginal strands in the representation of Western music history, and to draw in still others, perhaps in some future version of this series, and elsewhere—the musical cultures of Latin America for one example, whose absence is lamented by Murata, and the representation of the Middle Ages in their truly cosmopolitan aspect, for another.

This series of books remains at its core the conception and the work of Oliver Strunk. Its revision is the achievement of the editors of the individual volumes, most of whom have in turn benefited from the advice of numerous colleagues working in their fields of specialization. Participating in such a broadly collaborative venture has been a most gratifying experience, and an encouraging one in a time that is sometimes marked by a certain agonistic temper.

The initiative for this revision came in 1988 from Claire Brook, who was then music editor of W. W. Norton. I am indebted to her for granting me the privilege of organizing it and for our fruitful planning discussions at the outset. Her thoughts about the project are manifested in the outcome in too many ways to enumerate. Her successor Michael Ochs has been a dedicated and active editor, aiming always for the highest standards and expediting with expertise the complex tasks that such a project entails.

Leo Treitler
Lake Hill, New York

INTRODUCTION

$\mathcal{W}$hen the original edition of *Source Readings in Music History* appeared in 1950, the nineteenth-century portion of its contents focused exclusively on Romantic phenomena; when the later paper edition of this fascicle appeared, it was quite appropriately titled *The Romantic Era*. Music scholarship in Oliver Strunk's generation habitually treated "Romanticism" as synonymous with the century as a whole (when indeed it dealt with the nineteenth century at all).[1] By now, however, most musicologists would argue that a more nuanced view is necessary. It is not that we have devised a finer grid for discriminating musical style periods within the century: on the contrary, even the latest studies agree—whether with conviction or resignation—that musical style remained "romantic" until something "modernist," or perhaps "impressionist," arrived on the scene.[2]

But there is more to the history of music than the history of compositional styles. Subsuming a whole century under one label fails us in at least two dimensions. Culturally, it speaks only to the preoccupations of the composer/ artist circle and not very accurately to the interests or beliefs of the era as a whole—a kind of historical representation that Jacques Barzun once described as "all butter and no bread."[3] It is the genius who is the principal denizen of the Romantic world, and we are not even sure, in most cases, to what extent the audience shared the beliefs and enthusiasms of that personage. More significantly, the label "Romantic" ignores the enormous social and intellectual changes that occurred during the course of the century, such as the emergence of middle-class cultural dominance, the development of positivism and histori-

1. Only a few years later, during his presidency of the American Musicological Society, Strunk identified the nineteenth century, along with the Middle Ages, as the two periods most in need of study by musicologists. ("The Prospect Before Us," a talk delivered in observance of the Society's twenty-fifth anniversary; twenty-fifth annual meetings of the AMS, Chicago, December 27, 1959.)

2. Carl Dahlhaus calls this attribution a "bad blunder" but acknowledges its ubiquity and suggests no real alternative (*Nineteenth-Century Music*, trans. J. Bradford Robinson [Berkeley: University of California Press, 1989], p. 16). See also Rey M. Longyear, *Nineteenth-Century Romanticism in Music* (Englewood Cliffs, N.J.: Prentice-Hall, 1969) and Leon Plantinga, *Romantic Music: A History of Musical Style in Nineteenth-Century Europe* (New York: W. W. Norton, 1984). In literary scholarship, of course, Romanticism is understood as a phenomenon of some three or four decades, in part actually preceding the nineteenth century.

3. "The highbrow's culture is too likely to be a very thin slice of life—all butter and no bread—and as such incapable of standing by itself." Jacques Barzun, "Cultural History as a Synthesis," in *The Varieties of History: From Voltaire to the Present,* ed. Fritz Stern (New York, 1972), p. 393.

cism as the primary modes of intellectual inquiry, and the upending of Romantic idealism in Marxist (and other) materialist philosophies. Such events, together with the great cultural impact of the global empires that European nations had acquired by the end of the century, affected how music was produced and understood. Friedrich Blume argued that "Romanticism is no definable style but a spiritual attitude,"[4] and that attitude neither permeated all levels of culture nor lasted out the century.

None of this is to say that the Romantic literary and musical movement is no longer of interest as such. Its principal hallmark as a cultural-historical development was the rejection of Enlightenment rationalism and classical authority in favor of imagination, feeling, and transcendence. This predilection has permanently affected Western attitudes toward aesthetic experience and no doubt helped give rise to the gulf between the "two cultures" of the twentieth century. Wilhelm Heinrich Wackenroder describes his fictional young genius, Joseph Berglinger, as aspiring to something higher than "ordinary earthly tasks" such as, in particular, the "secret enervating poison" of the scientific and medical study practiced by Berglinger's father. This dichotomy, though transformed almost beyond recognition, can still be glimpsed in Hermann Helmholtz's commitment, on the one hand, to the scientific exploration of musical phenomena and his relief, on the other hand, that explaining their mysterious aesthetic power is not his task.

For the Romantics, of course, aesthetic experience was at the same time a spiritual, even religious, matter. "An art work," Wagner tells us, "is religion brought to life." Our pluralist sensibilities may be surprised by the intense association of Romanticism with Christianity—on the grounds that Christian faith merges us with the infinite. We may even find slightly shocking Jean Paul's assertion that, because of this association, Venus may be beautiful but the Madonna can be romantic. He juxtaposes Greek and Christian cultures directly, to the detriment of the former, in rejecting the classical models beloved of eighteenth-century art. Mazzini invokes the Gothic cathedral to exemplify the kind of cultural-religious expression that the music of the future might become. Margaret Fuller, in pondering what we can learn from the lives of great musicians, calls them "high-priests of sound" with a special connection to the higher realms.

Nor was Romanticism a democratic or *laissez-faire* aesthetic, despite its occasional rhetoric of egalitarianism.[5] In an argument that sounds remarkably up-to-date, Fuller laments the characteristic American resistance to the "love of greatness," dismissing the interest of some in reading the "simple annals of

---

4. Friedrich Blume, *Classic and Romantic Music: A Comprehensive Survey*, trans. M. D. Herter Norton (New York: W. W. Norton, 1970), p. 103.

5. That is, the claim that the social origins of the genius are irrelevant was characteristic of Romanticism, but the notion that Everyman could write music as valuable as the genius's was emphatically not. See Part III of Leonard B. Meyer, *Style and Music: Theory, History, and Ideology* (Philadelphia: University of Pennsylvania Press, 1989).

the poor" with the argument that genius is our only profitable object of study because it reveals to us what we might at our best become. Philistinism was regarded as a major cultural problem, with John Sullivan Dwight battling it in the pages of his *Journal* every bit as fervently as Schumann and his League of David. Dwight not only champions music education to combat philistine attitudes, he insists that, since the "simple masses" respond to "high-spiced advertisement" that finer instincts deplore, concert programming must be planned to edify the "truly musical" rather than entertain "the unmusical many."

Even so, the Romantic musical world was not a seamless garment, as Raphael Georg Kiesewetter observed in characterizing the period as the era of Beethoven and Rossini. The persistent debate over the respective merits of "playing North and singing South"—and contemporary participants were interested as much in the contrast of attitudes as of musical styles—surfaces again and again in texts about music. Jean Paul attributes the difference to climate and relative distance from Greece. With gentle irony and stylistic acumen, George Eliot puts the pro-North polemic into the mouth of her fictional musician, Klesmer, at the same time permitting one of her quintessential propertied philistines to complain of Klesmer's own music that it sounds "like a jar of leeches," without clear formal demarcations. With less subtlety but compensating heights of passion, the political activist Giuseppe Mazzini calls for a Hegelian synthesis, not only of German and Italian musical styles, but of their entire essences as oppositional cultures and philosophies. For Mazzini the classic "contest" between melody and harmony betokens another sort of rift that must be healed—that between individual and society. It is particularly interesting that both Mazzini and Wagner envision a future in which such racial and national differences—although seen to be absolute and of ancient standing— would be transcended in a universal humanist sensibility.

To a considerable extent, the North-South argument was fueled by the Romantic view of music as a matter of personal expression: innate differences could be expected to surface. The ideas, feelings, attitudes, and narratives that are suggested as falling within music's expressive purview—or thought to be useful in helping listeners understand music—are the feature of Romanticism that may be most alien to late twentieth-century academic sensibilities. Writers made widely differing claims about the relation of music to its composer, to its listener, and to objects in the world, and argued their positions energetically. At the same time, the variety of audiences and of purposes for which they wrote assured a spectrum of rhetorical styles that were often difficult to interpret and compare. Schumann, for instance, maintained that the familiar characters of *Don Giovanni* seem to exist and act unproblematically in Chopin's variations on Mozart's theme, winking at us from among the notes. E. T. A. Hoffmann urges that music not be concerned with the representation of definite emotions and events, but proceeds to read both narratives and dramatic scenarios freely, distinguishing the symphonies of Haydn, Mozart, and Beethoven according to the scenes they bring before the imagination. Even Berlioz, who devotes more space than most of his contemporaries to compositional shoptalk, does not balk at words like "depicts" in his discussion of Rossini's overture, and commends Beethoven for a symphonic movement in which an "illusion is complete." We see here quite normal ways of describing music before Eduard Hanslick made his fateful attempt to confine aesthetic discourse to philosophically appropriate channels. Hanslick's efforts, it must be said, were more efficacious in the long term than in his own era: the disputatious assortment of metaphoric, visual, and ascriptive languages remained the norm for most of the century.

Gender metaphors, whether celebrating sexual difference or (more often) anxious about its abrogation, simply abound from one end of the nineteenth century to the other, seeming sometimes to be the foundational trope for the culture as a whole. Such metaphoric systems are, of course, notorious for the mutability of their specific meanings and referents—Romantic gender is not the same as Victorian. But one of the most fascinating and characteristic aspects of their nineteenth-century manifestation is the almost ubiquitous association of music itself with the female or the feminine. Wagner is well known for the sensational mating, described in *Opera and Drama*,[6] of female music with male poetry. A more prim scenario is scripted in Mazzini's call for the rescue of both music and womanhood from prostitution, and as well in Dwight's related insistence that honor and modesty are "two qualities as inseparable in the artistic character as they are in woman." Most strikingly, in Wackenroder's story it is Joseph Berglinger, not any of his five *lumpen* sisters, who is "like a maiden" in the delicacy and musical sensibility of his inner life—which may serve as a reminder that gender stereotypes, where common enough to saturate a culture, have a life of their own independent of mere biology.

In pondering the almost obsessive concern with the "music of the future" that developed around mid-century, we become aware that other intellectual realms and movements beyond Romanticism affected what must otherwise seem a remarkably rarefied discourse. The anxiety of composers about their rightful place in the onflowing "mainstream" of music, which persisted nearly to our own generation, seems to emerge from the confluence of two strains: the overwhelming sense of history that marked nineteenth-century culture generally, and scientific theorizing about evolution as a mechanism for that very history. The promiscuous application of ideas about evolution to a wide variety of social, moral, and cultural processes was the common coin of intellectual life.[7] In such an atmosphere, it is scarcely surprising that Wagner struggled

6. See many passages throughout, but especially pt. 1, sec. 7 (*"Die Musik ist ein Weib"*), and pt. 3, sec. 4. In *The Artwork of the Future* Wagner uses an older trope, the Sister Arts, and thus treats dance, poetry, and music as female.

7. Many theorists of evolution—from Jean-Baptiste de Lamarck, Erasmus Darwin, and George-Louis Leclerc de Buffon in the eighteenth century to Charles Lyell and many others in the nineteenth—had offered their ideas to the scientific community and in many cases the public,

so mightily to prove that his innovations in music drama were part of a "necessary" evolutionary path that music must take; that Adolf Bernhard Marx assures us that music has completed all the "essential tasks" assigned to it in human history now that Beethoven has made "the last unquestionable progress" in the art; or that Mazzini simply assumes that the continued spiritual and political maturation of human societies will necessarily yield up post-Romantic music of a higher sort, ready to undertake a new and more solemn mission. Everything evolved, and most people (if not most scientists) understood evolution as a process that always operated for the better.

The same serene confidence prevailed as European and American scholars, musicians, and audiences increasingly confronted the alien musics of faraway parts of the world. In the later years of the century, groups of non-Western musicians were frequently brought in to perform at international expositions—indeed, whole "native" villages were sometimes set up for viewing, as though in a zoo.[8] By all accounts, Europeans and Americans alike were fascinated by these spectacles, but the intellectual framework that held the new ethnographic information was relentlessly evolutionary: each cultural type could be assigned a rung on the developmental ladder, leading inexorably to the advanced near-perfection of Western music, often exemplified by Wagner or Beethoven. Richard Wallaschek likens "savages" to children in the "mistakes and peculiarities" of their attempts at cultural production. His simile differs strikingly from Margaret Fuller's Romantic one, in which it is artists who are "the young children of our sickly manhood" in their uncalculating innocence and perfectibility.

Scientific thought also inflects the nationalism so characteristic of the era. While its emergence in music and in other cultural venues was intimately bound up with political developments in Europe that encouraged expressions of national identity and consciousness, it is also true that notions of characteristic national and racial difference were supported by contemporary anthropology, ethnology, and the variety of far-flung geographical explorations that accompanied empire. After all, composers did not simply mine their own cultural heritages for folk references in obviously patriotic gestures, they also explored innumerable exotic musical traditions, whether in hopes of experiencing something of the essence of those cultures or merely for novelty value. Such references occur at all levels of musical culture, proliferating in increasing variety as the century goes on.

The era's own understanding of such essences is captured well in Dwight's description of the National Peace Jubilee of 1869 as a successful expression of

---

well before Charles Darwin's publications appeared. Although it is Herbert Spencer's name that is principally associated with "social Darwinism," his ideas too had frequently been anticipated in efforts to explain or prescribe cultural change and to buttress the belief in progress that was the principal industry of the Victorian era.

8. One riveting account is offered by Stewart Culin in "Retrospect of the Folk-Lore of the Columbian Exposition," *Journal of American Folklore* 7 (1894): 51–59.

"the genius of a great, free People," whose planners had been determined "that it should be American in some sense which they could be proud of." American culture, already understood as uniquely heterogeneous even before the great waves of immigration, presented a puzzle to a society so committed to national essences. By the 1890s, when Dvořák visited the United States, certain anomalies were impossible to ignore. His European experience had taught him that "the music of the people, sooner or later, will . . . creep into the books of composers," but who *were* the American people? All races, Dvořák thought, have their distinctive musics, which they will recognize spontaneously "even if they have never heard them before," whence his confused but earnest suggestion that composers in the United States might exploit the music of Black people and American Indians as sources of a "truly American" musical language— never mind the characteristic confusion of race and nation. Here the essential ideal has become a desideratum rather than an expectation, an irresistible imperative to forge a homogeneity from a diverse population.

The music of African-Americans, emancipated from slavery only after midcentury, was commonly seen as an expression of the essential nature of a relatively unevolved—and therefore innocent and childlike—people apparently acquiescent in their enslavement. A dash of cold water is offered by Frederick Douglass's explanation of slave songs as noisy "tracers" required by overseers, or perhaps as coded communications about escape plans. Douglass himself is less interested in speculation about racial character than in the commonalities he heard between slave songs and the songs of the Irish during the famine of 1845 as expressions of human misery.

Early developments in scientific psychology also went a long way toward undermining essential tenets of Romantic faith by investigating the very powers of the soul that Romantics had deemed ineffable. "Emotion" for Edmund Gurney is a far cry from what it was for E. T. A. Hoffmann—just as far as Helmholtz's "nature" is from Wackenroder's. Or we might more properly say that under the sway of Romanticism, emotion was the preeminent aesthetic value and the guarantor of authenticity and individuality (we must demand, says Liszt, "emotional content in the formal container") while under positivism emotion itself became an object of study. Gurney is interested in *why* human beings are able to have emotional responses to patterns of notes, "by what alchemy abstract forms of sound . . . are capable of transformation into phenomena charged with feeling"—a question, incidentally, that also interested Hanslick. The answer, Gurney believes, is that evolution favors the exercise of musical skills, although peoples at different developmental "stages" are moved by music of strikingly different levels of quality. He guesses, for example, that the ancient Greeks were "spellbound by performances for the like of which we should probably tell a street-performer to pass on," as though emotional fastidiousness itself were an evolving genetic trait.

Similarly, Richard Wallaschek argues in his pioneering ethnomusicological study—in contradiction to other theorists who held that the aesthetic realm lay outside the scope of natural selection—that human societies develop musical abilities "as practical life-preserving and life-continuing activities." In other words, he maintains, as Gurney does, that musical activity has an evolutionary advantage. Although Wallaschek is no popularizer of simplistic views of evolution—his argument is for nurture over nature, for the view that individual talent is determined by the state of the culture into which a child is born rather than an innate, racially-determined ability—his Darwinian commitment can be seen in his insistence that primitive societies form a developmental "bridge," emotionally and psychologically as well as physically, between animal and human worlds.

•   •   •

Many of our authors, from E. T. A. Hoffman to Margaret Fuller to Richard Wallaschek, characterize the nineteenth century as preeminently *the* era of music. The claim is richly confirmed by the frequency with which music became a subject of study by newly developing sciences and was made a testing ground for theories, like evolution, that were at the center of discourse. For this reason an extraordinary number of nineteenth-century documents could claim our attention as students of the "living record" of music history that Strunk sought to compile. Many colleagues helped with the nearly impossible task of selection: I wish to thank Raphael Atlas, William Austin, Peter Bloom, Philip Bohlman, Reinhold Brinkmann, Malcolm Hamrick Brown, Scott Burnham, Marcis Citron, Jon Finson, Bea Friedland, Joseph Horowitz, Lawrence Kramer, Richard Kramer, Ralph Locke, Rena Mueller, Roger Parker, Harold Powers, Lee Rothfarb, Margaret Sarkissian, Maynard Solomon, R. Larry Todd, James Webster, and Elizabeth Wood, all of whom generously contributed suggestions, citations, offers of assistance, and even photocopies. My coworkers on the Strunk project, especially Wye Allanbrook, Robert Morgan, Gary Tomlinson, and Leo Treitler, were also invaluably and unflaggingly helpful. No volume however gargantuan could have contained so many generous offerings; in any event, my own education has been immensely enriched by them.

THE ROMANTIC ARTIST

1 Jean Paul

"The highest criticism is that which leaves an impression identical with the one called forth by the thing criticized. In this sense Jean Paul, with a poetic companion-piece, can perhaps contribute more to the understanding of a symphony or fantasy by Beethoven, without even speaking of the music, than a dozen of those little critics of the arts who lean their ladders against the Colossus and take its exact measurements."

Strange to say, this observation of Schumann's is not altogether wide of the mark. A self-taught amateur whose piano playing did not go beyond the improvisation of extravagant rhapsodies, Jean Paul responded almost as a clairvoyant to the poetic side of musical composition; a musical writer who never wrote on music, he exerted a compelling influence on the music and musical criticism of his time. By 1800, thanks to the musical episodes and allusions in his early novels, his name had become so closely identified with music in the minds of his readers that a sentimental ode by Andreas Kretschmer could win immediate and widespread popularity simply by being printed under the title "Jean Paul's Favorite Song." Two well-known writers on music sought him out and recorded their impressions of his personality—Johann Friedrich Reichardt, who spent an evening with him in 1796, and Ludwig Rellstab, who called on him in 1822 with a letter from Ludwig Tieck. For many of his contemporaries he was the literary counterpart of Beethoven. August Lewald, who knew them both, found that they had much in common and reports that the resemblance extended even to physical characteristics. "Beethoven was somewhat smaller," he wrote in 1836, "but one noticed at once the same powerful nature, the same indifference to external appearance, the same kindliness, the same simplicity and cordiality. If we look at their works we find the same profundity, the same sharp characterization, the same painting of details; quiet states of temperament are described and sudden outbursts of extreme passion; ideas that might have been drawn from the most commonplace reality alternate with the highest flights into the sublime. I am confident that I can rediscover in Beethoven's symphonies the Swedish country parson's Sunday (*Flegeljahre,*) the unfortunate's dream (*Herbst-Blumine,*) Natalia Aquilana's letter (*Siebenkäs,*) and the most magnificent episodes of the *Titan.* Only in Jean Paul's improvisation, however, did his kinship with Beethoven become truly evident."

The son of a musician whose father had been a musician before him, Jean Paul (properly Johann Paul Friedrich Richter) was born at Wunsiedel in the Bavarian Fichtelgebirge on March 21, 1763. After attending the university in Leipzig he lived for a time in Hof and later in Weimar; in 1804 he settled in Bayreuth, where he continued a resident until his death on November 14, 1825. Two of Jean Paul's shorter writings, *Quintus Fixlein* and *Des Feldpredigers Schmelzle Reise nach Flätz,* were translated into English by Carlyle.

FROM *Elementary Course in Aesthetics*
(2d ed., 1813)

22. THE NATURE OF ROMANTIC POETRY

THE SOUTHERN AND THE NORTHERN DISTINGUISHED

"The origin and character of all recent poetry is so readily derived from Christianity that one could quite as well call this poetry Christian as romantic." With this assertion the author of the present paragraphs opened fire some years ago;[1] refuted and instructed, however, by more than one worthy critic of the arts, he has felt called upon to alter some details, removing them as one might remove a suburb to protect a fortification or a city as a whole. The first question is: Wherein does the romantic style[2] differ from the Greek? Greek images, stimuli, motives, sensations, characters, even technical restrictions are easily transplanted into a romantic poem without the latter's surrendering on this account its universal spirit; in the other direction, however, the transplanted romantic stimulus finds no congenial place in the Greek art work, unless it be a stimulus of the exalted sort, and then only because the exalted, like a borderline divinity, links the romantic with the antique. Even the so-called modern irregularity, for example that of the Italian opera or the Spanish comedy, may—since mere technique has not the power to divide the spiritual sphere of poetry into an old world and an American new one—be pervaded and animated with the spirit of Antiquity; this is nicely supported by the observation of Bouterwek,[3] who says that Italian poetry, for all its lack of ideas, through its clarity, simplicity, and grace follows and approaches the Greek model more nearly than any other modern sort, and this though the Italian forms have traveled further from the Greek than either the German or the English. And with this correct observation Bouterwek refutes that other one of his,[4] according to which romanticism is precisely to be found in an un-Greek community of the serious, indeed tragic, and the comic. For this is as little a necessary characteristic of the romantic, where it is often absent, as its opposite is of the antique, where it is frequently present, for example, in Aristophanes, who sternly and crassly blends the exaltation of the choruses with the humiliation of the gods them-

TEXT: *Vorschule der Aesthetik. Sämtliche Werke*, pt. 1, vol. 11 (Weimar, 1935), 75–81. Translation by Oliver Strunk, using the notes of Eduard Berend, the editor of this volume of Jean Paul's collected works.

1. The first edition of the *Vorschule* was published in 1804.
2. Schiller calls it the *modern*, as though everything written since Grecian times were modern and new, irrespective of whether one or two thousand years old; likewise the *sentimental*, an epithet which the romanticists Ariosto and Cervantes would not have taken over-seriously. [Au] In Schiller's "Über naive und sentimentalische Dichtung," first published in *Die Horen* for 1795 and 1796.
3. *Geschichte der Poesie und Beredsamkeit* (Göttingen, 1801–19), vol. 2, p. 544
4. In his review of the *Vorschule*.

selves, as though blending an intensification of an emotion with its comic relaxation.

Rather let us ask feeling why, for example, it calls even a countryside romantic. A statue, through its sharp, closed outlines, excludes everything romantic; painting begins to approach it more closely through its groups of human figures and, without them, attains it in landscapes, for example in those of Claude.[5] A Dutch garden seems only to deny everything romantic, but an English one, reaching out into the indefinite landscape, can surround us with a romantic countryside, that is, with a background of imagination set free amid the beautiful. What is it, further, that confers on the following poetic examples their romantic stamp? In the tragedy *Numantia* of Cervantes, the citizens, in order not to fall victims to hunger and the Romans, dedicate themselves in a body to a common death. When they have carried this out and the empty city is strewn with corpses and funeral pyres, Fame appears on the walls and proclaims to the enemy the suicide of the city and the future brilliance of Spain. Again, in the midst of Homer, the romantic passage in which Jupiter surveys from Mount Olympus, at one time and under one sun, the warlike upwrought Trojan plain and the far Arcadian meadows, filled with men of peace.[6] Or, although it sparkles less brightly, the passage in Schiller's *Tell* in which the eye of the poet sweeps down from the towering chain of mountain peaks to the long, laughing wheatfields of the German lowlands.[7] In all these examples, the decisive element is not that of *exaltation*, which, as we have said, readily flows over into the romantic, but that of *expanse*.[8] Romanticism is beauty without bounds— the beautiful infinite, just as there is an exalted infinite. Thus Homer, in the example we have given, is romantic, while in the passage in which Ajax prays to the gods from the darkened battlefield, asking only for light,[9] he is merely exalted. It is more than a simile to call romanticism the wavelike ringing of a string or bell, in which the tone-wave fades into ever further distances, finally losing itself in us so that, while already silent without, it still resounds within. In the same way, the moonlight is at once a romantic image and a romantic example. To the Greeks, who defined things sharply, the half-light of the

5. Claude Lorrain (Claude Gellée), French landscape painter of the seventeenth century.
6. *Iliad*, 13.1.
7. *Wilhelm Tell*, act 3, sc. 3.
8. For musical illustrations of the application of this thoroughly romantic principle, see Liszt's *Ce qu'on entend sur la montagne* (after Victor Hugo), or the closing moments of Wagner's *Tristan und Isolde*:

In dem wogendem Schwall,	In the surging swell,
in dem tönendem Schall,	in the ocean of sound,
in des Welt-Atems	in the world-breath's
wehendem All—	drifting All,
ertrinken,	to drown,
versinken—	engulfed,
unbewußt	without thought—
höchste Lust!	highest bliss!

9. *Iliad*, 17.645.

romantic was so remote and foreign that even Plato, so much the poet and so close to the Christian upheaval, in treating a genuinely romantic-infinite subject—the relation of our petty finite world to the resplendent hall and starry roof of the infinite—expresses it only through the confined and angular allegory of a cave, from out which we chain-bound ones see passing in procession the shadows of the true beings who move behind us.[10]

If poetry is prophecy, then romanticism is being aware of a larger future than there is room for here below; romantic blossoms float about us, just as wholly unfamiliar sorts of seeds drifted through the all-connecting sea from the New World, even before it had been discovered, to the Norwegian shore.

Who is the author of this romanticism? Not in every land and century the Christian religion, to be sure; to this divine mother, however, all its others are somehow related. Two un-Christian varieties of romanticism, historically and climatically independent of one another, are those of India and the Edda. Old Norse romanticism, bordering more nearly on the exalted, finds for the ghostly Orcus in the shadowy realm of its climatically darkened and awe-inspiring natural environment, in its nights and on its mountains, a boundless spirit world in which the narrow sensual world dissolves and sinks from sight; here Ossian[11] belongs, with his evening and night pieces in which the heavenly nebulous stars of the past stand twinkling above the thick nocturnal mist of the present; only in the past does he find future and eternity.

Everything in his poem is music, but it is a distant and hence a doubled music, grown faint in endless space like an echo that enchants, not through its crudely faithful reproduction of a sound, but through its attenuating mitigation of it.

Hindu romanticism has as its element an all-enlivening religion which, through animism, has broken away the confines from the sensual world; this world has become as expansive as the spirit world itself, yet it is filled, not with mischievous spirits, but with cajoling ones, and earth and sky reach out toward one another as they do at sea. To the Hindu a flower is more alive than to the Norseman a man. To this, add the climate, that voluptuous bridal night of nature, and the Hindu himself, who, like the bee reposing in the honey-filled calix of the tulip, is swung to and fro by tepid west winds and takes his rest in a delightful rocking. Precisely for this reason, Hindu romanticism had inevitably to lose itself more and more in the magic of the senses, and if the moonlight and the echo are characteristics and images of other romantic kinds, the Hindu kind may be characterized by its dark perfume, the more so since this so frequently pervades its poetry and its life.

---

10. *Republic*, 7.514–521B.

11. Great as are the advantages of Ahlwardt's translation, thanks to the discovery of the purer text, it seems to me nonetheless that far too little of the praise that is its due has been accorded to the lightness, the fidelity, and the euphonies of the translation by Jung.[Au.] James Macpherson's pretended translations from "Ossian" had been translated into German by F. W. Jung in 1808 and by C. W. Ahlwardt in 1811.

Through its predilection for the exalted and the lyric, through its incapacity for drama and characterization—above all, through its Oriental mode of thought and feeling—Oriental poetry is related less to the Greek than to the romantic. This mode of thought and feeling—namely, the sense of the mortal futility of our night's shadows (shadows cast, not by a sun, but as though by moon and stars—shadows that the meager light itself resembles); the sense that we live our day of life under a total eclipse filled with horror and the flying things of night (like those eclipses in which the moon quite swallows up the sun and stands alone before it with a radiant ring)—this mode of thought and feeling, which Herder, the great delineator of the East, has so exactly painted for the North,[12] could but approach romantic poetry by the path by which a kindred Christianity quite reached and formed it.

We come at length to Christian romanticism, respecting which we must first show why in the South (particularly in Italy and Spain) it took on and created other forms than in the North, where, as was shown above, the very soil made of the heathen outer court a romantically Christian holy of holies. In its natural environment, and then because of manifold historic connections, the South presents an aspect so very different from the North that such reflections as derive romanticism from sources wholly distinct from Christian ones must be considered or corrected.

For the southerly and earliest variety, Bouterwek names these sources:[13] first, the heightened respect for womankind, brought in by the ancient Goths, then, the more spiritualized form of love.

But it was the Christian temple that gave shelter to romantic love, not the prehistoric German forest, and a Petrarch who is not a Christian is unthinkable. The one and only Mary ennobles every woman; hence, while a Venus can only be beautiful, a Madonna can be romantic. This higher form of love was or is precisely a blossoming and blooming from out Christianity, which, with its consuming hatred of the earthly, transformed the beautiful body into the beautiful soul that one might love the other—beauty, then, in the infinite. The name "Platonic love" is borrowed, notoriously, from another sort of love, from that pure unsullied friendship between youths in itself so innocent that the Greek lawgivers counted it a duty, so fanatical that the lover was punished for the errors of the loved one; here, then, simply directed toward another sex, we have again as with the ancient Goths the same deifying love, held—to prevent its profanation—as far as possible from nature, not the love that sanctifies through Christianity and clothes the loved one with the luster of romance.

The spirit of chivalry—which, apart from this, embroidered side by side upon its banners love and religion, *dame* and *Notre Dame*—and the Crusades, named sires of romanticism as second choices, these are children of the Christian spirit. . . . To enter the promised land, which two religions at once and the

12. Above all in his *Älteste Urkunde* (Riga, 1774), p. 95, and *Zerstreute Blätter,* Vol. 4 (Gotha, 1792), p. 131.
13. *Geschichte der Poesie und Beredsamkeit,* vol. 1, p. 22.

greatest being on earth had elevated for the imagination to a twilight realm of holy anticipation and to an isthmus between the first world and the second, to enter this land was to glorify oneself romantically and with two strengths, with valor and with faith, to make oneself master, literally and poetically, of one's baser earthly nature. What comparable result could the heroic ages and the voyages of the Argonauts bring forth?

As servants and silent creatures of romanticism we reckon further the ascending centuries which, allying all peoples more and more closely with one another, round off their sharp corners from without, while from within, through the rising sunlight of abstraction, like a form of Christianity, they break up more and more the solid material world. All this emboldens one to prophesy that, as time goes on, the writing of poetry will become more and more romantic, freer from rules or richer in them, that its separation from Greece will become wider and wider, and that the wings of its winged steed will so multiply that, precisely with the crowd, it will experience greater and greater difficulty in maintaining a steady course, unless, like Ezekiel's seraphim, it uses certain wings merely to cover its face.[14] But as for that, what concern have aestheticians and their prolegomena with time and eternity? Is only creeping philosophy to make progress, and soaring poetry lamely to gather rust? After three or four thousand years and their millions of *horae* is there to be no other division of poetry than Schiller's dull division of it into the *horae*[15] of the sentimental and the naïve? One might maintain that every century is romantic in a different way, just as one might, in jest or in earnest, place a different sort of poetry in every planet. Poetry, like all that is divine in man, is fettered to its time and place; at one time it must become Carpenter's Son and Jew, yet at another its state of abasement may begin on Mount Tabor and its transfiguration take place on a sun and blind us.[16]

Aside from this, it follows of itself that Christianity, although the common father of all romantic children, must in the South beget one sort of child, in the North another. The romanticism of the South—in Italy, climatically related to Greece—must blow more gently in an Ariosto, flying and fleeing less from the antique form, than that of the North in a Shakespeare, just as in turn the same southern variety takes on a different and orientally bolder form in torrid Spain. The poetry and the romanticism of the North is an aeolian harp through which the tempest of reality sweeps in melodies, its howlings resolved in tones, yet melancholy trembles on these strings—at times indeed a grief rends its way in.

---

14. Ezekiel, 1:11; Isaiah, 6:2.
15. Jean Paul is using the word *horae* (*Horen*) both in its literal sense and in reference to the periodical *Die Horen*, edited by Schiller and published monthly from 1795 to 1797. See note 2 above.
16. An ancient tradition makes Mount Tabor the scene of the Transfiguration. Matt. 17:1–9; Mark 9:2–10; Luke 9:28–36.

2 Wilhelm Heinrich Wackenroder

Born in Berlin in 1773, Wilhelm Heinrich Wackenroder was one of the first of the German romanticists. He was a fellow student of Ludwig Tieck's at Erlangen and Göttingen and inspired his friend with his own enthusiasm for the art of the Middle Ages. Wackenroder sought with romantic fervor to penetrate the mystery of music and emphasized in his writings the close relationship between religious feeling and artistic creation. This is the main theme of his *Herzensergiessungen eines kunstliebenden Klosterbruders* (1797). Wackenroder's premature death at the age of twenty-five was a great blow to Tieck, who completed and published his friend's posthumous *Phantasien über die Kunst für Freunde der Kunst* (1799).

The Remarkable Musical Life of the Musician Joseph Berglinger
(1797)

PART ONE

I have often looked backward and gathered in for my enjoyment the art-historical treasures of past centuries; but now my inclination impels me to tarry for once with the present time and to try my hand at the story of an artist whom I knew from his early youth and who was my most intimate friend. Alas, to my regret you soon departed this world, my Joseph, and not easily shall I find your like again! But I shall console myself by retracing in my thoughts the story of your genius, from the beginning, and by retelling it for those to whom it may give pleasure—just as, in happy hours, you often spoke of it to me at length, and just as I myself came inwardly to know you.

* * *

Joseph Berglinger was born in a little town in the south of Germany. His mother was taken from the world as she brought him into it; his father, already a somewhat elderly man, was a doctor of medical science in straitened circumstances. Fortune had turned her back on him, and it was only by dint of much perspiration that he got along in life with his six children (for Joseph had five sisters), the more so since he was now without a capable housekeeper.

TEXT: "Das merkwürdige musikalische Leben des Tonkünstlers Joseph Berglinger," from his *Herzensergiessungen eines kunstliebenden Klosterbruders* (Confessions of an Art-Loving Friar). *Kunstanschauung der Frühromantik*. ed. Andreas Müller (Leipzig, 1931), 89–105. Translation by Oliver Strunk.

The father had formerly been a tender and very kindhearted man who liked nothing better than to give such help, counsel, and alms as he could afford; after a good deed, he slept better than usual; deeply moved and grateful to God, he could long thrive on the good works of his heart; he nourished his spirit in preference with affecting sentiments. Indeed, one cannot but give way to a profoundly melancholy admiration when one contemplates the enviable simplicity of these souls who discover in the ordinary manifestations of a kindly heart a source of grandeur so inexhaustible that it becomes the whole heaven on earth that reconciles them to the world at large and preserves them in constant and comfortable contentment. When he considered his father, Joseph was entirely of this mind; but Heaven had once and for all so constituted him that he aspired steadily to something higher; he was not content with mere spiritual health or satisfied that his soul should carry out its ordinary earthly tasks—to work and to do good; he wanted it to dance as well in exuberant high spirits—to shout to Heaven, as to its source, for joy.

His father's temperament, however, comprised still other elements. He was a hardworking and conscientious doctor and had known no other diversion, his whole life long, than the curious knowledge of things hidden in the human body and the vast science of all the wretched ills and ailments of mankind. As often happens, this intensive study became a secret enervating poison which penetrated his very arteries and gnawed, in his breast, through many a responsive cord. To this was added his discontent with his wretched poverty, and finally his age. All these things served to undermine his former kindliness, for, where the soul is not strong, whatever a man comes into contact with is absorbed into his blood and alters his inner nature without his knowing it.

The children of the old doctor grew up under his care like weeds in a deserted garden. Joseph's sisters were some of them sickly, some of them feebleminded, and, in their dark little room, they led a pitiable and lonely life.

In such a family no one could have been more out of place than Joseph, whose whole life was a beautiful fantasy and a heavenly dream. His soul was like a delicate young tree whose seed a bird has dropped into a ruined wall, where, among the rough stones, it springs up like a maiden. He was always by himself, alone and quiet, feeding only on his inner fantasies; on this account, his father considered him too a little foolish and unbalanced. He was sincerely fond of his father and his sisters, but most of all he prized his inner life, keeping it secret and hidden from others. Thus one secretes a jewel casket, to which one gives no one the key.

Music had from the first been his chief joy. Occasionally he heard someone play the piano and could even play a little himself. In time, by means of this often-repeated pleasure, he developed himself in a way so peculiarly his own that his being became thoroughly musical and his temperament, lured on by the art, wandered about continually among the shady bypaths of poetic feeling.

An outstanding chapter in his life was a visit to the episcopal residence, whither a well-to-do relation, who lived there and had taken a fancy to him, carried him off for a few weeks. Here he was really in his element; his spirit was fascinated by beautiful music, thousand-sided, and, not unlike a butterfly, it fluttered about in the congenial breeze.

Above all he visited the churches to hear the sacred oratorios, cantilenas, and choruses resounding in the full blast of trumpet and trombone beneath the vaulted roofs; from inner piety, he often listened humbly on his knees. Before the music began, as he stood there in the tightly packed and faintly murmuring congestion of the crowd, it seemed to him as though he heard buzzing about him, unmelodiously confused, as at a great fair, the common-place and ordinary life of man; his brain was paralyzed with empty earthly trivialities. Full of expectation, he awaited the first sound of the instruments; as this now broke forth from out the muffled silence, long drawn and mighty as the sigh of a wind from heaven, and as the full force of the sound swept by above his head, it seemed to him as though his soul had all at once unfurled great wings: he felt himself raised up above the barren heath, the dark cloud-curtain shutting out the mortal eye was drawn, and he soared up into the radiant sky. Then he held his body still and motionless, fixing his gaze steadfastly on the floor. The present sank away before him; his being was cleansed of all the pettiness of this world—veritable dust on the soul's luster; the music set his nerves tingling with a gentle thrill, calling up changing images before him with its changes. Thus, listening to certain joyous and soul-stirring songs in praise of God, he seemed quite plainly to see David in his royal mantle, a crown upon his head, dancing toward him and shouting psalms before the Ark of the Covenant; he saw all his enthusiasm, all his movements, and his heart leapt in his breast. A thousand sensations latent within him were liberated and marvelously interwoven. Indeed, at certain passages in the music, finally, an isolated ray of light fell on his soul; at this, it seemed to him as though he all at once grew wiser and was looking down, with clearer sight and a certain inspired and placid melancholy, on all the busy world below.

This much is certain: When the music was over and he left the church, he thought himself made purer and more noble. His entire being still glowed with the spiritual wine that had intoxicated him, and he saw all passersby with different eyes. Now when he chanced to see a group of people standing together on the pavement and laughing or exchanging gossip, it made a quite peculiarly disagreeable impression on him. As long as you live, he thought, you must hold fast, unwavering, to this beautiful poetic ecstasy, and your whole life must be a piece of music. When he went to lunch at his relation's and had thoroughly enjoyed his meal in a company not more than usually hearty and jovial, it displeased him that he had let himself be drawn again so soon into the prosaic life and that his rapture had vanished like a gleaming cloud.

His whole life long he was tormented by this bitter dissension between his inborn lofty enthusiasm and our common mortal lot, which breaks in daily on our reveries, forcibly bringing us down to earth.

When Joseph was at a great concert he seated himself in a corner, without so much as glancing at the brilliant assembly of listeners, and listened with precisely the same reverence as if he had been in church—just as still and motionless, his eyes cast down to the floor in the same way. Not the slightest sound escaped him, and his keen attention left him in the end quite limp and exhausted. His soul, eternally in motion, was wholly a play of sounds; it was as though, liberated from his body, it fluttered about the more freely, or even as though his body too had become a part of his soul. Thus freely and easily was his entire being wound round with the lovely harmonies, and the music's foldings and windings left their impress on his responsive soul. At the lighthearted and delightful symphonies for full orchestra of which he was particularly fond, it seemed to him quite often as though he saw a merry chorus of youths and maidens dancing on a sunny meadow, skipping forward and backward, single couples speaking to each other in pantomime from time to time, then losing themselves again amid the joyous crowd. Certain passages in this music were for him so clear and forceful that the sounds seemed words. At other times again, the music called forth a wondrous blend of gladness and sadness in his heart, so that he was equally inclined to smile and weep—a mood we meet so often on our way through life, for whose expression there is no fitter art than music. And with what delight and astonishment he listened to that sort of music which, beginning like a brook with some cheery, sunny melody, turns imperceptibly and wonderfully, as it goes on, into increasingly troubled windings, to break at last into a loud and violent sob, or to rush by, as though through a wild chasm, with an alarming roar! These many-sided moods now all of them impressed upon his soul new thoughts and visual images, invariably corresponding—a wondrous gift of music, the art of which it may be said in general that the more dark and mysterious its language, the greater its power to affect us, the more general the uproar into which it throws all forces of our being.

The happy days that Joseph had spent in the episcopal residence came to an end at last, and he returned again to his birthplace and to his father's house. How sad was this return, how doleful and depressed he felt at being once more in a household whose entire life and strife turned only on the bare satisfying of the most essential physical needs and with a father who so little approved of his inclinations, who despised and detested all the arts as servants of extravagant desires and passions and as flatterers of the elegant world! From the very first it had displeased him that his Joseph had so fastened his heart on music; now that this inclination in the boy was growing by leaps and bounds, he made a determined and serious effort to convert him, from a harmful propensity for an art whose practice was little better than idleness and which catered merely to sensual excess, to medicine, as the most beneficent science and as the one most generally useful to the human race. He took great pains to instruct his son himself in its elementary principles and gave him books to read.

This was a truly distressing and painful situation for poor Joseph. Secretly he buried his enthusiasm deep in his breast, not to offend his father, and sought to compel himself, if possible, to master a useful science on the side. Yet in his soul there was a constant struggle. In his textbooks he could read one page ten times over without grasping what he read; unceasingly within, his soul sang its melodious fantasies on and on. His father was much distressed about him.

In secret his passionate love of music came to dominate him more and more. If for several weeks he heard no music, he became actually sick at heart; he noted that his feelings dried up, an emptiness arose within him, and he experienced a downright longing to be again inspired. Then even ordinary players, on church festival and consecration days, could with their wind instruments move him to feelings which they themselves had never felt. And as often as a great concert was to be heard in a neighboring town, he rushed out, ardent and eager, into the most violent snow, storm, or rain.

Scarcely a day went by without his calling sadly to mind those wonderful weeks in the episcopal residence, without his soul's reviewing the priceless things that he had heard there. Often he repeated to himself from memory the lovely and touching words of the sacred oratorio which had been the first that he had heard and which had made a particularly deep impression on him:

Stabat mater dolorosa	The sorrowful mother stood
Juxta crucem lacrymosa,	In tears beside the cross
Dum pendebat Filius	From which hung her Son.
Cujus animam gementem,	Her soul—lamenting,
Contristantem et dolentem,	Saddened and suffering—
Pertransivit gladius.	Was pierced by a sword.
O quam tristis et afflicta	O, how sad and dejected
Fuit illa benedicta	Was that blessed
Mater Unigeniti!	Mother of the Only-begotten!
Quae moerebat, et dolebat,	How she grieved, sorrowed,
Et tremebat, cum videbat	And trembled when she saw
Nati poenas inclyti.[1]	Her Son's punishment.

And so forth.

But alas for those enchanted hours, in which he lived as in an ethereal dream or had just come quite intoxicated from the enjoyment of a splendid piece of music; when they were interrupted for him—by his sisters, quarreling over a new dress, by his father, unable to give the eldest daughter enough money for her housekeeping or telling the story of a thoroughly wretched and pitiable invalid, or by some old beggar-woman, all bent over, coming to the door, unable to shield herself in her rags from the wintry frost—alas, there is in all the world no feeling so intensely bitter and heartrending as that with which Joseph was then torn. Dear God, he thought, is this the world as it is—and is it Thy will that I should plunge into the turmoil of the crowd and share the general misery? So it seems, and, as my father constantly preaches, it is the destiny and

---

1. *Stabat mater* is a sequence, assigned in the Roman liturgy to the Feast of the Seven Sorrows (September 15); its later polyphonic settings are also frequently used during Lent. Wackenroder is probably thinking of the setting by Pergolesi.

duty of man to share it, to give advice and alms, to bind up loathesome wounds, to heal odious diseases. And yet again an inner voice calls out to me quite clearly: "No! No! You have been born to a higher, nobler end!" With thoughts like these he often tormented himself for hours at a time, finding no way out; before he knew it, however, there vanished from his soul those unpleasant pictures which seemed to pull him by force into the mire of this life, and his spirit floated once more unruffled on the breeze.

In time he became thoroughly convinced that God had sent him into the world to become a really distinguished artist, and it may sometimes have occurred to him that, in view of the gloomy and confining poverty of his youth, Providence might be going to reward him all the more brilliantly. Many will consider it a novelesque and unnatural invention, but it is none the less strictly true that in his loneliness, from an ardent impulse of his heart, he often fell on his knees and prayed God to so guide him that he might some day become an altogether splendid artist in the sight of God and man. At this time, his pulse often violently agitated by the pressure of ideas directed steadily toward one point, he wrote down a number of shorter poems, setting forth his state of mind or the praise of music, and these, without knowing the rules, he set joyously to music after his childish heartfelt fashion. A sample of these songs is the following, a prayer which he addressed to music's sainted patron:

> See me comfortless and weeping,
> Solitary vigil keeping,
>   Saint Cecilia, blessed maid;
> See me all the world forsaking,
> On my knees entreaty making;
>   Oh, I pray thee, grant me aid.
>
> Let the hearts of men be captured,
> By my music's tones enraptured,
>   Till my power has no bound,
> And the world be penetrated,
> Fantasy-intoxicated,
>   By the sympathetic sound.

Perhaps for more than a year poor Joseph tormented himself, brooding alone over the step he wished to take. An irresistible force drew his spirit back to that splendid city which he regarded as his paradise, for he was consumed by the desire to learn his art there from the ground up. But it was his relations with his father that weighed particularly on his heart. Having no doubt observed that Joseph was no longer at all willing to apply himself seriously and industriously to his scientific studies, his father had indeed already half given him up, withdrawing himself into his displeasure which, with his advancing age, increased by leaps and bounds. He no longer paid much attention to the boy. Joseph, meanwhile, did not on this account give up his childlike feeling; he struggled continually against his inclination and still had not the heart to breathe, in his father's presence, a word of what he had to reveal. For whole days at a time he tortured himself by weighing one course against another, but he simply could not extricate himself from the horrible abyss of doubt; his ardent prayers were all to no avail—this almost broke his heart. To the utterly gloomy and distressed state of mind in which he was at this time, these lines, which I found among his papers, bear witness:

> Ah, what are these forces that surround me
> And in their embrace have tightly bound me,
> Calling me away—shall I obey them?
> Urging me from home—can I gainsay them?
> I must bear, though guiltless of transgression,
> Torture and temptation and oppression.

> That Thou'lt deign to save me, I implore Thee
> Bury me in earth, call me before Thee;
> Otherwise I cannot long withstand it,
> Must live at the will (if it demand it)
> Of that unknown force whose awful power
> Governs me more fully every hour.

From day to day his distress grew more and more acute, the temptation to escape to the splendid city stronger and stronger. But, he thought, will not Providence come to my aid—will it give me no sign at all? His suffering finally reached its highest peak when his father, in connection with some family disagreement, addressed him sharply in a tone quite different from his usual one, afterwards consistently repulsing him. Now the die was cast; from now on he turned his back on all doubts and scruples; he would now consider the matter no further. The Easter holiday was at hand; this he would celebrate with the others at home; but as soon as it was over—out into the wide world.

It was over. He awaited the first fine morning, for the bright sunshine seemed to lure him on as though by magic; then, early in the morning, he ran out of the house and away—one was used to this in him—but this time he did not come back. With delight and with a pounding heart he hastened through the narrow alleys of the little town; hurrying past everything he saw about him, he could scarcely keep from leaping into the open air. On one corner he met an old relation. "Why in such a hurry, cousin?" she asked. "Are you fetching vegetables for the table from the market again?" Yes, yes, called Joseph to himself, and, trembling with joy, he ran out through the gates.

But when he had gone a little distance into the country, he looked about and burst into tears. Shall I turn back, he thought. But he ran on, as though his heels were on fire, and wept continually, so that it looked as though he were running away from his tears. His way led now through many an unfamiliar village and past many an unfamiliar face; the sight of the unfamiliar world revived his courage, he felt strong and free—he came nearer and nearer—and at last—Heavens, what delight!—at last he saw lying before him the towers of the splendid city.

PART TWO

I return to my Joseph a number of years after we left him; he has become Capellmeister in the episcopal residence and lives in great splendor. His relation, having received him very cordially, has been the author of his good fortune, has seen to it that he was given the most thorough training in music, and has also more or less reconciled Joseph's father, little by little, to the step his son had taken. By exceptional application Joseph has worked his way up, to attain at length the highest rung of success that he could possibly wish.

Yet the things of this world change before our very eyes. On one occasion, after he had been Capellmeister for several years, he wrote me the following letter:

Dear Padre:

It is a miserable life I lead—the more you seek to comfort me, the more keenly I am aware of it.

When I recall the dreams of my youth—how blissfully happy I was in those dreams! I thought I wanted to give my fancy free rein continuously and to let out my full heart in works of art. But how strange and austere even my first years of study seemed to me—how I felt when I stepped behind the curtain! To think that all melodies (although they had aroused the most heterogeneous and often the most wondrous emotions in me) were based on a single inevitable mathematical law—that, instead of trying my wings, I had first to learn to climb around in the unwieldy framework and cage of artistic grammar! How I had to torture myself to produce a thing faultlessly correct with the machinelike reason of ordinary science before I could think of making my feelings a subject for music! It was a tiresome mechanical task. But even so, I still had buoyant youthful energy and confidence in the magnificent future. And now? The magnificent future has become the lamentable present.

What happy hours I spent as a boy in the great concert hall, sitting quietly and unnoticed in a corner, enchanted by all the splendor and magnificence, and wishing ever so ardently that these listeners might some day gather to hear my works, to surrender their feelings to me! Now I sit often enough in this same hall, even perform my works there, but in a very different frame of mind indeed. To think I could have imagined that these listeners, parading in gold and silk, had gathered to enjoy a work of art, to warm their hearts, to offer their feelings to the artist! If, even in the majestic cathedral, on the most sacred holiday, when everything great and beautiful that art and religion possess violently forces itself on them, these souls are not so much as warmed, is one to expect it in the concert hall? Feeling and understanding for art have gone out of fashion and become unseemly; to feel, in the presence of an artwork, is considered quite as odd and laughable as suddenly to speak in verse and rhyme in company, when one otherwise gets through one's life with sensible prose, intelligible to all. Yet for these souls I wear out my spirit and work myself up to do things in such a way that they may arouse feeling! This is the high calling to which I had believed myself born.

And when on occasion someone who has a sort of halfway feeling seeks to praise me and to commend me critically and to propound critical questions for me to answer, I am always tempted to beg him not to be at such pains to learn about feeling from books. Heaven knows, when I have enjoyed a piece of music—or any other delightful work of art—and my whole being is full of it, I should paint my feeling on the canvas with a single stroke, if only a single color could express it. I cannot bestow false praise, and I can bring forth nothing clever.

To be sure, there is a little consolation in the thought that perhaps—in some obscure corner of Germany to which this or that work of mine may penetrate some day, even though long after my death—there may be someone whom Heaven has made so sympathetic to my soul that he will feel on hearing my melodies precisely what I felt in writing them—precisely what I sought to put in them. A lovely idea, with which, no doubt, one may pleasantly deceive oneself for a time!

Most horrible of all, however, are those other circumstances with which the artist is hemmed in. To speak of all the loathsome envy and spiteful conduct, of all the untoward petty customs and usages, of all the subordination of art to the will of a court—to speak a word of this is repugnant to me; it is all so undignified, so humiliating to man's soul, that I cannot bring a syllable of it past my lips. A threefold misfortune for music that the mere existence of a work requires such a number of hands! I collect myself and lift up my entire soul to produce a great work—and a hundred unfeeling empty-headed fellows put in their word and demand this and that.

In my youth I thought to avoid the misery of earthly life; now, more than ever, I have sunk into the mire. This much seems certain, sad to say—for all our exertion of our spiritual wings we cannot escape this earth; it pulls us back by force, and we fall again into the common human herd.

They are pitiable artists, those I see about me, even the noblest ones so petty that, for conceit, they do not know what to do once a work of theirs has become a general favorite. Dear God, is not one half our merit due to art's divinity, to nature's eternal harmony, the other half to the gracious Creator who gave us the power to make use of this treasure? Those charming melodies which can call forth in us the most varied emotions thousandfold, have they not sprung, all of them, from the unique and wondrous triad, founded an eternity since by nature? Those melancholy feelings, half soothing, half painful, which music inspires in us, we know not how, what are they after all but the mysterious effect of alternating major and minor? Ought we not to thank our Maker if he now grants us just the skill to combine these sounds, in sympathy from the first with the human soul, so that they move the heart? Art, surely, is what we should worship, not the artist—he is but a feeble instrument.

You see that my ardor and my love for music are no less strong than formerly. And this is just the reason why I am so miserable in this . . . but I shall drop the subject and not annoy you further by describing all the loathsome reality about me. Enough—I live in a very impure atmosphere. How far more ideally I lived in those days when I still merely enjoyed art, in youthful innocence and peaceful solitude, than I do now that I practice it, in the dazzling glare of the world, surrounded only by silks, stars and crosses of honor, and people of culture and taste! What should I like? I should like to leave all this culture high and dry and run away to the simple shepherd in the Swiss mountains to play with him those Alpine songs which make him homesick wherever he hears them.

From this fragmentarily written letter one can realize in part the situation in which Joseph found himself. He felt neglected and alone amid the buzzing of the many unharmonious souls about him; his art was deeply degraded in his eyes in that, so far as he knew, there was no one on whom it made a lively impression, for it seemed to him created only to move the human heart. In many a dark hour he was in utter despair, thinking: How strange and singular is art! Is then its mysterious power for me alone—is it to all other men mere sensual pleasure and agreeable amusement? What is it really and in fact, if it is nothing to all men and something to me alone? Is it not a most absurd idea to make this art one's whole aim and chief business and to imagine a thousand wonderful things about its great effects on human temperament—about an art which, in everyday reality, plays much the same role as card-playing or any other pastime?

When such thoughts occurred to him, it seemed to him that he had been the greatest of visionaries to have striven so hard to make a practical artist of himself for the world. He hit on the idea that the artist should be artist for himself alone, to his own heart's exaltation, and for the one or two who understand him. And I cannot call this idea wholly incorrect.

But I must sum up briefly the remainder of my Joseph's life, for my memories of it are beginning to depress me.

For a number of years he continued to live on in this way as Capellmeister, and, as time went on, his discouragement increased, as did his uneasy realization that, for all his deep feeling and intimate understanding of art, he was of no use to the world, less influential than a common tradesman. Often and regretfully he recalled the pure ideal enthusiasm of his boyhood and with it how his father had tried to make a doctor of him so that he might lessen man's misery, heal the unfortunate, and thus make himself useful in the world. This had perhaps been better, he thought more than once.

His father, meanwhile, had at his age grown very weak. Joseph wrote regularly to his eldest sister and sent her something toward his father's support. He could not bring himself to pay him an actual visit and felt that this would be beyond him. He became more despondent; his life was far spent.

On one occasion he had performed in the concert hall a new and beautiful piece of music of his own composition; it seemed the first time that he had made any impression on the hearts of his listeners. The general astonishment, the silent approval, so much more welcome than noisy applause, made him happy in the thought that this time he had perhaps been worthy of his art; once more he was encouraged to begin work anew. But when he went out on to the street, a girl, dressed very miserably, crept up and sought to speak to him. Heavens, he cried; it was his youngest sister and she was in a wretched state. She had run on foot from her home to bring him the news that his father was about to die and had insistently demanded to speak with him before the end. At that, the music in his breast broke off; in a heavy stupor he made his preparations and set off in haste for his birthplace.

The scenes which took place at his father's bedside I shall not describe. But let the reader not believe that there were any melancholy long-drawn-out debates; without wasting many words they understood each other fully—in this respect, indeed, it seems that nature mocks us generally, men never understanding one another properly until these critical last moments. At the same time, he was smitten to the heart by all that he saw. His sisters were in the most deplorable circumstances; two of them had fallen from grace and run away; the eldest, to whom he regularly sent money, had wasted most of it, letting his father starve; in the end his father died miserably before his eyes; alas, it was horrible, the way his poor heart was wounded through and through and torn to bits. He did what he could for his sisters and went home, for his affairs recalled him.

For the impending Easter festival he was to write a new Passion music; his envious rivals were eagerly awaiting it. Yet, as often as he sat down to work, he burst into a flood of tears; his tortured heart would not let him recover himself. He lay deeply depressed, buried among the leavings of this world. At length, by an effort, he tore himself free, stretching out his arms to heaven in an impassioned prayer; he filled his soul with the most sublime poetry, with a full and exultant hymn, and, in a marvelous inspiration, but still violently shaken emotionally, he set down a Passion music which, with its deeply affecting melodies, embodying all the pains of suffering, will forever remain a masterpiece. His soul was like that of the invalid who, in a strange paroxysm, exhibits greater strength than the healthy man.

But after he had performed the oratorio in the cathedral on Easter Sunday, straining himself to the utmost in feverish agitation, he felt faint and exhausted. Like an unhealthy dew, a nervous weakness attacked all his fibers; he was ill for a time and died not long afterwards, in the bloom of his years.

Many a tear have I offered to his memory, and a strange feeling comes over me when I review his life. Why did Heaven ordain that the struggle between his lofty enthusiasm and the common misery of this earth should make him unhappy his whole life long and in the end tear quite apart the twofold nature of his mind and body?

The ways of Providence are hidden from us. But let us marvel once again at the diversity of those inspired beings whom Heaven sends into the world to serve the arts.

A Raphael brought forth in all innocence and artlessness works of the utmost ingenuity in which we see revealed the whole of Heaven; a Guido Reni, leading a wild gambler's life, created the gentlest and most sacred paintings; an Albrecht Dürer, a simple citizen of Nuremberg, in that same cell in which his wicked wife abused him daily, produced with the antlike industry of the mechanic artworks highly spiritual in content; yet Joseph, in whose harmonious music lies such mysterious beauty, differed from them all.

Alas, his lofty fantasy was what destroyed him. Shall I say that he was perhaps created rather to enjoy art than to practice it? Those in whom art works silently and secretly, like an inner genius, not hindering their doings upon earth—are they perhaps more fortunately constituted? And must the ceaselessly inspired one, if he would be true artist, perhaps not weave his lofty fantasies, like a stout strand, boldly and firmly into this earthly life? Indeed, is not perhaps this incomprehensible creative power something altogether different and—as it now seems to me—something still more marvelous and godlike than the power of fantasy?

The spirit of art is and remains for man eternally a mystery, and he grows dizzy when he seeks to plumb its depths; at the same time, it is eternally an object for his highest admiration, as must be said of all the great things in this world.

•   •   •

But after these recollections of my Joseph I can write no more. I conclude my book—in the hope that it may have served to awaken good ideas in some one or other of my readers.

3 Margaret Fuller

Sarah Margaret Fuller Ossoli, born in Massachusetts in 1810, was a critic, teacher, and feminist. She was an intellectual prodigy as a child and became especially well known for the brilliance of her conversation. For five years in Boston she conducted "conversations" for women, to encourage their participation in cultural and intellectual life. A member of the American transcendentalist movement, she edited *The Dial,* the transcendentalists' magazine, from 1840 to 1842 and published in its pages many pieces of her own writing.

In 1844 Fuller moved to New York, where she became the literature and arts critic of Horace Greeley's *New York Tribune.* She continued as a foreign correspondent for that newspaper after moving to Italy a few years later, remaining there when revolution broke out in Rome. Her manuscript history of that revolution was lost in the 1850 shipwreck off Fire Island, New York, that also claimed Fuller's life.

Fuller's essay is an extended meditation on the lives of artistic geniuses and the lessons those lives may hold for us. While not a book review, the argument focuses on five actual composer biographies and uses extended quotations from them to illustrate her points. Fuller does not give complete citations for the books she discusses, but they may be identified as follows: Friedrich Schlichtegroll's *Mozarts Leben* (1794) in a French translation by Bombet (a pseudonym of Marie-Henri Beyle, who also used the pseudonym Stendhal); Johann Nikolaus Forkel's *Über Johann Sebastian Bachs Leben, Kunst und Kunstwerke* (1802), in an English translation (1820); Bombet's *Vies de Haydn, de Mozart et de Métastase* (1814); Anton Schindler's *Biographie von Ludwig van Beethoven* (1840); and an unidentified life of Handel, which may have been John Mainwaring's *Memoirs of the Life of the Late George Frederick Handel* (1760) since she characterizes it as being "in the style of the days of Addison and Steele." Only the introduction and conclusion of the long essay are given here.

FROM Lives of the Great Composers, Haydn, Mozart, Handel, Bach, Beethoven
(1841)

The lives of the musicians are imperfectly written for this obvious reason. The soul of the great musician can only be expressed in music. This language is so much more ready, flexible, full, and rapid than any other, that we can never expect the minds of those accustomed to its use to be expressed by act or word, with even that degree of adequacy, which we find in those of other men. They are accustomed to a higher stimulus, a more fluent existence. We must read them in their works; this, true of artists in every department, is especially so of the high-priests of sound.

Yet the eye, which has followed with rapture the flight of the bird till it is quite vanished in the blue serene, reverts with pleasure to the nest which it finds of materials and architecture, that, if wisely examined, correspond entirely with all previously imagined of the songster's history and habits. The biography of the artist is a scanty gloss upon the grand text of his works, but we examine it with a deliberate tenderness, and could not spare those half-effaced pencil marks of daily life.

In vain the healthy reactions of nature have so boldly in our own day challenged the love of greatness, and bid us turn from Boswellism[1] to read the record of the village clerk. These obscure men, you say, have hearts also, busy lives, expanding souls. Study the simple annals of the poor, and you find there, only restricted and stifled by accident, Milton, Calderon, or Michel Angelo. Precisely for that, precisely because we might be such as these, if temperament and position had seconded the soul's behest, must we seek with eagerness this spectacle of the occasional manifestation of that degree of development which we call hero, poet, artist, martyr. A sense of the depths of love and pity in our obscure and private breasts bids us demand to see their sources burst up somewhere through the lava of circumstance, and Peter Bell has no sooner felt his first throb of penitence and piety, than he prepares to read the lives of the saints.

Of all those forms of life which in their greater achievement shadow forth what the accomplishment of our life in the ages must be, the artist's life is the fairest in this, that it weaves its web most soft and full, because of the material most at command. Like the hero, the statesman, the martyr, the artist differs from other men only in this, that the voice of the demon within the breast

TEXT: *The Dial: A Magazine for Literature, Philosophy, and Religion* 2, no. 2 (October 1841): 148–151, 202–3. I am grateful to Ora Frishberg Saloman for assistance in identifying the five composer biographies listed above.

1. James Boswell (1740–1795) is best known as the biographer of Samuel Johnson.

speaks louder, or is more early and steadily obeyed than by men in general. But colors, and marble, and paper scores are more easily found to use, and more under command, than the occasions of life or the wills of other men, so that we see in the poet's work, if not a higher sentiment, or a deeper meaning, a more frequent and more perfect fulfilment than in him who builds his temple from the world day by day, or makes a nation his canvass and his pallette.

It is also easier to us to get the scope of the artist's design and its growth as the area where we see it does not stretch vision beyond its power. The Sybil of Michel Angelo indeed shares the growth of centuries, as much as Luther's Reformation, but the first apparition of the one strikes both the senses and the soul, the other only the latter, so we look most easily and with liveliest impression at the Sybil.

Add the benefits of rehearsal and repetition. The grand Napoleon drama could be acted but once, but Mozart's Don Giovanni presents to us the same thought seven times a week, if we wish to yield to it so many.

The artists too are the young children of our sickly manhood, or wearied out old age. On us life has pressed till the form is marred and bowed down, but their youth is immortal, invincible, to us the inexhaustible prophecy of a second birth. From the naive lispings of their uncalculating lives are heard anew the tones of that mystic song we call Perfectibility, Perfection.

Artist biographies, scanty as they are, are always beautiful. The tedious cavil of the Teuton cannot degrade, nor the sultry superlatives of the Italian wither them. If any fidelity be preserved in the record, it always casts new light on their works. The exuberance of Italian praise is the better extreme of the two, for the heart, with all its blunders, tells truth more easily than the head. The records before us of the great composers are by the patient and reverent Germans, the sensible, never to be duped Englishman, or the sprightly Frenchman; but a Vasari[2] was needed also to cast a broader sunlight on the scene. All artist lives are interesting. And those of the musicians, peculiarly so to-day, when Music is *the* living, growing art. Sculpture, Painting, Architecture are indeed not dead, but the life they exhibit is as the putting forth of young scions from an old root. The manifestation is hopeful rather than commanding. But music, after all the wonderful exploits of the last century, grows and towers yet. Beethoven, towering far above our heads, still with colossal gesture points above. Music is pausing now to explain, arrange, or explore the treasures so rapidly accumulated; but how great the genius thus employed, how vast the promise for the next revelation! Beethoven seems to have chronicled all the sobs, the heart-heavings, and god-like Promethean thefts of the Earth-spirit. Mozart has called to the sister stars, as Handel and Haydn have told to other spheres what has been actually performed in this; surely they will answer through the next magician.

---

2. Giorgio Vasari (1511–1574), Italian painter and architect, and author of *Lives of the Most Eminent Italian Architects, Painters and Sculptors* (1550).

The thought of the law that supersedes all thoughts, which pierces us the moment we have gone far in any department of knowledge or creative genius, seizes and lifts us from the ground in Music. "Were but this known all would be accomplished" is sung to us ever in the triumphs of Harmony. What the other arts indicate and Philosophy infers, this all-enfolding language declares, nay publishes, and we lose all care for to-morrow or modern life in the truth averred of old, that all truth is comprised in music and mathematics.

> By one pervading spirit
> Of tones and numbers all things are controlled,
> As sages taught where *faith* was found to merit
> Initiation in that mystery old.
> —Wordsworth, "Stanzas on the power of sounds"

A very slight knowledge of music makes it the best means of interpretation. We meet our friend in a melody as in a glance of the eye, far beyond where words have strength to climb; we explain by the corresponding tone in an instrument that trait in our admired picture, for which no sufficiently subtle analogy had yet been found. Botany had never touched our true knowledge of our favorite flower, but a symphony displays the same attitude and hues; the philosophic historian had failed to explain the motive of our favorite hero, but every bugle calls and every trumpet proclaims him. He that hath ears to hear, let him hear!

Of course we claim for music only a greater rapidity, fulness, and, above all, delicacy of utterance. All is in each and each in all, so that the most barbarous stammering of the Hottentot indicates the secret of man, as clearly as the rudest zoophyte the perfection of organized being, or the first stop on the reed the harmonies of heaven. But music, by the ready medium, the stimulus and the upbearing elasticity it offers for the inspirations of thought, alone seems to present a living form rather than a dead monument to the desires of Genius.

·　·　·　·　·

In three respects these artists, all true artists, resemble one another. Clear decision. The intuitive faculty speaks clear in those devoted to the worship of Beauty. They are not subject to mental conflict, they ask not counsel of experience. They take what they want as simply as the bird goes in search of its proper food, so soon as its wings are grown.

Like nature they love the work for its own sake. The philosopher is ever seeking the thought through the symbol, but the artist is happy at the implication of the thought in his work. He does not reason about "religion or thorough bass." His answer in Haydn's, "I thought it best so." From each achievement grows up a still higher ideal, and when his work is finished, it is nothing to the artist who has made of it the step by which he ascended, but while he was engaged in it, it was all to him, and filled his soul with a parental joy.

They do not criticise, but affirm. They have no need to deny aught, much less one another. All excellence to them was genial; imperfection only left room for new creative power to display itself. An everlasting yes breathes from the life, from the work of the artist. Nature echoes it, and leaves to society the work of saying no, if it will. But it will not, except for the moment. It weans itself for the moment, and turns pettishly away from genius, but soon stumbling, groping, and lonely, cries aloud for its nurse. The age cries *now,* and what an answer is prophesied by such harbinger stars as these at which we have been gazing. We will engrave their names on the breastplate, and wear them as a talisman of hope.

4 George Eliot

The novels of Mary Ann Evans (1819–1880), who used the pen name George Eliot, are particularly celebrated for their intellectual and historical depth, their moral sensibility, and the acuteness of their social descriptions. *Daniel Deronda,* her last novel, is no exception. Its principal historical material is the Zionist movement and the social situation of Jews in England; its moral themes are responsibility and kinship. Music plays an important role, as it frequently does in Eliot's work, as an index of character. In the two excerpts given here, two very different young women sing for the distinguished musician Julius Klesmer and encounter two very different responses.

The scenes reveal Eliot's keen understanding of the musical mores and debates of the day: the famed philistinism of the English, the entrapment of young women like Gwendolen Harleth in meaningless musical study for largely decorative purposes, the battle between German Wagnerian music and Italian music and the ideology underlying that dispute. There is also, Eliot makes clear, the persistent tinge of anti-Semitism; nearly all of the characters in the novel who are represented as genuine, natural musicians are Jewish, and Klesmer's very name means "musician" in Yiddish. The model for the composer / pianist Klesmer may have been Anton Rubinstein, whom Eliot met in Weimar during a visit to Liszt, or may, indeed, have been Liszt himself.

FROM *Daniel Deronda*

(1878)

"Ah, here comes Herr Klesmer," said Mrs. Arrowpoint, rising; and presently bringing him to Gwendolen, she left them to a dialogue which was agreeable

TEXT: Cabinet edition (Edinburgh and London: Blackwood, 1878), portions of chaps. 5 and 39.

on both sides, Herr Klesmer being a felicitous combination of the German, the Sclave, and the Semite, with grand features, brown hair floating in artistic fashion, and brown eyes in spectacles. His English had little foreignness except its fluency; and his alarming cleverness was made less formidable just then by a certain softening air of silliness which will sometimes befall even Genius in the desire of being agreeable to Beauty.

Music was soon begun. Miss Arrowpoint and Herr Klesmer played a four-handed piece on two pianos which convinced the company in general that it was long, and Gwendolen in particular that the neutral, placid-faced Miss Arrowpoint had a mastery of the instrument which put her own execution out of the question—though she was not discouraged as to her often-praised touch and style. After this every one became anxious to hear Gwendolen sing; especially Mr. Arrowpoint; as was natural in a host and a perfect gentleman, of whom no one had anything to say but that he had married Miss Cuttler, and imported the best cigars; and he led her to the piano with easy politeness. Herr Klesmer closed the instrument in readiness for her, and smiled with pleasure at her approach; then placed himself at the distance of a few feet so that he could see her as she sang.

Gwendolen was not nervous: what she undertook to do she did without trembling, and singing was an enjoyment to her. Her voice was a moderately powerful soprano (someone had told her it was like Jenny Lind's), her ear good, and she was able to keep in tune, so that her singing gave pleasure to ordinary hearers, and she had been used to unmingled applause. She had the rare advantage of looking almost prettier when she was singing than at other times, and that Herr Klesmer was in front of her seemed not disagreeable. Her song, determined on beforehand, was a favourite aria of Bellini's, in which she felt quite sure of herself.

"Charming!" said Mr. Arrowpoint, who had remained near, and the word was echoed around without more insincerity than we recognise in a brotherly way as human. But Herr Klesmer stood like a statue—if a statue can be imagined in spectacles; at least, he was as mute as a statue. Gwendolen was pressed to keep her seat and double the general pleasure, and she did not wish to refuse; but before resolving to do so, she moved a little towards Herr Klesmer, saying, with a look of smiling appeal, "It would be too cruel to a great musician. You cannot like to hear poor amateur singing."

"No, truly; but that makes nothing," said Herr Klesmer, suddenly speaking in an odious German fashion with staccato endings, quite unobservable in him before, and apparently depending on a change of mood, as Irishmen resume their strongest brogue when they are fervid or quarrelsome. "That makes nothing. It is always acceptable to see you sing."

Was there ever so unexpected an assertion of superiority? at least before the late Teutonic conquests? Gwendolen coloured deeply, but, with her usual presence of mind, did not show an ungraceful resentment by moving away immediately; and Miss Arrowpoint, who had been near enough to overhear (and also to observe that Herr Klesmer's mode of looking at Gwendolen was more conspicuously admiring than was quite consistent with good taste), now with the utmost tact and kindness came close to her and said—

"Imagine what I have to go through with this professor! He can hardly tolerate anything we English do in music. We can only put up with his severity, and make use of it to find out the worst that can be said of us. It is a little comfort to know that; and one can bear it when everyone else is admiring."

"I should be very much obliged to him for telling me the worst," said Gwendolen, recovering herself. "I daresay I have been extremely ill taught, in addition to having no talent—only liking for music." This was very well expressed considering that it had never entered her mind before.

"Yes, it is true; you have not been well taught," said Herr Klesmer, quietly. Woman was dear to him, but music was dearer. "Still, you are not quite without gifts. You sing in tune, and you have a pretty fair organ. But you produce your notes badly; and that music which you sing is beneath you. It is a form of melody which expresses a puerile state of culture—a dangling, canting, see-saw kind of stuff—the passion and thought of people without any breadth of horizon. There is a sort of self-satisfied folly about every phrase of such melody: no cries of deep, mysterious passion—no conflict—no sense of the universal. It makes men small as they listen to it. Sing now something larger. And I shall see."

"Oh, not now—by-and-by," said Gwendolen, with a sinking of heart at the sudden width of horizon opened round her small musical performance. For a young lady desiring to lead, this first encounter in her campaign was startling. But she was bent on not behaving foolishly, and Miss Arrowpoint helped her by saying—

"Yes, by-and-by. I always require half an hour to get up my courage after being criticised by Herr Klesmer. We will ask him to play to us now: he is bound to show us what is good music."

To be quite safe on this point Herr Klesmer played a composition of his own, a fantasia called *Freudvoll, Leidvoll, Gedankenvoll*[1]—an extensive commentary on some melodic ideas not too grossly evident; and he certainly fetched as much variety and depth of passion out of the piano as that moderately responsive instrument lends itself to, having an imperious magic in his fingers that seemed to send a nerve-thrill through ivory key and wooden hammer, and compel the strings to make a quivering lingering speech for him. Gwendolen, in spite of her wounded egoism, had fulness of nature enough to feel the power of this playing, and it gradually turned her inward sob of mortification into an excitement which lifted her for the moment into a desperate indifference about her own doings, or at least a determination to get a superiority over them by laughing at them as if they belonged to somebody else. Her eyes had become brighter, her cheeks slightly flushed, and her tongue ready for any mischievous remarks.

1. "Joyful, Sorrowful, Thoughtful."

"I wish you would sing to us again, Miss Harleth," said young Clintock, the archdeacon's classical son, who had been so fortunate as to take her to dinner, and came up to renew conversation as soon as Herr Klesmer's performance was ended. "That is the style of music for me. I never can make anything of this tip-top playing. It is like a jar of leeches, where you can never tell either beginnings or endings. I could listen to your singing all day."

"Yes, we should be glad of something popular now—another song from you would be a relaxation," said Mrs. Arrowpoint, who had also come near with polite intentions.

"That must be because you are in a puerile state of culture, and have no breadth of horizon. I have just learned that. I have been taught how bad my taste is, and am feeling growing pains. They are never pleasant," said Gwendolen, not taking any notice of Mrs. Arrowpoint, and looking up with a bright smile at young Clintock.

Mrs. Arrowpoint was not insensible to this rudeness, but merely said, "Well, we will not press anything disagreeably:" and as there was a perceptible outrush of imprisoned conversation just then, and a movement of guests seeking each other, she remained seated where she was, and looked round her with the relief of the hostess at finding she is not needed.

. . . . .

About four o'clock wheels paused before the door, and there came one of those knocks with an accompanying ring which serve to magnify the sense of social existence in a region where the most enlivening signals are usually those of the muffin-man. All the girls were at home, and the two rooms were thrown together to make space for Kate's drawing, as well as a great length of embroidery which had taken the place of the satin cushions—a sort of *pièce de résistance* in the courses of needlework, taken up by any clever fingers that happened to be at liberty. It stretched across the front room picturesquely enough, Mrs. Meyrick bending over it at one corner, Mab in the middle, and Amy at the other end. Mirah, whose performances in point of sewing were on the makeshift level of the tailor-bird's, her education in that branch having been much neglected, was acting as reader to the party, seated on a camp-stool; in which position she also served Kate as model for a title-page vignette, symbolising a fair public absorbed in the successive volumes of the Family Tea-table. She was giving forth with charming distinctness the delightful Essay of Elia, *The Praise of Chimney-Sweeps*, and all were smiling over the "innocent blacknesses," when the imposing knock and ring called their thoughts to loftier spheres, and they looked up in wonderment.

"Dear me!" said Mrs. Meyrick; "can it be Lady Mallinger? Is there a grand carriage, Amy?"

"No—only a hansom cab. It must be a gentleman."

"The Prime Minister, I should think," said Kate, drily. "Hans says the greatest man in London may get into a hansom cab."

"Oh, oh, oh!" cried Mab. "Suppose it should be Lord Russell!"

The five bright faces were all looking amused when the old maid-servant bringing in a card distractedly left the parlour-door open, and there was seen bowing towards Mrs. Meyrick a figure quite unlike that of the respected Premier—tall and physically impressive even in his kid and kerseymere, with massive face, flamboyant hair, and gold spectacles: in fact, as Mrs Meyrick saw from the card, *Julius Klesmer.*

Even embarrassment could hardly have made the "little mother" awkward, but quick in her perceptions she was at once aware of the situation, and felt well satisfied that the great personage had come to Mirah instead of requiring her to come to him; taking it as a sign of active interest. But when he entered, the rooms shrank into closets, the cottage piano, Mab thought, seemed a ridiculous toy, and the entire family existence as petty and private as an establishment of mice in the Tuileries. Klesmer's personality, especially his way of glancing round him, immediately suggested vast areas and a multitudinous audience, and probably they made the usual scenery of his consciousness, for we all of us carry on our thinking in some habitual *locus* where there is a presence of other souls, and those who take in a larger sweep than their neighbours are apt to seem mightily vain and affected. Klesmer was vain, but not more so than many contemporaries of heavy aspect, whose vanity leaps out and startles one like a spear out of a walking-stick; as to his carriage and gestures, these were as natural to him as the length of his fingers; and the rankest affectation he could have shown would have been to look diffident and demure. While his grandiose air was making Mab feel herself a ridiculous toy to match the cottage piano, he was taking in the details around him with a keen and thoroughly kind sensibility. He remembered a home no larger than this on the outskirts of Bohemia; and in the figurative Bohemia too he had had large acquaintance with the variety and romance which belong to small incomes. He addressed Mrs. Meyrick with the utmost deference.

"I hope I have not taken too great a freedom. Being in the neighbourhood, I ventured to save time by calling. Our friend Mr. Deronda mentioned to me an understanding that I was to have the honour of becoming acquainted with a young lady here—Miss Lapidoth."

Klesmer had really discerned Mirah in the first moment of entering, but with subtle politeness he looked round bowingly at the three sisters as if he were uncertain which was the young lady in question.

"Those are my daughters: this is Miss Lapidoth," said Mrs. Meyrick, waving her hand towards Mirah.

"Ah," said Klesmer, in a tone of gratified expectation, turning a radiant smile and deep bow to Mirah, who, instead of being in the least taken by surprise, had a calm pleasure in her face. She liked the look of Klesmer, feeling sure that he would scold her, like a great musician and a kind man.

"You will not object to beginning our acquaintance by singing to me," he added, aware that they would all be relieved by getting rid of preliminaries.

"I shall be very glad. It is good of you to be willing to listen to me," said Mirah, moving to the piano. "Shall I accompany myself?"

"By all means," said Klesmer, seating himself, at Mrs. Meyrick's invitation, where he could have a good view of the singer. The acute little mother would not have acknowledged the weakness, but she really said to herself, "He will like her singing better if he sees her."

All the feminine hearts except Mirah's were beating fast with anxiety, thinking Klesmer terrific as he sat with his listening frown on, and only daring to look at him furtively. If he did say anything severe it would be so hard for them all. They could only comfort themselves with thinking that Prince Camaralzaman,[2] who had heard the finest things, preferred Mirah's singing to any other:—also she appeared to be doing her very best, as if she were more instead of less at ease than usual.

The song she had chosen was a fine setting of some words selected from Leopardi's grand Ode to Italy:—

> *O patria mia, vedo le mura e gli archi*
> *E le colonne e i simulacri e l'erme*
> *Torri degli avi nostri—*

This was recitative: then followed—

> *Ma la gloria non vedo—*

a mournful melody, a rhythmic plaint. After this came a climax of devout triumph—passing from the subdued adoration of a happy Andante in the words—

> *Beatissimi voi,*
> *Che offriste il petto alle nemiche lance*
> *Per amor di costei che al sol vi diede—*

to the joyous outburst of an exultant Allegro in—

> *Oh viva, oh viva:*
> *Beatissimi voi*
> *Mentre nel mondo si favelli o scriva.*[3]

2. Qamar-al-Zaman, a character in *The Arabian Nights;* the Meyrick girls' nickname for Daniel Deronda.

3.
> O my country, I see the walls and arches,
> The columns and statues and the
> Towers of our forefathers . . .
>
> But I do not see glory . . .
>
> Blessed are you
> Who offered your breast to enemy lances
> For love of those who gave you life . . .
>
> Hail to you,
> Most blessed
> As long as men shall speak or write.
>   (Giacomo Leopardi, "All'Italia" (1818), *Canti*, vol. 1.)

When she had ended, Klesmer said after a moment—

"That is Joseph Leo's[4] music."

"Yes, he was my last master—at Vienna: so fierce and so good," said Mirah, with a melancholy smile. "He prophesied that my voice would not do for the stage. And he was right."

"*Con*tinue, if you please," said Klesmer, putting out his lips and shaking his long fingers, while he went on with a smothered articulation quite unintelligible to the audience.

The three girls detested him unanimously for not saying one word of praise. Mrs. Meyrick was a little alarmed.

Mirah, simply bent on doing what Klesmer desired, and imagining that he would now like to hear her sing some German, went through Prince Radzivill's[5] music to Gretchen's songs in the Faust, one after the other, without any interrogatory pause. When she had finished he rose and walked to the extremity of the small space at command, then walked back to the piano, where Mirah had risen from her seat and stood looking towards him with her little hands crossed before her, meekly awaiting judgment; then with a sudden unknitting of his brow and with beaming eyes, he put out his hand and said abruptly, "Let us shake hands: you are a musician."

4. Leo is, like Klesmer himself, an invention of Eliot's.
5. Anton Heinrich Radziwill (1775–1833), composer and patron of music; his *Goethes Faust* was composed in 1819.

THE MUSIC OF THE FUTURE

5 Giuseppe Mazzini

An Italian patriot and revolutionary who was continually under sentence for conspiring to overthrow absolutist governments, Giuseppe Mazzini (1805–1872) spent much of his life abroad in exile, living sometimes in France, sometimes in Switzerland, and for a considerable time in England. His mind was seldom far from Italy, however, and he was a prolific essayist and propagandist for the unification of the Italian states and their liberation from foreign domination.

Mazzini's writings in the early nineteenth century look beyond Romanticism to a time when the energies of art and of culture as a whole would be turned toward the cause of political liberation and human moral development. In this process, he argued, national styles must fall away, leaving behind a genuinely European art. His *Filosofia della musica,* first published in a Parisian journal, presents an agenda for composers of the future along these lines, urging a synthesis of the best aspects of both warring musical factions, North and South.

In a later note to this text (1867), Mazzini celebrated the major operas of Giacomo Meyerbeer, proclaiming that here was discovered the prophet and precursor (though not yet the fulfillment) of the music of the future.

FROM *Philosophy of Music*
(1836)

Let us return to music, taking consolation for the terrible condition of current taste in the hopes emanating from this divine art, despite the depths to which it has currently sunk. Music, like woman, is so holy with anticipation and purification, that even when men sully it with prostitution, they cannot totally obliterate the aura of promise that crowns it. Even in the midst of that music which today we condemn, there is still a ferment of life that foretells new destinies, a new development, a new and more solemn mission. The image of beauty and of eternal harmony appears in it in fragments, but still it does appear. You might say that an angel, out of the abyss into which he has been thrown, still manages to address us as if from paradise. Perhaps in the future it will fall to woman and to music to carry a broader responsibility for resurrection than has so far been anticipated. Perhaps to music first, because music, speaking to all humanity in a single voice, will have the responsibility of initiating an idea which in turn will be interpreted and developed by the other arts. Music is the faith of a world whose poetry is one and the same as its philosophy. And great eras begin with faith. In any case, the initiative for the new musical

TEXT: *Filosofia della musica, e Estetica musicale del primo Ottocento, testi scelti* . . . , ed. Marcello de Angelis (Florence: Guaraldi, 1977), pp. 48–61, 76–77. Translation by Yvonne Freccero, with Giovanna Bellesia and John Sessions.

synthesis will come, unless I am mistaken, from Italy. The only possible contender would be Germany. But Germany, intent these days on applied knowledge, and weary from a long stretch of centuries spent in the strictly theoretical sphere of abstraction, has been forced inevitably into a reaction all the more violent for its late arrival, against the tendency toward mysticism that has dominated it totally until now. And the power to initiate an era in an art that is more spiritual than any other is forbidden to those who make common cause with materialism and even actively embrace it. Among us, these days, movement can only go in the opposite direction, and therefore we are in the very best condition for creation. Because whatever one may say—and although the Italians, a great many at least, even now deny it—surely all or almost all the origins of great things must arise from Italy.

Let us suppose that there is a rebirth of faith, that materialism is at an end, and that analysis, which is in sole control these days, has been confined to the role it was meant to fulfill, which is the verification and step-by-step application of a synthesis. Let us suppose that tastes evolve from the exhausted mission of the eighteenth century toward the ultimate future of the nineteenth. Let us suppose a holy enthusiasm, and a public ready for the artist—a condition without which there is nothing to be hoped for—which path should genius choose? For which problem should it seek the solution? And what will be these tendencies of the musical era that awaits initiation?—in other words, where are we? What limits have we reached? Only the knowledge of current tendencies, of limits reached, of the philosophical terms that define art, can reveal for us what is to be done, the secret of future art.

Inclinations are about as infinite as the talents that surround us, but a closer look reveals that they are all secondary and confined to questions of *form*, interesting in a superficial way, rather than focussing on the intimate life, the substance, the idea that is the soul of music. As far as the latter is concerned we find that all tendencies are reduced to two; all things are organized, properly speaking, into two primary groups, centering around two sovereign elements.

These are the two eternal elements of all things, the two principles constantly in operation, and one or the other of them is foremost in all the problems that have wearied the human mind for thousands of years; the two terms that in all matters end up in conflict, and whose continuing development in two converging lines, from century to century, define the subject matter of history: man and humanity, individual thought and social thought.

Hovering between these two principles, today as always, are science or systematic thought and Art which is its manifestation. Of the two tendencies produced by these terms, one makes the individual its center and revolves around him, while the other forgets the individual and obliterates him in the vast reaches of a concept of universal unity. One is nourished on analysis, the other on synthesis—both are exclusive and self-contained, and they have perpetuated to this day a controversy that divides human forces and impedes progress, since one, denying a common purpose to individual actions, is dragged into ruin through analysis of a materialist sort and the other, having lost itself in the paths of an unapplied synthesis, evaporates into vagueness, into the indefinite, into a sphere of mysticism unconducive to real achievements. Whoever settles this argument, bringing the two tendencies together in one purpose without repudiating either of the original terms, will have solved the problem. Eclecticism, which in recent times has misled the best minds, has done nothing but delineate the problem.

Demonstration of these two tendencies—in philosophy, in history, in literature, in the physical sciences, in all branches of intellectual development—is not within the scope of this work. Readers may do it for themselves, because it has never been more evident than today.

But in music, where, as I have said, the action of this general law has never been noticed, neither observed nor suspected, these tendencies are nevertheless even more noticeable than elsewhere. *Melody* and *harmony* are the two generative elements. The first represents individuality, the other social thought. In the perfect accord of these two basic terms of all music—and then in the consecration of this accord to a sublime purpose or a holy mission—lies the secret of Art, the concept of a European music which, consciously or unconsciously, we all invoke.

These days, corresponding to the two tendencies that hinge on one or the other of these elements, are two schools, two camps, you might say two distinct zones: the North and the South, German and Italian music. I know of no other music that exists by itself, independent in its essential concept from these two, nor do I believe that anyone else, even allowing for the delusions of patriotic pride, can find one.

Italian music is *melodic*[1] in the highest degree. Since the time when Palestrina translated Christianity into tones, and initiated the Italian school with his melodies, it has assumed and maintained this characteristic. The spirit of the Middle Ages breathes in it and inspires it. *Individuality*, meanwhile, as a theme that finds in Italy a more deeply felt and more vigorous expression than anywhere else, has generally speaking inspired our music, and dominates it entirely. The ego reigns, despotic and alone. It indulges itself; it obeys every whim of a will that brooks no opposition; it goes where it will and is spurred on by desire. Rational and consistent standards, a life that moves in a single

---

1. I am speaking of *predominant* characteristics in this rapid sketch of Italian and German music. Neither school could concentrate on one element so that the other were excluded, remaining subdued and almost supplementary. In Italian music, and particularly in the time of living masters, *harmony* often invades the work and outstrips its rival, just as in German music, particularly in Beethoven, *melody* often rises in divine expression above the characteristic harmony of the school. But these usurpations are only apparent; being brief, they interrupt but do not eliminate the domination of the other.

It is useless to point out the misunderstanding of someone who confuses *melody* with human intonation, and *harmony* with instrumentation. Obviously, even instrumentation can be *melodic*, and indeed it is most of the time in Rossini. [Au.]

direction, thoughtfully directed toward a purpose, these do not exist. What do exist are the powerful sensation, the rapid and violent outburst.

Italian music surrounds itself with concrete objects, receives the sensations that come from them, then sends them back embellished, made divine. Lyrical to the point of frenzy, passionate to the point of intoxication, volcanic like the land where it was born, brilliant as the sun that shines on that land, it darts about rapidly, paying little or no attention to whys and wherefores or to transitions, bounding from one thing to another, from sentiment to sentiment, from thought to thought, from ecstatic joy to disconsolate grief, from laughter to tears, from anger to love, from heaven to hell—and always with power and emotion, always stirred up in some way, a life with twice the intensity of other lives, a heart that beats feverishly. To it belongs inspiration: boundless inspiration, an inspiration that is eminently *artistic* rather than religious. Sometimes it prays—and when it glimpses a ray of light from heaven, from the soul, when it feels a breath of the great universe and prostrates itself in adoration, it is sublime. Its prayer is that of a saint, of someone in rapture, but briefly, and you feel that if it bows its head, the very next moment it may lift it in an attitude of freedom and independence; you feel that it has bent under the force of a passing enthusiasm, not the habit of an ingrained religious sentiment.

Religious beliefs live on a faith in something that exists beyond the visible world, on a longing for the infinite, and on a purpose and a mission that invade all of life and are apparent in the least little act. But Italian music has faith only in itself, has no purpose other than itself. *Art for Art* is the supreme rubric of Italian music. Hence the lack of unity, hence its fragmented, disconnected, and spasmodic progress. It hoards secrets of power that, if honed toward an end, would stir up all creation to achieve it. But where is this end? The lever is lacking the fulcrum, there is no bond to link the thousands of sensations represented by its melodies. Like Faust, it can say: I have traversed the entire universe in my flight; but in bits and pieces, analyzing one thing after another— but the soul, and the God of the universe, where are they?

For such music, as for every period, or people, or discipline that in the course of development represents and idolizes *individuality,* there necessarily had to appear a man who would sum up everything within himself, becoming its symbol and bringing it to completion.

And along came Rossini.

Rossini is a Titan, a powerful and daring Titan. Rossini is the Napoleon of a musical era. Careful examination reveals that Rossini has accomplished in music what romanticism accomplished in literature. He has decreed the independence of music. He has disavowed the principle of authority which the inept masses want to impose on the creative artist, and he has proclaimed the omnipotence of genius. When he came along the old rules weighed heavily on the head of the *artist,* just as theories of imitation and the stale Aristotelian unities of classicism stayed the hand of anyone who tried to write dramas or poems. And he became the champion of all those who groaned but did not dare to free themselves from that tyranny. He called for revolt, and he dared. That is supreme praise; perhaps if he had not dared—if when the graybeards croaked, *don't do it,* he had not had the courage to reply, *I will do it*—there would now be no hope for the rebirth of music out of the torpor that threatened to overtake it and make it sterile. Gathering inspiration from the fine effort of Mayer,[2] and from the genius that was stirring in his soul, Rossini broke the spell and ended the long slumber: music was saved. Because of him, we can talk today of a European musical initiative. Because of him we can, without presuming, have faith that this initiative will come from Italy and nowhere else.

It is no use, however, to exaggerate or misunderstand Rossini's role in the progress of the art; the mission he undertook does not escape the confines of the era which we declare extinct, or nearly so. It is a mission for a genius who *summarizes* but does not *initiate.* He did not change or destroy the long-standing characteristics of the Italian school: he reconsecrated them. He did not introduce a new element that abolished or dramatically changed the old one, he raised its dominant element to the highest possible level of development; he pushed it to its ultimate consequence; he reduced it to a formula and once more placed it on the throne from which the pedants had driven it, without considering that whoever destroys something has the responsibility to replace it with something better. And all those who still look on Rossini as the creator of a school or era of music, as the leader of a radical revolution in taste and in the destiny of art, are mistaken. They forget the condition music was in just before Rossini; they make the same mistake that was made about literary romanticism by those who wanted to find in it a faith, an organic theory, a new literary synthesis: what is worse, they perpetuate the past while proclaiming the future.

Rossini did not create, he restored. He rebelled, not against the generative element, not against the fundamental concept of Italian music, but rather on behalf of that concept, fallen into oblivion as it was through its loss of vitality; he rebelled against the dictates of the scholars and the servility of their disciples, and against the vacuum both groups conspired to create. He innovated, but more in *form* than in *substance,* more in his method of development and use of material than in underlying principle. He found new manifestations of the thought of the era; he translated it in a thousand different ways; he crowned it with such detailed work, with such fertile additions, with such decorative art, that while a few may be his peers none could outdo him. He exemplified and developed this thought and goaded it this way and that until it was exhausted. He did not surpass it.[3] More powerful in fantasy than in profound thought or

2. Apparently Johann Simon Mayr (1763–1845), whose operas were influential on Rossini's.
3. Yet he did surpass it occasionally: he exceeded it perhaps in *Moses* [i.e., *Mosè in Egitto*]; he went beyond, certainly, in the third act of *Otello,* that divine work, which belongs entirely to the new era, because of its height of dramatic expression, the aura of destiny that breathes through it, its amazing unity of inspiration. But I am speaking of a genre, of a predominant concept, not of one scene or one act, but of the entire work of Rossini. Certainly he anticipated the social music,

feeling, a genius of freedom rather than of synthesis, he may have glimpsed but did not embrace the future. Perhaps also he lacked that single-mindedness and high purpose that keeps its gaze on the generations to come rather than on its contemporaries; he sought fame, not glory; he sacrificed the god to the idol; he worshipped the effect, not the intent, not the mission. He was left with the ability to form a sect, but not to found a faith.

Where is the new element in Rossini, where the foundation of a new school? Where is there a single concept that dominates his artistic life, that unites his series of compositions into an epic? We must look for it in every scene, or rather in every piece, in every *motive* in his music; not in the system, not in his works, not in his entire output. The edifice he has erected, like that of Nimrod,[4] rends the sky; but there is within it, as in Nimrod's, a confusion of languages. *Individuality* is seated at the summit: free, unrestrained, fantastic, represented by a brilliant *melody,* palpable, unambiguous, like the sensation that suggested it.

Everything in Rossini is conspicuous, defined, prominent; the indefinite, the delicately shaded, the ethereal, which would seem to belong more particularly to the nature of music, have given way, almost taken flight, before the invasion of an impulsive style—sharp, assertive, provocative, tangible. You might say that Rossini's melodies were carved in bas-relief. You might say they had all been poured out from the artist's imagination under a Neapolitan summer sky, at noon, when the sun floods everything, when it beats down vertically and eliminates the body's shadow. It is a music without shade, without mysteries, without dusk. It gives expression to decisive passions decisively felt—anger, grief, love, vengeance, jubilation, despair—and all are set forth so that the soul of the listener is entirely passive: subjugated, spellbound, immobilized. There are few if any gradations of feeling, there is no breath of the invisible world around us. The instrumentation often hints at an echo of this world and appears to look at infinity; but almost always it retreats, *it is individualized,* and it too becomes melody. Rossini and the Italian school whose various explorations and systems he brought together and fused into one, together represent man without God, individual powers not harmonized by a supreme law, not ordered by a single purpose, not consecrated to an eternal faith.

German music proceeds along a different road. There you have God without man, his image on earth, an active and progressive creature called on to expound the thought whose symbol is the earthly universe. There you find temple, religion, altar, and incense; but the faith lacks its worshiper and its

---

the musical drama of the future. Where is there a genius who, coming at the end of an era, is not on occasion illuminated by the rays of the era about to come, who does not anticipate its thought for a few moments? But between the presentiment and the feeling, between instinctively intuiting an era and initiating it, is as great a difference as that which separates reality from uncertain hope. [Au.]

4. Nimrod (Genesis 10:8–12), "the first potentate on earth," whose empire included the city of Babel.

priest. *Harmonic* in the highest degree, it represents *social* thought, the general concept, the *idea,* but without the *individuality* that translates thought into action, that develops the idea in its various applications, that sets forth and symbolizes the idea. The ego is lost. The soul lives, but a life not of this world. As in a life of dreams, when the senses are silent and the spirit looks into another world, where everything is lighter, and the pace more rapid, and all the images float in the infinite, German music lulls our instincts and material powers and lifts up the soul, through vast lands, unknown but vaguely remembered—faint, revealed to you as if you had glimpsed them in your first infant visions, between maternal caresses, so that the tumult and the joys and sorrows of the earth vanish.

This music is supremely elegiac: a music of remembered desires, of melancholy hopes and of a sadness that cannot be comforted by human lips; a music of angels who have wandered from their heavenly dwelling. Its home is infinity, for which it longs. Like Northern poetry, where it is not led astray by the influence of a foreign school and preserves its primitive nature, German music passes lightly over earthly fields, skims over the material world, but keeps its eyes turned to heaven. You might say it only places a foot on the ground in order to leap. You might say it is like a young girl born for smiles who has not found an answering smile, one full of the spirit of love who has not found anything mortal that merits being loved, and who dreams of another heaven, another universe, in which there would be the form of a being who would answer her love, who would respond to her virgin smile, and whom she would adore without coming to know.

And this form, this type of immortal beauty, appears and reappears every so often in German music, but imaginary, vague, lightly outlined. Its melody is brief, hesitant, fleetingly drawn; and while Italian melody defines, integrates, and forces an emotion upon you, in this music it appears veiled, mysterious, barely enough to leave you with a memory and the need to recreate it, to recompose the image for yourself. The one drags you forcefully to the ultimate limits of passion, the other points the way and then leaves you. German music is a music of preparation, a deeply religious music, although of a religion that has no creed and so no active faith to be translated into deeds; no martyrdom, no victory. It stretches around you a chain of tone-gradations, masterfully linked; it embraces you with a musical wave of chords that soothe you, comfort you, awaken the heart. It rouses the imagination, rouses whatever faculties you possess: to what end?—the music ends and you sink back into the real world and the prosaic life that teems around you, bringing with you the awareness of a different world, seen from a distance but indeterminate—the sense of having touched the primal mysteries of a great initiation, never begun so no longer strong in will, no longer firm against the assaults of fortune. Italian music lacks the sanctifying concept of all efforts: the moral thought that stimulates the forces of the mind, the blessing of a mission. German music lacks the energy to carry it out, the actual instrument of the conquest; it lacks, not the sentiment, but the concrete form of the mission. Italian music is rendered barren by materialism; German music is uselessly consumed in mysticism.

Thus the two schools proceed as distinct and jealous rivals, and they remain, the one school preferred in the North, the other in the South. And the music we propose, European music, will not exist until the two are fused into one and take on a social purpose—until united in the awareness of unity, the two elements that today form two worlds join together to inspire one. The sanctity of the faith that distinguishes the German school will bless the power of action that vibrates in the Italian school, and musical expression will combine the two basic terms: individuality and the thought of the universe—God and man.

Is this a utopia?

Even Rossini's music was a utopia in the days of Guglielmi and Piccinni.[5] Even the hugely synthesizing poetry of Alighieri[6] was utopian, at a time when the art was confined to the ballads of the Provençal troubadours and the clumsy works of Guittone.[7] Who in those days would have predicted that a poet would arise who would join heaven and earth in his poems, whose language, form, and power would all burst forth out of nothing, thanks to his genius; who would concentrate in his verses the whole soul of the Middle Ages as well as the idea of the era to come; who would make of one poem a national and religious monument, visible to the most distant generations, a poet who, five centuries before its first indications and tentative developments, would impart to his works and incarnate in his life the principle of the Italian mission in Europe? Would the prediction have found believers or mockers in Italy? Yet Dante did appear and did lay the foundations; and from his works today are drawn the norms that regulate our reborn literature, and later, when Dante's works have readers more worthy of them, there will emerge the origin of entirely other concepts and omens of Italian destiny.

And when I pause at sunset, my soul weary of the present and disconsolate about the future, when I stand before one of those churches to which traditional ignorance has given the name Gothic, and contemplate the soul of Christianity pouring out of the building, and prayer arching up, winding around the spires of the columns, hurling itself over the pinnacles into the sky, and the blood of martyrs mixed with the colors of hope displayed to God like a pledge of faith through the long glazed windows, and the believer's spirit wandering in its longing for the infinite, under the deep and mysterious vaults of the cathedral, and the spirit of Christ descending from the immense dome to the sanctuary, spreading around the vast walls and embracing the entire church with his love and benediction, peopling it with his apostles, his saints and confessors to tell the faithful about the Christian tradition, the persecutions

---

5. Pier Alessandro Guglielmi (1728–1804) and Niccolò Piccinni (1728–1800), Italian opera composers.
6. That is, Dante Alighieri (1265–1321): medieval poet, author of *The Divine Comedy.*
7. Probably Guittone d'Arezzo (c. 1230–1294), whose obscure style of writing was characteristic of Italian poetry before the *dolce stil nuovo* and Dante.

endured, the examples of virtue, resignation, and sacrifice, and from time to time thundering out his laws upon the organ—well, then—and no matter how vast a mission the era will impose—I do not despair of art, neither of its power nor of the miracles that genius will draw forth from it.

What? A synthesis, an era, a religion is sculptured in stone: architecture has been able to summarize the dominant thought of eighteen centuries in a cathedral—can music not do as much? If the idea of a social art or literature is not rejected, why hesitate at the idea of a social music? The synthesis of an era is expressed in all its art forms, and its spirit dominates them all, especially synthetic and religious music which surpasses all the others by its very nature. Music begins where poetry leaves off, and proceeds directly according to general formulae while its sister arts must move from specific cases and subjects to reach that point. Will music, which is the algebra of the immanent soul of humanity, alone remain inaccessible to the European synthesis, a stranger in its own time, a lone flower plucked out of the crown that the universe weaves for its creator? And in the land of Porpora and Pergolesi, in the land that gave Martini to *harmony* and Rossini to *melody,* can we doubt that a genius will arise who will unite two schools and purify them by interpreting in notes the thought of which the nineteenth century is the initiator?

That genius will appear. When the time is ripe and there are believers to venerate creative works, he will most certainly appear. It is not for me to say how or by what path he will reach his goal. The ways of genius are hidden, like those of God who inspires him. Criticism can and should anticipate his birth—in general terms—and it should declare what the urgent needs of the time are, and how great. It should prepare the people and clear the way for him—nothing more; nor do I intend to overstep these limits.

Today I urge emancipation from Rossini and the musical era he represents. I urge us to believe that he did not begin a school but ended one—that a school has ended when, driven to its ultimate consequences, it has exhausted all of the vitality that has carried it to that point, and that whoever persists in the footsteps of Rossini is condemned to be no more than a satellite—more or less splendid, but forever a satellite. I urge us to believe that to be renewed music must become *spiritualized,* that to resurrect its strength it must be reconsecrated to a mission. For music not to be ruined by the useless or the strange it needs to connect, to unite this mission with the general mission of the arts of the era, and seek its character in the era itself. In other words, music must become social and identify with the progressive movement of the universe. And I urge you to believe that today it is not a question of perpetuating or restoring an *Italian school* but of deriving *from Italy* the foundations of a *European school of music.*

·   ·   ·   ·   ·

But . . . musical reform will be accomplished. When a school or a trend or an era is exhausted, when a course has been run and nothing remains but to retrace it, reform is imminent, inevitable, and certain, because human ability cannot retreat. Young artists should prepare themselves, like devotees of religious mysteries, for the initiation of a new school of music. We are at a *vigil of arms,* as soldiers used to assemble in silence and solitude, meditating on what they must undertake, on the breadth of the mission to which they must dedicate themselves the next day, and in the generous and fervent hope of a new dawn.

Young artists must exalt themselves with the study of national songs, of patriotic stories and the mysteries of poetry and of nature, to a broader horizon than that offered by the rule books and the ancient canons of art. Music is the fragrance of the universe, and to deal with it properly the artist must be immersed in love, in faith, in the study of the harmonies that float on earth and in the heavens, in the thought of the universe. He must become familiar with the music of the great, not just the great of one country, or one school, or one time, but with the great of all countries, all schools, and all times. Not to analyze and dissect them with the cold and ancient doctrines of the music professors, but to gather into himself the creative and unifying spirit that moves through these works; not to imitate them narrowly and slavishly, but to emulate them freely, linking each new work to theirs.

Young artists should sanctify their souls with enthusiasm, with the breath of that eternal poetry that materialism has hidden but not banished from our land, worshipping art as something holy, a link between man and heaven. They should adore art, establishing for it a high social purpose, dedicating it to moral regeneration, cherishing it in their breasts and in their life, bright, pure, uncontaminated by commerce, or frivolity, or by the many excrescences that spoil the beautiful world of creation. Inspiration will descend on them like an angel of life and harmony, and their tombs will be emblazoned with the blessings of the grateful generations who have benefited, something that is worth more than a thousand honors, more than anything, just as virtue outweighs fortune's riches, and self-regard is greater than praise, and love greater than all earthly power.

6 Richard Wagner

The Artwork of the Future belongs to the most critical period in Richard Wagner's life, the first years of his exile and of his residence in Zurich, the years between the end of his work on *Lohengrin* (1847) and the beginning of his work on the *Ring* (1853). During this lull in his artistic productivity, Wagner endeavored to come to terms with the problem of the opera and with himself;

the results of this soul-searching are his three capital essays—*Art and Revolution* (1849), *The Artwork of the Future* (1850), and *Opera and Drama* (1852)—and in a larger sense, the great music dramas of his maturity and old age. Three times, later on, he attempted to summarize the contents of these essays—first in *A Communication to My Friends* (1852), then in *"Music of the Future"* (1860), finally in *On the Destiny of Opera* (1869); in 1879, near the end of his life, he returned to the problem once more in a series of three further essays—*On the Writing of Poetry and Music, On the Writing of Operatic Poetry and Music in Particular,* and *On the Application of Music to the Drama.*

It is well known that the three major essays of Wagner's earlier years in Zurich were written under the immediate influence of the philosopher Ludwig Feuerbach (1804–1872), author of *The Essence of Christianity* (1841), whose repeated attacks upon orthodox theology had attracted the interest of Karl Marx and Friedrich Engels and had made him, somewhat to his astonishment, the idol of the "Young German" intellectuals sympathetic to the uprisings of 1849. In his autobiography, Wagner tells us himself that his acquaintance with Feuerbach's reputation dates from his last years in Dresden; traces of Feuerbach's influence have even been detected in Wagner's *Jesus of Nazareth,* a dramatic synopsis sketched at just this time. As to *The Artwork of the Future,* this essay owes its very title to Feuerbach's *Principles of the Philosophy of the Future* (1843), and in its original edition as a separate monograph it was introduced by a letter from Wagner to Feuerbach, beginning: "To no one but you, my dear sir, can I dedicate this work, for with it I give you back your own property."

In later life, after his conversion to Arthur Schopenhauer and to a more prudent political philosophy, Wagner did what he could to play down the revolutionary character of his earlier writings and to represent his youthful enthusiasm for Feuerbach as an unimportant passing phase. This is already evident to some extent in the summary incorporated in his *"Music of the Future."* It became still more evident with the publication of the third and fourth volumes of his *Collected Writings* in 1872; here the dedication to Feuerbach is silently suppressed, while the foreword to the third volume contains this apologia: "From my reading of several of the works of Ludwig Feuerbach, which held a lively interest for me at the time, I had taken over various designations for concepts which I then applied to artistic ideas to which they could not always clearly correspond. Herein I surrendered myself without critical reflection to a brilliant author who appealed to my mood of the moment, particularly in that he bade farewell to philosophy (in which he believed himself to have discovered nothing but disguised theology) and addressed himself instead to a view of human nature in which I was persuaded that I could recognize again the artistic man I had had in mind. Thus there arose a certain reckless confusion, which revealed itself in a hastiness and lack of clarity in the use of philosophical schemes." Wagner then goes on to criticize his earlier use of Feuerbach's terminology, particularly of the expressions "willfulness" *(Willkür)* and "instinct" *(Unwillkür),* for which he now suggests the substitution, by the reader, of Schopenhauer's "will" *(Wille)* and "conscious will" *(Verstandeswille).* Still more exaggerated is Wagner's account of his relation to Feuerbach in his posthumously published autobiography: "Before long," he says, "it had already become impossible for me to return to his writings, and I recall that his book *On the Essence of Religion,* which appeared soon after this, so repelled me by the monotony of its title that when Herwegh opened it for me I clapped it shut before his eyes." How far from the truth this is, can be gathered from Wagner's letter of June 8, 1853, addressed to the imprisoned Röckel, his fellow revolutionary, and accompanied by a copy of the book in question: "Feuerbach's book is to a certain extent a résumé of all that he has hitherto done in the field of philosophy. It is not one of his really celebrated works, such as *The Essence of Christianity* or *Thoughts upon Death and Immortality,* but it is a shortcut to a complete knowledge of his mental development and of the latest results of his speculations. I should be glad to think of you as strengthened and encouraged by contact with this clear, vigorous mind."

In *A Communication to My Friends,* speaking of the contradictions between his new theories and his earlier scores, Wagner has this to say: "The contradictions to which I refer will not even exist for the man who has accustomed himself to look at phenomena from the point of view of their development in time. The man who, in judging a phenomenon, takes this developmental factor into consideration will meet with contradictions only when the phenomenon in question is an unnatural, unreasonable one, set apart from space and time; to disregard the developmental factor altogether, to combine its various and clearly distinguishable phases, belonging to different times, into one indistinguishable mass, this is in itself an unnatural, unreasonable way of looking at things, one that can be adopted by our monumental-historical criticism, but not by the healthy criticism of a sympathetic and sensitive heart. . . . Critics who make a pretence of judging my artistic activity as a whole have sometimes proceeded in this uncritical, inattentive, and insensitive way; taking as relevant to their judgment views on the nature of art which I had made known from a standpoint arrived at only after a gradual and deliberate development, they have applied these views to the very artworks in which the natural developmental process that led me to the standpoint in question began. . . . It does not occur to them at all, when they compare the newly acquired standpoint with the older one left behind, that these are in fact two essentially different points of view, each one of them logically developed in itself, and that it would have been much better to have explained the new standpoint in the light of the old one than it was to judge the one abandoned in the light of the one adopted."

Wagner's objection is well taken. Yet later on, as we have seen, he was himself guilty of an uncritical procedure very similar to the one complained of here. Wagner too endeavored to combine two clearly distinguishable phases of his development, the middle and the late, into one indistinguishable mass. But whereas his critics had sought, as he puts it, "to kill two flies at one blow," Wagner seeks to prove the essential identity of two points of view that are essentially opposed.

Friedrich Wilhelm Nietzsche, in his *Genealogy of Morals* (1887), sums up Wagner's dilemma with telling irony: "Think of the enthusiasm with which Wagner formerly followed in the footsteps of the philosopher Feuerbach: Feuerbach's expression 'healthy sensuality'—to Wagner, as to many Germans ('Young Germans,' they called themselves), this sounded in the thirties and forties like the word of redemption. Did he finally *learn* a different view? For it seems at least that at the end he wished to *teach* a different one."

FROM *The Artwork of the Future*
(1850)

MAN AND ART IN GENERAL

Nature, Man, and Art

As man is to nature, so art is to man.

When nature had of itself developed to that state which encompassed the conditions for man's existence, then man arose of himself; once human life engenders of itself the conditions for the appearance of the artwork, the artwork comes into being of itself.

Nature begets and shapes aimlessly and instinctively, according to need, hence of necessity; this same necessity is the begetting and shaping force in human life; only what is aimless and instinctive arises from genuine need, and only in need lies the cause of life.

Natural necessity man recognizes only in the continuity of natural phenomena; until he grasps this continuity, he thinks nature willful.

From that moment in which man became sensible of his divergence from nature and thereby took the first step of all in his development as man, freeing himself from the unconsciousness of natural animal life to pass over into conscious life—when he thus placed himself in opposition to nature and when, as an immediate result of this, his sense of his dependence on nature led to the development in him of thought—from that moment, as the first assertion of consciousness, error began. But error is the father of knowledge, and the history of the begetting of knowledge from error is the history of the human race from the myth of primeval time to the present day.

Man erred from the time when he placed the cause of natural phenomena outside the state of nature itself, assumed for material phenomena an ideal origin, namely a willful origin of his own conceiving, and took the infinite continuity of nature's unconscious and purposeless activity for the purposeful behavior of will's noncontinuous, finite manifestations. Knowledge consists in the correction of this error, this correction in the perception of necessity in those phenomena for which we had assumed a willful origin.

Through this knowledge nature becomes conscious of self—to be precise, in man, who arrived at his knowledge of nature only through his distinction between self and nature, which he thus made an object. But this distinction disappears again at the moment when man recognizes nature's state as identical with his own; recognizes the same necessity in all that genuinely exists and

TEXT: *Das Kunstwerk der Zukunft. Sämtliche Schriften und Dichtungen*, 6th ed., Leipzig, 1912–14. Wagner divides the essay into five chapters; the present abridged translation includes chapter 1, sections 1 and 6; chapter 2, section 4 abbreviated; chapter 4, abbreviated. Translation by Oliver Strunk.

lives, hence in human existence no less than in natural existence; and recognizes not only the connection of the natural phenomena with one another, but also his own connection with them.

If, through its connection with man, nature attains now to consciousness, and if the activity of this consciousness is to be human life itself—as though a representation, a picture, of nature—then human life itself attains to understanding through science, which makes of human life in turn an object of experience. But the activity of the consciousness won through science, the representation of the life made known through this activity, the copy of its necessity and truth is *art*.[1]

Man will not be that which he can and should be until his life is a faithful mirror of nature, a conscious pursuit of the only real necessity, *inner natural necessity*, not a subordination to an *outer* imagined *force*, imitating imagination, and hence not necessary but *willful*. Then man will really be man; thus far he has always merely existed by virtue of some predicate derived from religion, nationality, or state. In the same way, art too will not be that which it can and should be until it is or can be a faithful, manifestly conscious copy of genuine man and of the genuine, naturally necessary life of man, in other words, until it need no longer borrow from the errors, perversities, and unnatural distortions of our modern life the conditions of its being.

Genuine man, therefore, will not come into being until his life is shaped and ordered by true human nature and not by the willful law of state; genuine art will not live until its shapings need be subject only to the law of nature and not to the despotic caprice of fashion. For just as man becomes free only when he becomes joyously conscious of his connection with nature, so art becomes free only when it has no longer to be ashamed of its connection with life. Only in joyous consciousness of his connection with nature does man overcome his dependence on it; art overcomes its dependence on life only in its connection with the life of genuine, free men.

•   •   •   •   •

A STANDARD FOR THE ARTWORK OF THE FUTURE

It is not the individual mind, striving through art for fulfillment in nature, that has the power to create the art work of the future; only the collective mind, satisfied in life, has this power. But the individual can form an idea of it, and it is precisely the character of his striving—his striving for *nature*—which prevents this idea from being a mere fancy. He who longs to return to nature and who is hence unsatisfied in the modern present, finds not only in the totality of nature, but above all in *man's nature*, as it presents itself to him historically, those images which, when he beholds them, enable him to reconcile himself to life in general. In this nature he recognizes an image of all future things, already formed on a small scale; to imagine this scale expanded to its

---

1. Art in general, that is, or the art of the future in particular. [Au.]

furthest compass lies within the conceptual limits of the impulse of his need for nature.

History plainly presents two principal currents in the development of mankind—the *racial-national* and the *unnational-universal.* If we now look forward to the completion of this second developmental process in the future, we have plainly before our eyes the completed course of the first one in the past. To what heights man has been able to develop, subjected to this first, almost directly formative influence—insofar as racial origin, linguistic affiliation, similarity of climate, and the natural character of a common native land permitted him to yield unconsciously to nature's influence—we have every reason to take the keenest pleasure in acknowledging. In the natural morality of all peoples, insofar as they include the normal human being—even those cried down as rawest—we learn for the first time to recognize the truth of human nature in its full nobility, its genuine beauty. Not *one* genuine virtue has been adopted by any religion whatever as a divine command which had not been included of itself in this natural morality; not *one* genuinely human concept of right has been developed by the later civilized state—and then, unfortunately, to the point of complete distortion!—which had not already been given positive expression in this natural morality; not *one* discovery genuinely useful to the community has been appropriated by later culture—with arrogant ingratitude!—which had not been derived from the operation of the native intelligence of the guardians of this natural morality.

That *art* is not an *artificial* product—that the need of art is not one willfully induced, but rather one native to the natural, genuine, unspoiled human being—who demonstrates this more strikingly than precisely these peoples? Indeed, from what circumstance could our mind deduce the demonstration of art's necessity, if not from the perception of this artistic impulse and its splendid fruits among these naturally developed peoples, among the people in general? Before what phenomenon do we stand with a more humiliating sense of the impotence of our frivolous culture than before the art of the *Hellenes?* To this, to this art of all-loving Mother Nature's favored children, those most beautiful human beings whose proud mother holds them up to us, even in these nebulous and hoary days of our present fashionable culture, as an undeniable and triumphant proof of what she can do—to the splendid art of the Greeks we look, to learn from intimate understanding of it how the artwork of the future must be constituted! Mother Nature has done all she could—she has borne the Hellenes, nourished them at her breasts, formed them through her maternal wisdom; now she sets them before us with maternal pride and out of maternal love calls to us all: "This I have done for you; now, out of love for yourselves, do what you can!"

Thus it is our task to make of *Hellenic* art the altogether *human* art; to remove from it the conditions under which it was precisely a *Hellenic,* and not an altogether *human* art; to widen the *garb of religion,* in which alone it was a communal Hellenic art, and after removing which, as an egoistic individual art species, it could no longer fill the need of the community, but only that of luxury—however beautiful!—to widen this garb of the specifically *Hellenic religion* to the bond of the religion of the future—that of *universality*—in order to form for ourselves even now a just conception of the artwork of the future. Yet, unfortunate as we are, it is precisely the power to close this bond, this *religion of the future,* that we lack, for after all, no matter how many of us may feel this urge to the artwork of the future, we are *singular* and *individual.* An artwork is religion brought to life; religions, however, are created, not by the artist, but by the *folk.*

Let us, then, be content that for the present—without egoistic vanity, without wishing to seek satisfaction in any selfish illusion whatsoever, but with sincere and affectionate resignation to the hope for the artwork of the future—we test first of all the nature of the art varieties which today, in their dismembered condition, make up the present general state of art; that we brace ourselves for this test by a glance at the art of the Hellenes; and that we then boldly and confidently draw our conclusions as to the *great universal artwork of the future!*

• • • • •

THE ART OF TONE

The sea divides and connects the continents; thus the art of tone divides and connects the two extreme antitheses of human art, the arts of dancing and of poetry.

It is man's *heart;* the blood, circulating from this center, gives to the flesh, turned outward, its warm, lively color—at the same time it nourishes the brain nerves, tending inward, with waves of resilient energy. Without the activity of the heart, the activity of the brain would remain a mere mechanical performance, the activity of the body's external organs equally mechanical and unfeeling. Through the heart, the intellect is made sensible of its relation to the body as a whole—the mere man of the senses attains to intellectual activity.

But the organ of the heart is *tone,* and its artistically conscious speech is the *art of tone.* This is the full, flowing heart-love that ennobles sensual pleasure and humanizes spiritual thought. Through the art of tone, the arts of poetry and dancing understand each other; in the one there blend in affectionate fusion the laws governing the manifestations natural to the others—in the one the will of the others becomes instinctive will, the measure of poetry and the beat of dancing become the inevitable rhythm of the heartthrob.

If music receives from its sister arts the conditions of its manifestation, it gives these back to them, made infinitely beautiful, as the conditions of their manifestation; if dancing supplies music with its law of motion, music returns it in the form of rhythm, spiritually and sensually embodied as a measure for ennobled and intelligible movement; if poetry supplies music with its meaningful series of clear-cut words, intelligibly united through meaning and measure as material bodies, rich in idea, for the consolidation of its infinitely fluid tonal element, music returns this ordered series of quasi-intellectual, unfulfilled speech-sounds—indirectly representative, concentrated as image but not yet as immediate, inevitably true expression—in the form of *melody,* directly addressed to feeling, unerringly vindicated and fulfilled.

In musically animated *rhythm* and *melody,* dancing and poetry regain their own being, sensually objectified and made infinitely beautiful and capable; they recognize and love each other. But rhythm and melody are the *arms* with which Music encircles her sisters in affectionate entwinement; they are the *shores* by means of which she, the *sea,* unites two continents. Should the sea recede from the shores, should the abysmal waste spread out between it and them, no jaunty sailing ship will any longer range from the one continent to the other; they will forever remain divided—unless mechanical inventions, perhaps railroads, succeed in making the waste passable; then, doubtless, one will also pass clean across the sea in steamships; the breath of the all-animating breeze will give place to the puff of the machine; what difference need it make that the wind naturally blows eastward?—the machine clatters westward, precisely where we wish to go; thus the ballet maker sends across the steam-conquered sea of music to the poetry continent for the program of his new pantomime, while the stage piece fabricator fetches from the dancing continent as much leg seasoning as he happens to need to liven up a stale situation. Let us see what has happened to Sister Music since the death of all-loving Father *Drama!*

Not yet may we give up our figure of the *sea* as music's being. If *rhythm* and *melody* are the shores at which the tonal art meets with and makes fruitful the two continents of the arts primevally related to it, then tone itself is the primeval fluid element, and the immeasurable expanse of this fluid is the sea of *harmony.* Our eye is aware only of its surface; its depth only our heart's depth comprehends. Up from its bottom, dark as night, it spreads out to its mirroring surface, bright as the sun; from the one shore radiate on it the rings of rhythm, drawn wider and wider—from the shadowy valleys of the other shore rises the longing breeze which agitates the placid surface in waves of melody, gracefully rising and falling.

Into this sea man dives to yield himself again, radiant and refreshed, to the light of day; he feels his heart expand with wonder when he looks down into these depths, capable of unimaginable possibilities, whose bottom his eye is never to fathom, whose fathomlessness fills him accordingly with astonishment and forebodings of the infinite. This is the depth and infinity of nature itself, which veils from man's searching eye the impenetrable mystery of its budding, begetting, and longing, precisely because the eye can comprehend only what has become visible—the budded, the begotten, the longed for. This nature is in turn none other than the *nature of the human heart itself,* which encompasses the feelings of love and longing in their most infinite being, which is itself love and longing, and which—since in its insatiable longing it desires itself alone—grasps and comprehends itself alone.

• • • • •

But in nature everything immeasurable seeks its measure, everything limitless draws limits for itself, the elements concentrate themselves at last as definite phenomena; thus also the boundless sea of Christian longing found the new coastland against which it might break its impatience. There on the far horizon, where we had fondly imagined the entrance into the limitless heaven-space, always sought but never found, there at last the boldest of all navigators discovered land—inhabited by peoples—actual, blissful land. Through his discovery the wide ocean was not only measured, but also made for mankind an inland sea about which the coasts spread themselves out only in inconceivably wider circles. But if Columbus taught us to sail the ocean and thus to connect all the earth's continents; if through his discovery the shortsighted national man has, from the point of view of world history, become the all-seeing universal man—has become man altogether; so through the hero who sailed the wide shoreless sea of absolute music to its limits were won the new undreamed-of coasts which now no longer divide this sea from the old primevally human continents, but *connect* them for the newborn fortunate artistic humanity of the future. This hero is none other than—*Beethoven.*[2]

When Music freed herself from the round of her sisters—just as her frivolous sister, Dancing, had taken from her the rhythmic measure—she took with her from her brooding sister, Poetry, as an indispensable, immediate life condition, the *word;* not by any means, however, the human creative, ideally poetic word, but only the materially indispensable word, the concentrated tone. If she had relinquished the rhythmic beat to her parting sister, Dancing, to use as she pleased, she now built herself up solely through the word, the word of Christian faith, that fluid, spineless, evanescent thing which soon, gladly and unresistingly, placed itself altogether in her power. The more the word took refuge in the mere stammering of humility, the mere lisping of implicit, childlike love, the more inevitable was Music's recognition of her need to shape herself from the inexhaustible depths of her own fluid being. The struggle for such a shaping is the building up of *harmony.*

Harmony grows from the bottom up as a true column of related tonal materials, fitted together and arranged in strata laid one above another. The ceaseless changing of such columns, constantly rising up anew, each one adjoining another, constitutes the sole possibility of absolute harmonic movement on a horizontal plane. The perception of the need to care for the beauty of this movement on a horizontal plane is foreign to the nature of absolute harmony; harmony knows only the beauty of the changing play of the colors of its columns, not the charm of their orderly arrangement as perceived in time—for this is the work of rhythm. The inexhaustible many-sidedness of this changing

---

2. See *Oper und Drama,* chap. 1, sec. 5 (or, as translated by William Ashton Ellis [*Richard Wagner's Prose Works* (London, 1893)], Part I, pp. 70–71) where Wagner returns to this comparison of Beethoven to Columbus and develops it further.

play of colors is, on the other hand, the eternally productive source from whence harmony, in boundless self-satisfaction, derives the power to present itself unceasingly as new; the breath of life, moving and animating this restless change—which, in its turn is willfully self-conditioning—is the nature of tone itself, the breath of the impenetrable, all-powerful longing of the heart. The realm of harmony, then, knows no beginning or end; is like the objectless and self-consuming fervor of the temperament which, ignorant of its source, remains itself alone; is desiring, longing, raging, languishing—*perishing*, that is, dying without having satisfied itself in an object—dying, in other words, without dying; and hence, again and again, returns to self.

As long as the word was in power, it ruled beginning and end; when it sank to the fathomless bottom of harmony, when it remained only a "groaning and sighing of the soul"—as at the fervent height of Catholic church music—then, at the topmost stratum of those harmonic columns, the stratum of unrhythmic melody, the word was willfully tossed as though from wave to wave, and harmony, with its infinite possibilities, had now to lay down for itself self-derived laws for its finite manifestation. The nature of harmony corresponds to no other capacity of man as artist; it sees itself reflected, neither in the physically determined movements of the body, nor in the logical progression of thought; it can conceive its just measure, neither, as thought does, in the recognized necessity of the world of material phenomena, nor, as bodily movement does, in the presentation, as perceived in time, of its instinctive, richly conditioned character; it is like a natural force, apprehended, but not comprehended, by man. From out its own fathomless depths, from an outer—not inner—necessity to limit itself for positive finite manifestation, harmony must shape for itself the laws it will obey. These laws of harmonic succession, based on relationship, just as the harmonic columns, or harmonies, were themselves formed from the relationship of tonal materials, combine now as a just measure, which sets a beneficial limit to the monstrous range of willful possibilities. They permit the widest possible selection from out the sphere of harmonic families, expand to the point of free choice the possibility of connections through elective relationship with members of distant families, demand above all, however, a strict conformity to the house rules of the family momentarily chosen and an implicit acceptance of them for the sake of a salutary end. To postulate or to define this end—in other words, the just measure of the expansion of the musical composition in time—lies beyond the power of the innumerable rules of harmonic decorum; these, as that part of music which can be scientifically taught or learned, while they can separate the fluid tonal mass of harmony, dividing it into bounded smaller masses, cannot determine the just measure of these bounded masses in time.

If music, grown to harmony, could not possibly go on to derive from itself its law of expansion in time, once the limiting power of speech had been swallowed up, it was obliged to turn to those remnants of the rhythmic beat that dancing had left behind for it; rhythmic figures had to enliven the harmony;

their alternation, their return, their division and union had to affect the fluid expanse of harmony as the word had originally affected tone, concentrating it and bringing it to a definitely timed conclusion. This rhythmic enlivening, however, was not based on any inner necessity, crying out for purely human presentation; its motive power was not the man of feeling, thought, and will as he reveals himself in speech and bodily movement, but an *outer* necessity which harmony, demanding an egoistic conclusion, had made its own. This rhythmic alternation and shaping, not motivated by an inner necessity, could therefore be enlivened only according to willful laws and discoveries. These laws and discoveries are those of *counterpoint.*

Counterpoint, in its various progeny, normal and abnormal, is the artificial play of art with art, the mathematics of feeling, the mechanical rhythm of egoistic harmony. With its discovery abstract music was so pleased that it gave itself out as the one and only absolute and self-sufficient art—as the art owing its existence, not to any human need whatever, but simply to *itself,* to its divine and absolute nature. Quite naturally, the willful man considers himself the one man absolutely justified. Music, to be sure, owed to its arbitrary will alone only its seeming independence, for these tone-mechanical, contrapuntal pieces of art handiwork were altogether incapable of filling a *spiritual need.* In its pride, then, music had become its own direct antithesis; from a concern of the *heart* it had become a concern of the *mind,* from an expression of the boundless spiritual longing of the Christian it had become a balance sheet of the modern money market.

The living breath of the human voice, eternally beautiful and instinctively noble as it burst forth from the breast of the living folk, always young and fresh, blew this contrapuntal house of cards to the four winds. The *folk tune,* still true to self in undistorted grace—the *song* with positive limits, intimately entwined and one with poetry—lifted itself up on its elastic pinions into the regions of the scientifically musical world, with its need for beauty, and announced a joyous redemption. This world wished once more to set forth *men,* to cause men—not reeds—to sing; to this end it took possession of the folk tune and constructed from it the *operatic aria.* Just as the art of dancing had taken possession of the folk dance, to refresh itself, as it required, at this source and to employ it, as fashion dictated, in artistic combination, so also the elegant art of opera dealt with the folk tune; it now grasped, not the *whole* man, to indulge him artistically to the full according to his natural need, but only the *singing* man—and in the tune he sang, not the folk poem with its innate creative power, but only the melodious tune, abstracted from the poem, to which it now adapted as it pleased fashionably conventional, intentionally meaningless literary phrases; it was not the throbbing heart of the nightingale, but only its throbbing throat, that it understood and sought to imitate. Just as the art dancer trained his legs in the most varied and yet most uniform bends, twists, and whirls to vary the folk dance, which he could not of himself develop further, so the art singer trained his throat in endless ornaments and scrollwork of all sorts to paraphrase and change the tune taken from the lips of the folk, which he could from its nature never create anew; thus the place which contrapuntal cleverness had vacated was taken only by a mechanical dexterity of another kind. Here we need not characterize at greater length the repulsive, indescribably disgusting perversion and distortion of the folk tune as manifested in the modern operatic aria—for it is in point of fact only a mutilated folk tune, not by any means an original invention—as, in derision of all nature, of all human feeling, it frees itself from any linguistically poetic basis and, as a lifeless, soulless toy of fashion, tickles the ear of the idiotic world of the opera house; we need only admit with sorrowful sincerity that our modern public actually takes it for the whole of music.

But remote from this public and the makers and sellers of fashionable wares who serve it, the innermost being of music was to soar up from its bottomless depths, with all the undiminished abundance of its untried capacity, to a redemption in the radiance of the universal, *single* art of the future, and was to take this flight from that bottom which is the bottom of all purely human art—that of *plastic bodily movement,* represented in musical *rhythm.*

If, in the lisping of the stereotyped Christian word, eternally and eternally repeated to the point of utter thoughtlessness, the *human voice* had at length completely taken refuge in a merely sensual and fluid tone device by means of which alone the art of music, wholly withdrawn from poetry, continued to present itself, the tone devices, mechanically transmitted at its side as voluptuous accompaniments of the art of dancing, had developed an increasingly heightened capacity for expression. To these devices, the bearers of the dance tune, *rhythmic melody* had been assigned as an exclusive possession, and since, in their combined effect, these readily absorbed the element of Christian harmony, all responsibility for music's further development *from within itself* devolved on them. The *harmonized dance* is the basis of the richest artwork of the modern *symphony.* This dance made in its turn an appetizing morsel for the counterpoint machine, which freed it from its obedient devotion to its mistress, the corporeal art of dancing, and caused it now to leap and turn at *its* command. Yet the warm life breath of the natural folk tune had only to inspire the leather harness of this dance, trained up in counterpoint, and it became at once the living flesh of the humanly beautiful artwork. This artwork, in its highest perfection, is the *symphony of Haydn, Mozart, and Beethoven.*

In the symphony of *Haydn,* the rhythmic dance melody moves with all the fresh serenity of youth; its interweavings, dissolvings, and recombinings, though carried out with the utmost contrapuntal skill, reveal themselves scarcely any longer as products of a thus skillful process, but rather as proper to the character of a dance governed by highly imaginative rules, so warmly are they permeated by the breath of genuinely and joyously human life. The middle movement of the symphony, in a more moderate tempo, we see assigned by Haydn to the swelling breadth of the simply melodious folk tune; following the rules of melos peculiar to singing, he expands this, intensifying it in higher flights and enlivening it in repetitions many-sided in their expression. The melody thus conditioned was elemental to the symphony of *Mozart,* with his wealth of song and delight in singing. He inspired his instruments with the ardent breath of the *human voice,* to which his genius was overwhelmingly inclined. The rich, indomitable tide of harmony he brought to bear on melody's heart, as though restlessly anxious to give synthetically to the purely instrumental melody that depth of feeling and fervor which, in the innermost heart, makes of the natural human voice an inexhaustible source of expression. As to all those things in his symphonies which lay more or less remote from the satisfying of this, his primary aim, if Mozart to a certain extent merely dispatched them with uncommonly skillful contrapuntal treatment according to the traditional usage, becoming stable even in him, he intensified the capacity of the purely instrumental for singing expression to such a point that it could encompass, not only serenity and placid easy intimacy, as had been the case with Haydn, but also the whole depth of the heart's infinite longing.

The immeasurable capacity of instrumental music for the expression of impulses and desires of elemental intensity was opened up by *Beethoven.* He it was who released to unrestricted freedom the innermost being of Christian harmony, that fathomless sea so boundlessly vast, so restlessly mobile. Borne by instruments alone, the *harmonic melody*—for thus we must call the melody isolated from the spoken line, to distinguish it from the rhythmic dance melody—was capable of the most unlimited expression and of the widest possible treatment. In long connected sequences and in larger, smaller, indeed smallest fragments, it became, under the poetic hands of the master, the sounds, syllables, words, and phrases of a language which could express the unheard, the unsaid, the unuttered.

• • • • •

What inimitable art Beethoven employed in his C-minor Symphony to guide his ship out of the ocean of endless longing into the harbor of fulfillment! He succeeded in intensifying the expression of his music almost to the point of moral resolve, yet was unable to proclaim this resolve itself. Without moral support, after each exertion of will, we are alarmed at the prospect that we may quite as well be headed, not for victory, but for relapse into suffering; indeed, such a relapse must seem to us rather more necessary than the morally unmotivated triumph, which—not a necessary achievement, but a willful gift of grace—can hence not lift us up or satisfy us *morally,* after the longing of the heart, as we require.

Who was less satisfied by this victory than Beethoven himself, may we presume? Was he tempted to another of this kind? The thoughtless army of his imitators, no doubt, who, having survived the tribulation of minor, concoct continual triumphs for themselves out of the glorious jubilation of major—but not the chosen master who was in his works to write the *world history of music.*

With reverent awe he refrained from plunging himself again into that sea of boundless and insatiable longing, bending his steps rather toward those light-hearted, vigorous beings whom he saw jesting, dancing, and wooing in the green meadows at the edge of the fragrant woods, spread out under sunny skies. There, in the shadow of the trees, to the rustling of the foliage and the familiar rippling of the brook, he made a salutary covenant with nature; there he felt himself a man, his longing driven back into his breast before the power of the sweet inspiring *prospect*. In gratitude to this prospect, in faith and all humility, he named the single movements of the composition thus inspired for the scenes from life whose aspect had summoned them forth; the whole he called *Recollections of Country Life*.

And yet they were in truth no more than recollections—images, not immediate and concrete reality. Toward this reality, however, he was impelled with all the force of necessary artist's longing. To give his tonal forms that concentration, that immediately perceptible, sure, and concrete solidity, which, to his joy and comfort, he had observed in natural phenomena—this was the generous spirit of that joyous urge that created for us the incomparably magnificent A-major Symphony. All violence, all longing and storming of the heart, have turned here to the rapturous exuberance of joy which carries us along in bacchanalian insistence through all the realms of nature, through all the streams and seas of life, self-confidently exultant everywhere we tread to the bold measure of this human dance of the spheres. This symphony is the very *apotheosis of the dance;* it is the highest being of the dance, the most blissful act of bodily movement, ideally embodied, as it were, in tone. Melody and harmony fill out together the bony frame of rhythm with firm human figures, slender and voluptuous, which almost before our eyes, here with supple giant limbs, there with delicate elastic flexibility, join the round to which the immortal melody sounds on and on, now charming, now bold, now serious,[3] now boisterous, now thoughtful, now exultant, until, in the last whirling of desire, a jubilant kiss brings to an end the last embrace.

And yet these blissful dancers were but tonally represented, tonally imitated beings! Like another Prometheus, forming men from *clay (Thon)*, Beethoven had sought to form men from *tone (Ton)*. Neither from clay nor tone, however, but from both substances at once must man, the likeness of life-giving Zeus, be created. If the creatures of Prometheus were present to the *eye* alone, Beethoven's were so only to the *ear. But only there where eye and ear mutually assure each other of his presence do we have the whole artistic man.*

Where indeed should Beethoven have found those beings to whom he might

3. To the rhythm of the second movement, solemnly striding along, a secondary theme lifts up its longing plaint; about that rhythm, whose steady step is heard unceasingly throughout the whole, this yearning melody entwines itself, as does about the oak the ivy, which, but for its encircling of the powerful trunk, would curl and wind chaotically along the ground, luxuriantly forlorn, but which now, as a rich ornament of the rough oak's bark, gains sure and substantial form from the solidity of the tree itself. With what want of discernment this deeply significant discovery of Beethoven's has been exploited by our modern composers of instrumental music, with their eternal "secondary theme-making." [Au.]

have offered his hand across the element of his music? Those beings with hearts so open that he might have let the all-powerful stream of his harmonious tones flood into them? With forms so vigorously beautiful that his melodious rhythms might have *borne* them, not *tread* them underfoot? Alas, no brotherly Prometheus, who might have shown such beings to him, came to his help from any side! He had himself to begin by discovering the *land of the man of the future.*

From the shores of dancing he plunged again into that endless sea from out whose depths he had once saved himself on these same shores, into the sea of insatiable heart's longing. But on this stormy voyage he set out aboard a strong-built ship, firmly joined as though by giant hands; with a sure grasp he bent the powerful tiller; he *knew* his journey's goal and was resolved to reach it. What he sought was not the preparation of imaginary triumphs for himself, not to sail back idly into the home port after boldly surmounted hardships; he sought to bound the limits of the ocean, to find the land which needs must lie beyond the watery wastes.

Thus the master forced his way through the most unheard-of possibilities of absolute tonal language—not by hurriedly stealing past them, but by proclaiming them completely, to their last sound, from his heart's fullest depths—until he reached that point at which the navigator begins to sound the sea's depths with his lead; at which he touches solid bottom at ever increasing heights as the strands of the new continent reach toward him from afar; at which he must decide whether to turn about into the fathomless ocean or whether to drop anchor in the new banks. But it was no rude hankering for the sea that had urged the master on to this long voyage; he wished and had to land in the new world, for it was to this end that the voyage had been undertaken. Resolutely he threw out his anchor, and this anchor was the *word.* This word, however, was not that willful, meaningless word which the fashionable singer chews over and over as the mere gristle of the vocal tone; it was the necessary, all-powerful, all-uniting word in which the whole stream of full heartfelt emotion is poured out; the safe harbor for the restless wanderer; the light lighting the night of endless longing; the word redeemed humanity proclaims from out the fullness of the world's heart; the word which Beethoven set as a crown upon the summit of his creations in tone. This word was— "*Joy!*" And with this word he called to all mankind: "*Be embraced, ye countless millions! And to all the world this kiss!*" And *this* word will become the language of the *artwork of the future.*

This *last symphony* of Beethoven's is the redemption of music out of its own element as a *universal art.* It is the *human* gospel of the art of the future. Beyond it there can be no *progress,* for there can follow on it immediately only the completed artwork of the future, *the universal drama,* to which Beethoven has forged for us the artistic key.

Thus from within itself music accomplished what no one of the other arts was capable of in isolation. Each of these arts, in its barren independence, helped itself only by taking and egoistic borrowing; not one was capable of being *itself* and of weaving from within itself the all-uniting bond. The art of tone, by being wholly *itself* and by moving from within its own primeval element, attained strength for the most tremendous and most generous of all self-sacrifices—that of self-control, indeed of self-denial—thus to offer to its sister arts a redeeming hand. Music has proved itself the *heart,* connecting head and limbs, and, what is not without significance, it is precisely music which, in the modern present, has spread to so unusual an extent through every branch of public life.

To form a clear conception of the *thoroughly inconsistent* spirit of this public life, we must consider, first of all, *that it was by no means a collective effort of the artists, as a body, and the public—indeed not even a collective effort of the musical artists themselves*—which brought to completion that tremendous process which we have just seen take place; *quite the other way, it was purely a superabundant artist individual* who individually absorbed the spirit of that collectivity wanting in the public, who actually began, indeed, by producing this collectivity in himself, out of the abundance of his own being, joined to the abundance of musical possibility, as something he himself longed for as an artist. We see that this wondrous creative process, as it is present in the symphonies of Beethoven as an increasingly determining, living force, was not only achieved by the master in the most complete isolation, but actually was not *understood* at all—or rather, was *misunderstood* in the most shameful way— by the company of artists. The forms in which the master proclaimed his artistic, world-historical struggle remained for the composers of his and the succeeding age mere *formulas,* passing through mannerism into fashion, and although no composer of instrumental music was so much as able to reveal the slightest originality, even in these forms, there was not one who lacked the courage to keep on writing symphonies and similar pieces, not one who even suspected that the *last* symphony had already been *written.*[4] Thus too, we have had to stand by while Beethoven's great voyage of world discovery—that unique, altogether inimitable feat which we saw accomplished in his "Symphony of Joy" as the final and boldest venture of his genius—was after the event reundertaken, with the most idiotic naïveté, and, without hardship, suc-

4. He who specifically undertakes to write the history of instrumental music since Beethoven will no doubt have within this period to report on isolated phenomena, capable, assuredly, of arousing a particular and interested attention. But he who considers the history of the arts from a point of view as broad as is here necessary has to restrict himself to its chief moments alone; whatever departs from or derives from these moments he must leave out of account. And the more unmistakably such isolated phenomena reveal great talent, the more strikingly do precisely these phenomena prove—in view of the general sterility of the whole artistic impulse behind them—that, once there has been expressed in their particular art variety what Beethoven expressed in music, whatever is left to be discovered has to do with technical procedures, perhaps, but not with the living spirit. In the great universal artwork of the future it will be possible to keep on making new discoveries forever—but not in the individual art variety which, after having been conducted into universality as music was by Beethoven, perseveres in its isolated development. [Au.]

cessfully weathered. A new genre, a "symphony with choruses"—this was all one saw in it. Why should not this or that composer also write his Symphony with Choruses? Why should not "God the Lord" be resoundingly praised at the end, after He has helped to conduct the three preliminary instrumental movements to the most facile of possible conclusions?[5] Thus Columbus discovered America only for the fulsome petty profiteering of our time.

•   •   •   •   •

You exert yourselves to no purpose when, to still your own childishly egoistic longing for productivity, you seek to deny the destructive, world-historical, musical significance of Beethoven's last symphony; not even the stupidity which enables you actually to misunderstand the work can save you! Do as you please; take no notice of Beethoven whatever, grope after Mozart, gird yourselves with Bach, write symphonies with or without voices, write masses, oratorios—those sexless operatic embryos!—make songs without words, operas without texts; you produce nothing that has real life in it. For behold—you do not have the *faith!*—the great faith in the necessity of what you do! You have only the faith of the foolish—the superstitious faith in the possibility of the necessity of your egoistic willfulness!

Surveying the busy desolation of our musical art world; becoming aware of the absolute impotence of this art substance, for all its eternal ogling of itself; viewing this shapeless mess, of which the dregs are the dried-up impertinence of pedantry, from which, for all its profoundly reflecting, ever-so-musical, self-arrogated mastery, can finally rise to the broad daylight of modern public life, as an artificially distilled stench, only emotionally dissolute Italian opera arias or impudent French cancan dance tunes; appraising, in short, this complete creative incapacity, we look about us fearlessly for the great destructive stroke of destiny which will put an end to all this immoderately inflated musical rubbish to make room for the artwork of the future, in which genuine music will in truth assume no insignificant role, to which in this soil, however, air and room to breathe are peremptorily denied.[6]

•   •   •   •   •

5. An allusion to Mendelssohn's *Lobgesang*.
6. Lengthily though I have spoken here about the nature of music, in comparison with the other art varieties (a procedure fully justified, I may add, by the peculiar character of music and by the peculiar and truly productive developmental process resulting from this character), I am well aware of the many-sided incompleteness of my discussion; not one book, however, but many books would be needed to lay bare exhaustively the immorality, the weakness, the meanness of the ties connecting our modern music and our modern life; to explore the unfortunate overemotional side of music, which makes it subject to the speculation of our education maniacs, our "improvers of the people," who seek to mix the honey of music with the vinegar-sourish sweat of the mistreated factory worker as the one possible mitigation of his sufferings (somewhat as our sages of the state and bourse are at pains to stuff the servile rags of religion into the gaping holes in the policeman's care of society); and finally to explain the saddening psychological

FUNDAMENTALS OF THE ARTWORK OF THE FUTURE

If we consider the situation of modern art—insofar as it is actually *art*—in relation to public life, we recognize first of all its complete inability to influence this public life in accordance with its high purpose. This is because, as a mere cultural product, it has not grown out of life, and because, as a hothouse plant, it cannot possibly take root in the natural soil and natural climate of the present. Art has become the exclusive property of an artist class; it gives pleasure only to those who *understand* it, requiring for its understanding a special study, remote from real life, the study of *art connoisseurship*. This study and the understanding it affords are thought today to be within the reach of everyone who has the money to pay for the art pleasures offered for sale; yet if we ask the artist whether the great multitude of our art amateurs are capable of understanding him in his highest flights, he can answer only with a deep sigh. And if he now reflects on the infinitely greater multitude of those who must remain cut off, as a result of the influence of our social conditions, unfavorable from every point of view, not only from the understanding, but even from the enjoyment of modern art, the artist of today cannot but become conscious that his whole artistic activity is, strictly speaking, only an egoistic self-complacent activity for activity's sake and that, in its relation to public life, his art is mere luxury, superfluity, and selfish pastime. The disparity, daily observed and bitterly deplored, between so-called culture and the lack of it is so monstrous, a mean between them so unthinkable, their reconciliation so impossible, that, granted a minimum of honesty, the modern art based on this unnatural culture would have to admit, to its deepest shame, that it owed its existence to a life element which in turn could base *its* existence only on the utter lack of culture in the real mass of humanity. The one thing that, in this, its allotted situation, modern art should be able to do—and, where there is honesty, does endeavor to do—namely, *to further the diffusion of culture*—it cannot do, for the simple reason that art, to have any influence on life, must be itself the flowering of a *natural* culture—that is, of one that has grown up from below—and can never be in a position to rain down culture from above. At best, then, our cultured art resembles the speaker who seeks to communicate with a people in a language which it does not understand—all that he says, his most ingenious sayings above all, can lead only to the most laughable confusions and misunderstandings.

Let us first make apparent how modern art is to proceed if it would attain *theoretically* to the redemption of its uncomprehended self from out of its isolated situation and to the widest possible understanding of the public; how this redemption can become possible only through the *practical* mediation of the public will then be readily apparent of itself.

---

phenomenon that a man may be not only cowardly and base, but also *stupid*, without these qualities preventing him from being a perfectly respectable musician. [Au.]

• • • • •

Man as artist can be fully satisfied only in the union of all the art varieties in the *collective* artwork; in every *individualization* of his artistic capacities he is *unfree,* not wholly that which he can be; in the collective artwork he is *free,* wholly that which he can be.

The *true* aim of art is accordingly *all-embracing;* everyone animated by the true artistic impulse seeks to attain, through the full development of his particular capacity, not the glorification of *this particular capacity,* but the glorification *in art of mankind in general.*

The highest collective artwork is the *drama;* it is present in its *ultimate completeness* only when *each art variety, in its ultimate completeness,* is present in it.

True drama can be conceived only as resulting from the *collective impulse of all the arts* to communicate in the most immediate way with a *collective public;* each individual art variety can reveal itself as *fully understandable* to this collective public only through collective communication, together with the other art varieties, in the drama, for the aim of each individual art variety is fully attained only in the mutually understanding and understandable cooperation of all the art varieties.

7 Adolf Bernhard Marx

Adolf Bernhard Marx (1795?–1866) was well regarded as a music critic and pedagogue, although in the twentieth century he is remembered chiefly as a music theorist. In addition to his critical writing for the *Berliner allgemeine musikalische Zeitung,* which he founded, and his critical and biographical work on Beethoven, Marx devoted much of his career to the preparation of books intended for his students at the University of Berlin or for popular musical education: most notably, his four-volume *Lehre von der musikalischen Komposition* (1837–47) and the briefer, simplified *Allgemeine Musiklehre* (1839).

A. B. Marx is remembered particularly as the coiner of the term *Sonatenform* and for his detailed discussions of compositional procedures used in such movements (see Reading 17, pp. 181–89). He was one of the earliest writers to expound on notions of musical form, and his treatment of the subject became a model for later theorists. In particular, Marx saw the basis of form in the shaping of thematic statements and their alternation with transitional sections; as a result he insisted upon a three-part conceptualization of sonata form, as opposed to the customary two-part model based on harmonic process.

Marx's more philosophical or abstract book, *Die Musik des neunzehnten Jahrhunderts und ihre Pflege,* is also profoundly concerned with music pedagogy. Here, rather than technical matters, he explores the ethical, moral, and historical imperatives of proper teaching.

FROM *The Music of the Nineteenth Century*
(1854)

THE FUTURE

Where do we stand? Whither are we going in our art? May we expect of it new revelations, a new circle of ideas, and a new phase of development; or what destiny awaits it in the further existence of nations?

To these questions we have been led by the contemplation of the present state of music.

But it may be asked: Are we, short-sighted mortals, able to penetrate the future? May not those apparitions which we persuade ourselves to be signs of the future turn out mere idle dreams, possibly to be convicted of their fallacy by the very next day, and laughed to scorn, with all their cares and hopes and preparations, by the bright splendour of to-morrow's rising sun?

I ask, in reply: Can we evade this question of the future? Is it possible for us, even if we had the wish, to confine our thoughts to that moment of time which we term the present; and which, whilst we are naming it, disappears already in the stream of the past; leaving us to the next moment of time, which just now belonged to the future, but has become present, until it shall have passed away as swiftly as the former? To him who labours, the future is an inseparable continuation of the present: his work of yesterday was intended for to-day, and continues to live, together with him and the work which this day has brought forth. To the contemplating mind also, the present and future appear as an uninterrupted current of causes and consequences, and the knowledge of the past and present serves it as a light into the future. In this point of view it is, that the history of the different arts, as well as of the nations, is a truly divine revelation of the eternal guide, Reason: inasmuch as it discloses to us that unalterable law of causes and consequences, that inexorable decree of necessity, according to which all that has come into being and all that has happened, continue to operate upon the times and acts that follow. This alone constitutes the spiritual connexion, the significancy and value of our existence.

TEXT: *The Music of the Nineteenth Century, and Its Culture: Method of Musical Instruction,* trans. of *Die Musik des neunzehnten Jahrhunderts und ihre Pflege,* by August Heinrich Wehrhan (London, 1855), pp. 80–86.

The life of every individual being, as well as that of the nations, the life of the human mind, in all its forms of belief, of art and of science, is subject to and obeys the eternal call "onwards!" Imbecility and hypocrisy alone are reactionary; these alone dare to command "stillstand" (which would be living death), or preach "retrogression," or hope for and try to bring about the restoration of that which has passed away. Yesterday never returns, for it is the preceding condition of to-day; and whether you blame or acquiesce in to-day, it will be followed in unalterable sequence by to-morrow, in which it will continue to live and operate in all its plenitude. It is thus with the life of individuals and nations, it is the same in the state, in the family, and in the arts.

In order to convince every one of the necessity of progress in art, it is sufficient to refer to a simple practical observation, which proves the utter impossibility of remaining stationary, or successfully imitating the productions of a previous period of art, even if they should have remained ever so interesting and dear to us. What musician or amateur is not, even to this day, enchanted with Haydn's symphonies, so full of youthful freshness and unsurpassed in their charming innocence and playful sprightliness? In vain have teachers and critics from time to time urged that other composers should attempt the same style of music. The thing is simply impossible. To original and honest minds the request itself is objectionable, whilst those willing to imitate or repeat—these Pleyels, Wanhalls, and others of the same stamp[1]—have served up nothing but coarse and tasteless fare. We observe and are delighted at the careless ease and playfulness with which 'father' Haydn makes his bassoon and flute dance along, or perform what else he wishes them to do; and yet not one of our instrumentalists has attempted the same thing without becoming vulgar or baroque. So also has Mozart been imitated by hundreds of opera composers (his Magic Flute has led to "magic bells," "magic fiddles," and "magic bassoons;" his Papageno to *Larifaris*), but by no one more faithfully than by the burgomaster Wolfram, of Teplitz, who, some thirty years ago, was even greeted as a "second" Mozart. Who knows anything about Wolfram nowadays? We must go forwards, because we cannot recede.

To go forwards is a matter of necessity; how, and whither, are questions which could be solved with equal certainty, if we were fully acquainted with all the preceding circumstances, causes, and connexions. Proportionate to the knowledge and circumspection with which we approach the boundary between the present and the future, will be the clearness of our view beyond it, unless narrow prejudices or paltry timidity obscure our sight. But we never can close our eyes to that enigma. The onward pressure of life itself constrains us to put that question, and to answer it as well as we are able. Those ardent disciples of our art who prophecy of a "music of the future" may err, more or less, in certain

1. Ignace Joseph Pleyel (1757–1831), composer and piano maker; Johann Baptist Vanhal (1739–1813), composer and music teacher.

things; but they cannot be mistaken in the presentiment that the mind must move onwards. They burn with the thirst of life, and they feel the impulse and courage to obey the true command of life—"march on!" They see before them a hopeful future, full of new enjoyments and new revelations, not knowing whether much or little of it shall fall within the circle of their life. The future beyond, is their own by faith; as it was to those champions of liberty, who, with the ever true and glorious shout, *"L'arenir est à nous,"* marched on to victory—or death.

For there is another alternative, also, which we must look boldly in the face. Immortality does not belong to any individual being: neither does immortality belong to any individual art, but only to the spirit which calls it forth out of itself, now in this form of manifestation, and now in another, as its necessary expression and the characteristic element of its life. This we observe everywhere. Nations have gone down, together with their arts and sciences; so ancient Egypt, India, Assyria, all Asia, once so crowded with nations and highly adorned with works of art. Perished is that unparalleled national drama of Æschylus, and every attempt to restore it to life (like those made formerly by Caccini and his associates, and of late by Mendelssohn) has proved a mockery, a caricature devoid of all those elements—the cosmology, religion, traditions, and manners of the Greek nation, and even the sublime site of representation by the side of the steep cliff of the Acropolis, and under the serene and luminous sky of Hellas—which imparted life and reality to the original. The epos has died away with the ancient traditions; the plastic art of Greece has disappeared with the gods that peopled Olympus and the youthful, joyous, and beautiful race of the Hellenes. It was not the want of creative power that made the Buonarottis and Thorwaldsens[2] inferior to the Ancients; but it was the difference of soil and clime; the want of that serenity and mildness of the atmosphere which makes existence a pleasure; of that youthful innocence and freshness, and that pure sensuous susceptibility which roused the Greeks to delight in the mutual contemplation of the beauty of their well-formed limbs; of that perfection of bodily form exhibited in their martial games, their dances and religious processions; of that fulness of existence which had not yet ascetically divided itself into an abstract mind and a contaminated and shame-deserving body, but which in godlike images idealized itself, and, thus idealized, became its own admirer.

And yet we do not look back with sorrow or childish regret. That rich existence had lived its time; and terminated after it had fully satisfied the youthful spirit of mankind, filling even to overflow the temples and market places, the streets and groves, until the "marble population" left living beings scarcely room to walk. To that people, existing so entirely in and for the

---

2. Buonarotti: Michelangelo Buonarroti (1475–1564); Bertel Thorvaldsen (ca. 1770–1844), Danish sculptor active in Rome, a prominent Neoclassicist.

sunny outer world, music was merely a means of making language more sonorous, just as the acoustic vases in their theatres served to increase the resonance of sound. But when the spirit retired from the outer to the mystic inner world of the soul, then musical art became its place of abode and its proper organ.

And should we tremble, if, having groped its way and lived through this region of twilight and deeply hidden mysteries, our satiated spirit—now or at some future time—should seek for new gratification and a new existence in some other sphere? What those Hellenes created still exists and will exist for ever in the spirit of mankind; it does not cease to elevate and adorn also our existence, as long as we find sense and room for it. More it cannot be to us, for we have lived and grown beyond the deification of the bodily man, beyond the legends and traditions of little Hellas, and the fated *future* of the ancients, veiled in awe and mystery. And so, also, all that the sweet strains of sound have ever whispered and sung to us will live and move for ever in the soul of mankind, even though the human spirit should find another form of revelation than that which we call music. And if, now or hereafter, the spirit should in fresh youth proceed to reveal itself in new forms, even then those flattering strains will still remain the echoes of the soft confessions of the heart, a balm and comfort after the heat and toil of the day; they will adorn, as now, our public festivals, and wing the foot for dance or battle. No more will be required of them, if such a time arrive, nor any more accepted.

And here my sympathizing heart—for I feel with them—turns to the faithful band of those who, even in the face of this momentous "if," are drawn with irresistible force towards the altar of our art, and feel constrained to cling to it, although it be deserted by the people—not from choice, but of necessity, and in obedience to the spirit's call that draws them onwards to some other sphere. It was not love of gain, or thirst for fame—the spurious artist's idols—which brought you to the altar; nor is it indolence, or ostentatious pride in what you have acquired and learnt, or a stubborn refusal to open your eyes to the dawning light of the new day, which keeps you there. It was the disposition of your mind—you do not know who tuned its strings—which led you there; and there creative love has kindled in your bosom, there is the focus of your thoughts and visions, and there one of those eternal melodies has vibrated through your heart. You could not and cannot help prophesying those visions which grew up flaming in your spirit; and having once begun, you must persist, although the wave of time is rolling past your sanctuary. You cannot "limp after strange gods," in whom you have no faith, and whom you do not love; neither can you make "concessions," and fancy that by falsely putting Yes and No together, and sacrificing at two different altars, you will be able surreptitiously to serve the cause of truth. You must proclaim what dwells within your soul, *or* cease to speak. To the world you are "foolishness and an offence;" but the poet has sung of you:

Sagt es Niemand, nur den Weisen,
Weil die Menge gleich verhöhnet,
Das Lebend'ge, will ich preisen,
Das nach Flammentod sich sehnet.[3]

Your love and faithfulness alone remain your consolation and reward. The chattering multitude passes by, heedless of you; except, perhaps, that here and there a contemplative wanderer will look with transitory emotion upon that fidelity which will not leave even the grave of its devotion and affection; as, in the times of youthful and victorious Christianity, the last small bands of unbelievers, though chased from place to place, clung to the broken altars of their gods. You are the witnesses of sunken glory; your works remain to testify of your sincerity and of the immortality of that idea by which you were inspired. Then dedicate those works, as Æschylus did of old, to "time," to a discerning future; convinced that, if you sink into the grave to be forgotten for a period, like Sebastian Bach, that last evangelist, the following century will recognise you in your real being and truthfulness. But still your faithful service must not and cannot stop the Dionysian march of the spirit through the mountain passes and deep gorges of existence. "Onwards!" the call resounds, and resounds without intermission.

•   •   •

Does it sound for our art also? And, if so, does it point to the present time or to the nearest future? Or shall a longer period elapse before our art shall be awakened to new achievements, and to a new phase of existence?

Let us, first of all, endeavour to determine more precisely the real significance of this question, and the moment when it will certainly press more imperatively for solution.

The art of sound will certainly never cease to delight sensuous man, and to call forth emotions in the feeling heart. For it is inborn to man, and constitutes a part of his nature; the man without music is an incomplete being. We may also rest assured that this art will always continue to find talents and followers in the repetition of favorite forms, and the application of such forms to subjects of a kindred nature. But this does not touch the real question as to the future of our art. The essence of art is CREATION, the realization of the ideal, and a consequent progress from that which already exists to that which remains still to be accomplished. It counts its epochs of existence by the successive revelation of these ideals: those who raise such heavenly forms from the undulating and life-breathing motion of general art have been inspired with creative power; to them alone pertains the epithet Divine—the name of Genius, so often lavished in vain. It is they alone in whom and through whom all progress is effected, in whom the future becomes reality, whilst it is the mission of *talent*

3. Tell it no one but the wise; / For the multitude would sneer—/ The Living Being will I prize / That yearns for death in flames. (Goethe, "Selige Sehnsucht," *West-Östlicher Divan*).

to spread those creations of genius over the breadth of life, to refresh and fructify every thing around them, and prepare it for the next creative epoch. So the waters of Egypt's one living stream are conducted over the whole country by means of canals, ditches, trenches, and water-wheels. A similar distribution is to be observed in the life of art.

The question of the future, therefore, relates to *new creations* produced by the power of genius. It starts from the last that have been revealed.

The last unquestionable progress in musical art is associated with the name of Beethoven; it is the spiritualization of instrumental music, by raising it to the sphere of definite conceptions and ideas. The question, taken strictly, is, whether another real progress has been effected since his time, or whether any further progress is still to be expected. To undertake to answer such a question must appear an act of great temerity, and yet an answer to it can be no longer refused. Every thinking man puts this question to himself, although he may not have the courage or feel called upon to answer it aloud.

One leading idea, which will assist us in the execution of this task, has already been established by the foregoing inquiries. It is this—that the different epochs of progress in art effected by the power of genius do not occur accidentally and irregularly, but appear to be regulated according to the strictest laws of reason and consistency. Art, like every other organism, develops itself according to the conditions and exigencies of its existence, and its creations are always in keeping with the actual condition and the wants of the human mind. It was impossible for Bach to treat his parts as individual and characteristic exponents, both of word and sentiment, until those parts had been made pliant and singable by the contrapuntists of the middle ages. Haydn had first to finish his childlike blissful play with the orchestra, before Beethoven was enabled to unlock the spiritual depths of this region of fairy life. Nowhere but in the sacerdotal service of the Catholic Church could Palestrina find his place, for therein lived his people and his Lord. Nothing, on the other hand, but the people's own song (Volkslied) could sound in opposition to it in our dear, liberated Germany, so long as the Reformation continued to be the work of the people, and formed an element of its existence; until that people turned away from its haughty rulers imbued with French manners, and clung for support and consolation to the "Word of God" alone, which Bach was sent to expound in its true power and fulness. The artist only gives form and expression to that which, although still void of shape and form, is already in existence amongst the people.

There is another point which must be kept well in sight, in order that the lines of demarcation between the past and future may not be obliterated. This is the remarkable phenomenon, that art—like life itself—appears periodically to return to certain ideas and forms; and yet progresses with these forms until they appear satisfactory and perfect, when it proceeds to others of a decidedly different nature. This phenomenon may be observed in individual artists, as well as in different nations and times. Thus, e. g. the simplest form of vocal music, the song, has been repeated by singers of all times and nations. Thus, also, the form of the musical drama may be traced far beyond the Greeks to the most ancient nations of Eastern Asia; it makes its appearance again in the 13th century (if not sooner), and once more in the 16th century, when its further cultivation is taken up by France, Italy, and Germany. Thus, also—to mention a special case—Bach's Chromatic Fantasia, and Beethoven's Fantasia with Orchestra and Chorus, as also his Ninth Symphony, are based upon the same idea. But in these cases there is only an apparent repetition, easily and clearly distinguishable, to a more searching eye, from the non-progressive or even retrogressive reproduction of previous forms. For, in the latter, we perceive as clearly the naked "repeat" (*Noch-Einmal*) of something that had before been, and has seen its day, and therefore is now void of life and truth, as we behold, in the former mode of revival, that unconscious dialectic power of the artistic mind which turns and works the same idea until it has brought it to full maturity and truth.

•   •   •

If we examine the past development of musical art from this point of view, we obtain at once a distinct perception of the different stages through which it has passed, and the tasks which remain still to be accomplished.

Looking at this development as a whole, and not in its details, it appears that music has completed all its essential tasks. After all that has been said in the preceding chapters, we can now pronounce the essential and ultimate object of every art to be this: that it shall reveal in its productions the spirit of man, and the essence of his life; and that all its forms shall be filled with this spirit. Thus the life of musical art must first manifest itself in a sensuous form, as a delightful sensuous exercise. This consciousness of sensuous delight must next raise itself to the higher, but still dim and uncertain, sphere of emotion. After this, the spoken word, the definite expression of the mind, had not only to be joined externally to the tune, but so entirely incorporated with it as to become music itself; whilst music, on the other hand, acquired a definite expression by the help of language. This new tongue of word and tone united was the condition and commencement of the musical drama, the opera. Finally, music had to endeavour, by itself alone, to seize and reveal so much of man's spiritual life as comes within its sphere. Further it cannot go; the near approach to the ultimate boundary is everywhere perceptible; music is no longer an isolated art, and people already begin to inquire and dispute about its power and right to receive and interpret, by itself alone, those revelations of the spirit.

MUSIC
CRITICISM

8 François-Joseph Fétis

Frédéric Chopin, at the time completely unknown in Paris, gave his first concert there on February 26, 1832, in the piano-maker Camille Pleyel's showrooms, then located at 9, rue Cadet. The concert was a grand success and led to his immediate celebrity in the French capital.

The varied offerings of the concert that are discussed here are typical of the period and remind us of the importance of the soirée as a musical institution. Reviews at the time rarely identify programs with precision, of course, and François-Joseph Fétis's is no exception. Though it is unsigned, the authoritative tone, the historical perspective (far more informative than Schumann's famous review of Chopin's Op. 2 [see pp. 102–3]), and the vocabulary—including the use of such a characteristic phrase as "autant d'étonnement que de plaisir," which he elsewhere applied to Berlioz—suggest that the author of the column is indeed the editor of the *Revue Musicale*.

In addition to the intrinsic interest both of the information offered here and of Fétis's recognition of Chopin's talent, students of the cultural history of music will also be struck by this very early positing of a spiritual opposition between Chopin and Beethoven that became a commonplace later in the century. Chopin himself would have been bemused by the cliché; he told Eugène Delacroix that Beethoven's music is obscure because "he turns his back on eternal principles" (*The Journal of Eugène Delacroix,* trans. Walter Pach [New York, 1948], p. 195; diary entry for 7 April 1849).

The Concert of Monsieur Chopin from Warsaw

(1832)

These days, to say of a pianist that he is highly talented, or even, if you wish, that he is *supremely talented,* is simply to say that he is the rival or the enemy of a few other artists of the first rank whose names come immediately to mind. To add that his compositions are very good is merely to suggest that they fall into a category analogous to that of the works of Hummel, for example, and of a small number of other celebrated composers. But with such praises it is difficult to give an idea of novelty or of originality because, except for a few nuances of style and niceties of structure, music by pianists is generally written in certain conventional forms that one may consider fundamental, forms that have been used again and again for more than thirty years. This is the great shortcoming of piano music, and even our most accomplished artists have been unable to eliminate it from their works.

TEXT: *Revue Musicale* (March 3, 1832): 38–39, translated by Peter Bloom, who also provided most of the introduction and the information in the notes.

But here we have a young man who, giving himself over to his natural inclinations and following no models whatsoever, has effected, if not a total resuscitation of piano music, at least a part of what we have so long been searching for in vain—that is, a plethora of original ideas of a sort nowhere else to be found. This is not by any means to say that M. Chopin is gifted with the powerful spirit of a Beethoven, nor that there is in Chopin's music anything of the majestic force that one finds in the music of that great man: Beethoven wrote music *for piano,* but here I am speaking of music *for pianists*—and it is in this realm that I find in M. Chopin's inspirations the sign of a formal renaissance that could eventually exercise enormous influence upon this branch of art.

At the concert he gave on the 26th of this [*recte* last] month in the salons of MM. Pleyel and Company, M. Chopin played a concerto that surprised listeners as much as it pleased them both because of the novelty of its melodic ideas and because of its virtuoso passages, its modulations, and its larger structural organization.[1] There is vitality in his melody, fantasy in his passage-work, and originality in everything. Too many colorful modulations, so much confusion in linking phrases that it sometimes seems as though one is hearing an improvisation rather than a written composition—these are the imperfections that are found intermingled with the virtues I have just mentioned. But they are the imperfections of the youthful artist, and they will disappear as he gains greater experience. Indeed, if M. Chopin's subsequent works fulfill the promise of his debut, we can be sure that he will enjoy a brilliant and well-deserved reputation.

As a performer, this young artist also merits great praise. His playing is elegant, relaxed, and graceful; it is marked by both brilliance and clarity. He draws little sound from the instrument and resembles in this respect the majority of the German pianists. But the study of this aspect of his art, which he has undertaken with M. Kalkbrenner, cannot fail to provide him with that important quality upon which the confidence to perform depends, and without which one cannot shape the natural sounds of the instrument.

Apart from the concerto I have just spoken about, two further, quite remarkable works were heard on the same evening. One was a string quintet, performed with the emotional energy and kaleidoscopic inspiration that distinguish the playing of M. Baillot. The other was a piece for six pianos written by M. Kalkbrenner and performed by the composer along with MM. Chopin, Stammati, Hiller, Osborne, and Sowinski.[2] This piece, in which the instruments are deployed with great artifice and whose style is eminently graceful and elegant, had already been heard several years ago, and with great success, in the

---

1. The E-Minor Concerto, the future Op. 11 (dedicated to Kalkbrenner). [Tr.]
2. The string quintet was Beethoven's in C Major, Op. 29 (Fétis, following contemporary usage, refers to the work as "un quintetto pour le violon"). The work for six pianos, originally scored for two, plus two violins, viola, cello, and double bass *ad libitum,* was an arrangement of Kalkbrenner's *Grande Polonaise, précédée d'une Introduction et d'une marche,* Op. 92. [Tr.]

salons of MM. Pleyel and Company. It gave no less pleasure this second time around.

A solo for oboe, performed by M. Brod with the aplomb for which he is justly renowned, and several works sung by M. Boulanger and Mlles Isambert and Toméoni, completed this musical soirée, one of the most agreeable that we have heard this year.[3]

3. Chopin also played his Variations on Mozart's *Là ci darem la mano,* Op. 2, with quintet or second-piano accompaniment, and, solo, selected Mazurkas and Nocturnes. Among the artists who contributed to the concert were the members of the Baillot Quintet (Pierre Baillot and Jean-Joseph Vidal, violin, Chrétien Urhan and Théophile Tilmant, viola, and Louis Norblin, cello), the oboist Henri Brod, and the pianists Friedrich Kalkbrenner, Ferdinand Hiller, George Osborne, Camille Stamaty, and Albert Sowinski, as well as the singers Ernest Boulanger (Nadia's and Lili's father) and Mesdemoiselles Toméoni and Isambert (whose first names are not recorded in the literature). For further information, see Jean-Jacques Eigeldinger, "Les Premiers Concerts de Chopin à Paris," in *Music in Paris in the Eighteen-Thirties,* ed. Peter Bloom (Stuyvesant, NY: Pendragon Press, 1987), pp. 251–297; and Joel-Marie Fauquet, *Les Sociétés de musique de chambre à Paris de la Restauration à 1870* (Paris: Aux Amateurs de livres, 1986). [Tr.]

9 Hector Berlioz

In 1856, on Hector Berlioz's election to the Institute, his friends were outraged and his enemies consoled by a malicious bon mot put into circulation by the music critic of the *Revue des deux mondes:* "Instead of a musician, the Institute has chosen a journalist." Yet a casual reader of the Parisian press of those days might almost have believed this true. Since 1823, Berlioz had been a regular contributor to one musical or literary review after another; by 1863, when he gave up his long-standing association with the *Journal des débats,* he had published more than 900 separate pieces—leading articles, letters from abroad, humorous sketches, fictitious anecdotes, imaginary conversations, *causeries* and *feuilletons* of every sort and description. Only a small part of this enormous production is assembled in his three volumes of collected writings—*Les soirées de l'orchestre* (1852), *Les grotesques de la musique* (1859), and *A travers chants* (1862); other pieces were salvaged in his *Voyage musical* (1844) and in the two volumes of his memoirs, printed in 1865 but not published until after his death.

"Music is not made for everyone, nor everyone for music"—this is perhaps the central article of Berlioz's critical creed, and in the essay translated below it recurs again and again with the persistence of an *idée fixe.* But in writing on *William Tell,* Berlioz also reveals many of the other facets of his critical personality—his preoccupation with the poetic and the picturesque, his capacity for enthusiasm and for indignation, his horror of the mediocre and his impatience with all that fails to measure up to the very highest standards, his contempt for

everything academic, his intense dissatisfaction with the commercial and offi-
cial aspects of musical life. Above all, he reveals his sense of justice and his
readiness to acknowledge merit, even in the camp of the enemy. From the first,
Berlioz had taken his stand with the opponents of Gioachino Rossini and "the
party of the dilettanti." But he has undertaken to review *William Tell* and he
does so without *parti pris* and without hypocrisy.

Rossini's *William Tell*
(1834)

[PART 1]

Tired of hearing perpetual criticism of his works from the point of view of
dramatic expression, still more tired, perhaps, of the blind admiration of his
fanatical adherents, Rossini has found a very simple means of silencing the one
and getting rid of the others. This has been to write a score—one seriously
thought out, considered at leisure, and conscientiously executed from beginning to end in accordance with the requirements imposed upon all time by
taste and good sense. He has written *William Tell*. This splendid work is thus
to be regarded as an application of the author's new theories, as a sign of those
greater and nobler capacities whose development the requirements of the sensual people for whom he has written until now have necessarily made impossible. It is from this point of view that we shall examine—without favor, but also
without the least bias—Rossini's latest score.

If we consider only the testimonials that it has earned, the applause that it
has called forth, and the conversions that it has made, *William Tell* has unques-
tionably had an immense success—a success that has taken the form of spontaneous admiration with some and of reflection and analysis with many others.
And yet one is obliged to admit that to this glory it has not been able to add
that other glory of which directors, and sometimes even authors, are more
appreciative than of any other—popular success, that is, box-office success.
The party of the dilettanti is hostile to *William Tell* and finds it cold and tiresome. The reasons for such a difference of opinion will become clear, we hope,
in the course of the examination of this important production which we invite
the reader to make with us. Let us follow the author step by step as he hurries
along the new path that he has chosen, one that he would have reached the
end of more rapidly and with a steadier pace if the force of deeply rooted
habit had not caused him to cast an occasional glance behind him. These rare
deviations once again bear out the old proverb: "In the arts one must take
sides; there is no middle ground."

TEXT: "Guillaume-Tell, de Rossini." *Gazette musicale de Paris.* vol. 1 (1834), pp. 326–27, 336–39,
341–43, 349–51. Berlioz's essay was not written until five years after the first performance of the
opera, which took place in Paris on August 3, 1829. Translation by Oliver Strunk.

For the first time Rossini has sought to compose an overture meeting the dramatic requirements recognized by every nation in Europe, Italy alone excepted. In making his debut in this style of instrumental music, entirely new to him, he has enlarged the form, so that his overture has in fact become a symphony in four distinct movements instead of the piece in two movements usually thought to be sufficient.

The first movement depicts most successfully, in our opinion, the calm of profound solitude, the solemn silence of nature when the elements and the human passions are at rest. It is a poetic beginning to which the animated scenes that are to follow form a most striking contrast—a contrast in expression, even a contrast in instrumentation, this first part being written for five solo violoncellos, accompanied by the rest of the cellos and contrabasses, while the entire orchestra is brought into play in the next movement, "The Storm."

In this, it seems to us, our author would have done well to abandon the square-cut rhythms, the symmetrical phrase structures, and the periodically returning cadences that he uses so effectively at all other times: "often a beautiful disorder is an effect of art," as an author says whose classical reserve is beyond question.[1] Beethoven proves this in the prodigious cataclysm of his pastoral symphony; at the same time he attains the end which the Italian composer lets us expect but does not give us. Several of the harmonic devices are remarkable and ingeniously brought in; among others, the chord of the minor ninth gives rise to effects that are indeed singular. But it is disappointing to rediscover in the storm scene of *William Tell* those staccato notes of the wind instruments which the amateurs call "drops of rain"; Rossini has already used this device in the little storm in the *Barber of Seville* and perhaps in other operas. In compensation he manages to draw from the bass drum without the cymbals picturesque noises in which the imagination readily rediscovers the reechoing of distant thunder among the anfractuosities of the mountains. The inevitable decrescendo of the storm is handled with unusual skill. In short, it is not arresting or overpowering like Beethoven's storm, a musical tableau which will perhaps remain forever unequalled, and it lacks that sombre, desolate character which we admire so much in the introduction to *Iphigenia in Tauris,* but it is beautiful and full of majesty. Unfortunately the musician is always in evidence; we never lose sight of him in his combinations, even in those which seem the most eccentric. Beethoven on the other hand has known how to reveal himself wholly to the attentive listener: it is no longer an orchestra that one hears, it is no longer music, but rather the tumultuous voice of the heavenly torrents blended with the uproar of the earthly ones, with the furious claps of thunder, with the crashing of uprooted trees, with the gusts of an exterminating wind, with the frightened cries of men and the lowing of the herds. This is terrifying, it makes one shudder, the illusion is complete. The emotion that Rossini arouses in the same situation falls far short of attaining the same degree of— But let us continue.

1. Boileau, *L'Art poétique*, Canto 2, line 72.

The storm is followed by a pastoral scene, refreshing in the extreme; the melody of the English horn in the style of the *ranz des vaches*[2] is delicious, and the gamboling of the flute above this peaceful song is ravishing in its freshness and gaiety. We note in passing that the triangle, periodically sounding its tiny pianissimo strokes, is in its right place here; it represents the little bell sounded by the flocks as they saunter quietly along while the shepherds call and answer with their joyful songs. "So you find dramatic meaning in this use of the triangle," someone asks us; "in that case, pray be good enough to tell us what is represented by the violins, violas, basses, clarinets, and so forth." To this I should reply that these are musical instruments, essential to the existence of the art, while the triangle, being only a piece of iron whose sound does not belong to the class of sounds with definite pitch, ought not to be heard in the course of a sweet and tranquil movement unless its presence there is perfectly motivated, failing which it will seem only bizarre and ridiculous.

With the last note of the English horn, which sings the pastoral melody, the trumpets enter with a rapid incisive fanfare on B, the major third in the key of G, established in the previous movement, and in two measures this B becomes the dominant in E major, thus determining in a manner as simple as it is unexpected the tonality of the Allegro that follows. This last part of the overture is treated with a *brio* and a verve that invariably excite the transports of the house. Yet it is built upon a rhythm that has by now become hackneyed, and its theme is almost exactly the same as that of the Overture to *Fernand Cortez*. The staccato figuration of the first violins, bounding from C-sharp minor to G-sharp minor, is a particularly grateful episode, ingeniously interpolated into the midst of this warlike instrumentation; it also provides a means of returning to the principal theme and gives to this return an irresistible impetuosity which the author has known how to make the most of. The peroration of the saucy Allegro has genuine warmth. In short, despite its lack of originality in theme and rhythm, and despite its somewhat vulgar use of the bass drum, most disagreeable at certain moments, constantly pounding away on the strong beats as in a *pas redoublé* or the music of a country dance, one has to admit that the piece as a whole is treated with undeniable mastery and with an élan more captivating, perhaps, than any that Rossini has shown before, and that the overture to *William Tell* is the work of an enormous talent, so much like genius that it might easily be mistaken for it.

[PART 2]

Act 1 opens with a chorus that has a beautiful and noble simplicity. Placid joy is the feeling that the composer was to paint, and it is difficult to imagine anything better, more truthful, and at the same time more delicate than the melody he has given to these lines:

2. A traditional Swiss melody, played on the alphorn, to gather cows.

> How clear a day the skies foretell!
> Come bid it welcome with a song!

The vocal harmonies, supported by an accompaniment in the style of the *ranz des vaches*, breathe happiness and peace. Towards the end of the piece, the modulation from G to E-flat becomes original because of the way in which it is presented and makes an excellent effect.

The *romance* that follows ("Hasten aboard my boat") does not seem to us to be on the same level. Its melody is not always as naive as it should be for the song of a fisherman of Unterwald; many phrases are soiled by that affected style that the singers with their banal embellishments have unfortunately put into circulation. Besides, one scarcely knows why a Swiss should be accompanied by two harps.

Tell, who has been silent throughout the introduction and the fisherman's first stanza, comes forward with a measured monologue full of character; it sets before us the concentrated indignation of a lover of liberty, deeply proud of soul. Its instrumentation is perfect, likewise its modulations, although in the vocal part there are some intervals whose intonation is quite difficult.

At this point the general defect of the work as a whole begins to make itself felt. The scene is too long, and since the three pieces of which it consists are not very different in their coloring, the result is a tiring monotony which is further accentuated by the silence of the orchestra during the *romance*. In general, unless the stage is animated by a powerful dramatic interest, it is seldom that this kind of instrumental inactivity does not cause a fatal indifference, at least at the Opéra. Aside from this, the house is so enormous that a single voice, singing way at the back of the stage, reaches the listener deprived of that warm vibrancy that is the life of music and without which a melody can seldom stand out clearly and make its full effect.

After the intoning of a *ranz des vaches* with its echoes, in which four horns in G and E represent the Alpine trumpet, an Allegro vivace revives the attention. This is a chorus, full of impassioned verve, and it would be admirable if the meaning of the text were just the opposite of what it actually is. The key is E minor and the melody is so full of alarm and agitation that at the first performance, not hearing the words, as usually happens in large theatres, I expected the news of some catastrophe—at the very least, the assassination of Father Melchthal. Yet, far from it, the chorus sings:

> From the mountains a summons
> To repose sounds a call;
> A festival shall lighten
> Our labors in the field.

It is the first time that Rossini has been guilty of this particular kind of incongruity.

After this chorus, which is the second in this scene, there follows an accompanied recitative and then a third chorus, *maestoso*, chiefly remarkable for the rare felicity of the scale from the B in the middle register to the high B which the soprano spreads obliquely against the harmonic background. But the action does not progress, and this defect is made still more glaring by a fourth chorus, rather more violent than joyous in character, sung throughout in full voice, scored throughout for full orchestra, and accompanied by great strokes of the bass drum on the first beat of each measure. Wholly superfluous from the dramatic point of view, the piece has little musical interest. Ruthless cuts have been made in the present score, yet great care has been taken to delete nothing here; this would have been too reasonable. Those who make cuts know only how to cut out the good things; in castrating, it is precisely the noblest parts that are removed. By actual count, then, there are four fully developed choruses here, to do honor to "the clear day" and "the rustic festival," to celebrate "labor and love," and to speak of "the horns that reecho close by the roaring torrents." This is an awkward blunder, especially at the beginning, this monotony in the choice of means, wholly unjustified by the requirements of the drama, whose progress it aimlessly brings to a standstill. It appears that the work has been dominated at many points by the same unfortunate influence which led the composer astray at this one. I say "the composer," for a man like Rossini always gets what he wants from his poet, and it is well known that for *William Tell* he insisted on a thousand changes which M. Jouy did not refuse him.

Lack of variety even affects the melodic style: the vocal part is full of repeated dominants, and the composer turns about the fifth step of the scale with tiresome persistence, as though it held for him an almost irresistible attraction. Here are some examples from Act 1. During the fanfare of the four horns in E-flat, Arnold sings:

> Have a care! Have a care!
> The approach of the Austrian tyrant
> Is announced by the horns from the mountain.

All these words are on a single note—B-flat. In the duet that follows, Arnold again resorts to this B-flat, the dominant in E-flat, for the recitation of two whole lines:

> Under the yoke of such oppression
> What great heart would not be cast down?

Further on, after the modulation to D minor, Tell and Arnold sing alternately on A, the dominant of the new key:

> TELL: Let's be men and we shall win!
> ARNOLD: What revenge can end these affronts?
> TELL: Ev'ry evil rule is unstable.

Against this obstinate droning of the dominant, the five syllables on D, F, and C-sharp at the ends of the phrases can barely be made out. The key changes to F, and the dominant, C, appears again immediately:

ARNOLD: Think of all you may lose!
TELL: No matter!
ARNOLD: What acclaim can we hope from defeat?

And later on:

ARNOLD: Your expectation?
TELL: To be victorious,
           And yours as well; I must know what you hope.

Nor is this all; the dominants continue:

> When the signal sounds for the combat,
> My friend, I shall be there.

The E-flat fanfare of the horns begins again and Tell exclaims:

> The signal! Gessler comes.
> Even now as he taunts us,
> Willing slave of his whim, are you waiting
> To entreat the disdain of a favoring glance?

These four lines are entirely on the dominant, B-flat. True to his favorite note, Tell again returns to it in order to say, near the end of the movement:

> The music calls; I hear the wedding chorus;
> Oh, trouble not the shepherds at their feast
> Nor spoil their pleasures with your sad lament!

A defect as serious as this does immense harm to the general effect of the fine duet. I say "fine," for despite this chiming of dominants, it is really admirable in all other respects: the instrumentation is treated with unusual care and delicacy; the modulations are varied; Arnold's melody ("Oh Mathilda, my soul's precious idol") is suave in the extreme; many of Tell's phrases are full of dramatic accents; and except for the music of the line "But at virtue's call I obey," the whole has great nobility.

The pieces that follow are all of them more or less noteworthy. We cite in preference the A minor chorus:

> Goddess Hymen,
> Thy bright feast day
> Dawns for us.

This would have a novel, piquant effect if it were sung as one has the right to demand that all choruses should be at the Royal Academy of Music. The pantomimic Allegro of the archers also has great energy, and several *airs de danse* are distinguished by their fresh melodies and the exceptional finish of their orchestration.

The grand finale which crowns the act seems to us much less satisfactory. The beginning brings in the voices and orchestra a return of the dominant pedal-points which have been absent for some time. After a few exclamations by the chorus of Swiss, one hears Gessler's soldiers:

> The hour of justice now is striking.
> The murd'rer be accursed!
> No quarter!

All this is recited on B, the dominant in E minor, which has already been used as a pedal by the basses of the orchestra during the first nineteen measures of the introduction. Confronted by this persistent tendency of the composer's to fall back on the most familiar and monotonous of musical formulas, one can only suppose it to be due to sheer laziness. It is very practical indeed to write a phrase for orchestra whose harmony turns about the two fundamental chords of the key and then, when one has a leftover bit of text to add to it, to set this to the dominant, the note common to the two chords—this saves the composer much time and trouble. After this introductory movement there follows a chorus ("Virgin, adored by ev'ry Christian"); the tempo is slow—I might say, almost dragging—and the piece is accompanied in a very ordinary fashion, so that its effect is to hold up the action and the musical interest most inappropriately. Little is added by the syllabic asides of the soldiers' chorus during the singing of the women:

> How they tremble with fright!
> Do as we bid!
> Your own lives are at stake!

The music for these words is neither menacing nor ironic: it is simply a succession of notes, mere padding to fill out the harmonies, expressing neither contempt nor anger. At length, when the women have finished their long prayer, Rudolf—Gessler's most ardent satellite—breaks out in a violent rage. The orchestra takes a tumultuous headlong plunge, the trombones bellow, the violins utter shrill cries, the instruments vie with one another in elaborating "the horrors of plundering and pillage" with which the Swiss are threatened; unfortunately, the whole is a copy of the finale of *La Vestale*. The figuration of the basses and violas, the strident chords of the brass, the incisive scales of the first violins, the syllabic accompaniment of the second chorus beneath the broad melody of the soprano—Spontini has them all. Let us add, however, that the *stretta* of this chorus contains a magnificent effect due wholly to Rossini. It is the syncopated descending scale for the whole chorus, singing in octaves, while trebles, flutes, and first violins forcefully sustain the major third E to G-sharp; against this interval the notes D-sharp, A, and F-sharp of the lower voices collide in violent agitation. This idea alone, in its grandeur and force, completely effaces all previous sections of the finale. These are now wholly forgotten. At the beginning one was indifferent—in the end one is moved; the author seemed to lack invention—he has redeemed himself and astonished us with an unexpected stroke. Rossini is full of such contrast.

[PART 3]

The curtain rises on Act 2. We are witnesses of a hunt; horses cross the stage at a gallop. The fanfare which we heard two or three times during the preceding act resounds again; it is differently scored, to be sure, and linked to a characteristic chorus, but it is a misfortune that so undistinguished a theme should be heard so frequently. The development of the drama imposed it, the musician will tell us. Nevertheless, as we have said before, Rossini might have obtained from his librettist a different arrangement of the scenes and thus have avoided these numerous chances for monotony. He failed to do so and, now that it is too late, he regrets it. Let us go on. Halfway through the chorus just mentioned there is a diatonic passage played in unison by the horns and the four bassoons that has an energy all its own, and the piece as a whole would be captivating were it not for the torture inflicted upon the listener who is at all sensitive by the innumerable strokes of the bass drum on the strong beats, whose effect is the more unfortunate since they again call attention to rhythmic constructions that are completely lacking in originality.

To all this I am sure that Rossini will reply: "Those constructions which seem to you so contemptible are precisely the ones that the public understands the most readily." "Granted," I should answer; "but if you profess so great a respect for the propensities of the vulgar, you ought also to limit yourself to the most commonplace things in melody, harmony, and instrumentation. This is just what you have taken care not to do. Why, then, do you condemn rhythm alone to vulgarity? Besides, in the arts, criticism cannot and should not take account of considerations of this kind. Am I on the same footing as an amateur who hears an opera once every three or four months, I who have occupied myself exclusively with music for so many years? Haven't my ears become more delicate than those of the student whose hobby it is to play flute duets on Sundays? Am I as ignorant as the shopkeeper on the Rue Saint-Denis? In a word, do you not admit that there is progress in music, and in criticism a quality that distinguishes it from blind instinct, namely taste and judgment? Of course you do. This being the case, the ease or difficulty with which the public understands new departures counts for little; this has to do with material results, with business, while it is art that concerns us. Besides, the public—especially in Paris— is not as stupid as some would like to think; it does not reject innovations if they are presented with the right sort of candor. The people who are hostile to innovations are—need I name them?—the *demi-savans*. No, frankly; excuses of this kind are unacceptable. You have written a commonplace rhythm, not because the public would have rejected another, but because it was easier and above all quicker to repeat what had already been used over and over again than to search for more novel and more distinguished combinations."

The distant "Bell Chorus," a contrast in style to the chorus that preceded it, seems to bear out this opinion of ours. Here the whole is full of charm—pure, fresh, and novel. The end of the piece even presents a chord succession whose effect is delightful, although the harmonies succeed one another in an order prohibited by every rule adopted since the schools began. I refer to the diatonic succession of triads in parallel motion which occurs in connection with the fourfold repetition of the line, "The night has come." A Master of Musical Science would call this kind of part-writing most incorrect: the basses and first sopranos are continually at the octave, the basses and second sopranos continually at the fifth. After the C major triad come those in B major and A minor and finally that in G major, the prevailing tonic. The agreeable effect resulting from these four consecutive fifths and octaves is due, in the first place, to the short pause that separates the chords, a pause sufficient to isolate the harmonies one from another and to give to each fundamental the aspect of a new tonic; in the second place, to the naïve coloring of the piece, which not only authorizes this infraction of a time-honored rule, but makes it highly picturesque. Beethoven has already written a similar succession of triads in the first movement of his heroic symphony; everyone knows the majestic nobility of this passage. Believe then, if you must, in absolute rules!

Hardly has this evening hymn died away like a graceful sunset when we are greeted with another return of the horn fanfare with its inevitable pedal point on the dominant:

> There sounds a call, the horn of Gessler.
> It bids us return; we obey it.

The chief huntsman and the chorus recite these two lines in their entirety on B-flat. Our earlier observations have here a more direct and a more particular application.

With the following number the composer begins a higher flight; this is quite another style. Mathilda's entrance is preceded by a long ritornello doubly interesting as harmony and as dramatic expression. There is real passion in this, and that feverish agitation that animates the heart of a young woman obliged to conceal her love. Then comes a recitative, perfect in its diction and admirably commented upon by the orchestra, which reproduces fragments of the ritornello. After this introduction follows the well-known *romance,* "Somber forests."

Rossini has, in our opinion, written few pieces as elegant, as fresh, as distinguished in their melody, and as ingenious in their modulations as this one: aside from the immense merit of the vocal part and the harmony, it involves a style of accompaniment for the violas and first violins that is full of melancholy, also—at the beginning of each stanza—a pianissimo effect for the kettledrum that rouses the listener's attention in a lively manner. One seems to hear one of those natural sounds whose cause remains unknown, one of those strange noises which attract our attention on a clear day in the deep forest and which redouble in us the feeling of silence and isolation. This is poetry, this is music, this is art—beautiful, noble, and pure, just as its votaries would have it always.

This style is sustained until the end of the act, and from henceforth marvel follows marvel. In the duet between Arnold and Mathilda, so full of chivalrous passion, we mention as a blemish the long pedal of the horns and trumpets on G, alternately tonic and dominant, the effect of which is at certain moments atrocious. Then too we shall reproach the composer for having blindly followed the example of the older French composers, who would have thought themselves disgraced if they had failed to bring in the trumpets at once whenever the words made any mention of glory or victory. In this respect Rossini treats us like the dilettanti of 1803, like the admirers of Sédaine and Monsigny.[3]

> Ah, return to war and to glory,
> Take wing and make me proud once more!
> One gains a name if one's a victor;
> The world will then approve my choice.

"Out with the obbligato fanfare," Rossini will have said on reading this in his libretto; "I am writing for France." Finally, it seems to us that this duet, which is developed at considerable length, would gain if there were no repetition of the motive which the two singers have together, "The one who adores you." Since the tempo of this passage is slower than the rest, the repetition necessarily brings with it two interruptions which break up the general pace and detract from the animated effect of the scene by prolonging it uselessly.

But from this point until the final chord of the second act, this defect does not recur. Walter and Tell enter unexpectedly; Mathilda takes flight, Arnold remains to listen to bitter reproaches on his love for the daughter of the Helvetian tyrant. Nothing could be more beautiful, more expressive, more noble than this recitative, both in the vocal parts and in the orchestra. Two phrases are particularly striking in the verity of their expression. One is Walter's counsel:

> Perhaps, though, you should alter
> And take the pains to know us better.

The other is Tell's apostrophe:

> Do you know what it is to feel love for one's country?

At length, the tragic ritornello of the trio is unfolded. Here we confess that, despite our role as critic and the obligations that it brings with it, it is impossible for us to apply the cold blade of the scalpel to the heart of this sublime creation. What should we analyze? The passion, the despair, the tears, the lamentations of a son horrified by the news of his father's murder? God forbid! Or should we make frivolous observations about details, quibble with the author over a *gruppetto* or a solo passage for the flute or an obscure moment in the second violin part? Not I! If others have the courage for it, let them attempt it. As for me, I have none at all—I can only join the crowd in shouting: "Beautiful! Superb! Admirable! Ravishing!"

But I shall have to be sparing of my enthusiastic adjectives, for I am going to need them for the rest of the act, which remains almost continuously on this same high level. The arrival of the three cantons affords the composer an opportunity to write three pieces in three wholly different styles. The first

3. The year in which Berlioz was born. Michel-Jean Sedaine (1719–1797), librettist, and Pierre-Alexandre Monsigny (1729–1817), composer, sustained a highly successful operatic collaboration during the 1760s and '70s.

chorus is in a strong, robust style which paints for us a working people with calloused hands and arms that never tire. In the second chorus and the chaste sweetness of its melody we recognize the timid shepherds; the expression of their fears is ravishing in its grace and naïveté. The fishermen from the canton of Uri arrive by boat from the lake while the orchestra imitates as faithfully as music can the movements and the cadenced efforts of a crew of oarsmen. Hardly have these latecomers disembarked when the three choruses unite in a syllabic ensemble, rapidly recited in half voice and accompanied by the pizzicati of the strings and an occasional muffled chord from the wind instruments:

> Before you, Tell, you see
> Three peoples as one band,
> Our rights our only arms
> Against a vile oppressor.

First recited by the chorus of fishermen and then taken up by the two other choruses, who mingle with it their exclamations and their laconic asides, this phrase is dramatically most realistic. Here is a crowd in which each individual, moved by hope and fear, can scarcely hold back the sentiments that agitate him, a crowd in which all wish to speak and each man interrupts his neighbor. Be it said in passing that the execution of this *coro parlato* is extremely difficult, a fact that may in part excuse the choristers of the Opéra, who usually recite it very badly indeed.

But Tell is about to speak and all grow silent—*arrectis auribus adstant.*[4] He stirs them, he inflames them, he apprises them of Melchthal's cruel death, he promises them arms; finally he asks them directly:

TELL: Do you agree to help?
CHORUS: We one and all agree.
TELL: You will join us?
CHORUS: We will.
TELL: Even in death?
CHORUS: We will.

Then, uniting their voices, they swear a grave and solemn oath to "the God of kings and of shepherds" to free themselves from slavery and to exterminate their tyrants. Their gravity under these circumstances, which would be absurd if they were Frenchmen or Italians, is admirable for a cold-blooded people like the Swiss, whose decisions, if less precipitate, are not lacking in steadfastness or in assurance of attainment. The movement becomes animated only at the end, when Arnold catches sight of the first rays of the rising sun:

ARNOLD: The time has come.
WALTER: For us this is a time of danger.
TELL: Nay, of vict'ry!
WALTER: What answer shall we give him?
ARNOLD: To arms!

4. "They stand by with attentive ears." Vergil, *Aeneid* 1. 152. [Fairclough, trans.].

ARNOLD ⎱
TELL   ⎬ To arms!
WALTER ⎰

Then the whole chorus, the soloists, the orchestra, and the percussion instruments, which have not been heard since the beginning of the act, one and all take up the cry: "To arms!" And at this last and most terrible war cry which bursts forth from all these breasts, shivering in the dawn of the first day of liberty, the entire instrumental mass hurls itself like an avalanche into an impetuous Allegro!

Ah, it is sublime! Let us take breath.

[PART 4]

We left Arnold in despair, thinking only of war and vengeance. His father's death, imposing new obligations upon him, has torn him abruptly from the attraction that had lured him little by little towards the ranks of his country's enemies. Filled with gloomy thoughts, his words to Mathilda at the beginning of Act 3 reveal his fierce and somber pre-occupation:

ARNOLD: I tarry to avenge my father.
MATHILDA: What is your hope?
ARNOLD: It is blood that I hope for;
    I renounce Fortune's favors all,
    I renounce all love and all friendship,
    Even glory, even marriage.
MATHILDA: And I, Melchthal?
ARNOLD: My father's dead.

The expression of these agitated sentiments dominates the whole of the long ritornello which precedes and prepares the entrance of the two lovers. After a short but energetic recitative, in which Arnold sings another five-measure phrase on a single note, an E, the great agitato aria of Mathilda begins.

At the outset, this piece is not as happy in its choice of melody and in its dramatic expression as we find it at the end. The composer seems to have begun it in cold blood and to have come to life by degrees as he penetrated his subject. The first phrase is what we might call "a phrase in compartments" (*une phrase à compartimens*); it belongs to that vast family of melodies consisting of eight measures, four of them on the tonic and as many on the dominant, examples of which occur at the beginning of nearly every concerto of Viotti, Rode, Kreutzer, and their imitators. This is a style in which each development can be foreseen well in advance; in composing this, his latest and perhaps his most important work, it would seem to us that Rossini ought to have abandoned it once and for all. Aside from this, the two lines that follow cry out for an expressive musical setting:

In my heart solitude unending!
Shall you never be at my side?

Rossini has failed to give it to them. What he has written is cold and common-place, despite an instrumentation that might have been less tortured in its superabundant luxuriousness. As though to efface the memory of this some-what scholastic beginning, the peroration is admirable in its originality, its grace, and its sentiment. The liveliest imagination could not have asked the composer for a style of declamation more truthful or more noble than that in which he has caused Mathilda to exclaim, with melancholy abandon:

> To the land of the stranger
> Whose shore you seek, I may not follow
> To offer you my tender care,
> And yet all my heart shall be with you,
> To all your woes it shall be true.

We are not as satisfied with the ensemble for the two voices which closes the scene. As the farewell of two lovers who separate, never to see each other again, it should have been heartbreaking; apart from Mathilda's chromatic vocalization on the word "Melchthal," it is only brilliant and overscored for the wind instruments, without contrasts or oppositions.

At the same time, it is greatly to be regretted—even if only because of the fine flashes of inspiration which we have mentioned—that the scene is entirely suppressed in the performances being given today. At present the act begins with the chorus of Gessler's soldiers, who are engaged in a brutal and arrogant celebration of the hundredth anniversary of the conquest of Switzerland and its addition to the German Empire.

After this there is dancing, of course; at the Opéra, an excuse for a ballet would be found, even in a representation of the Last Judgment. What difference does it make?—the *airs de danse,* all of them saturated with the Swiss melodic idiom, have rare elegance and are written with care (I except only the Allegro in G called the "Pas de soldats"). It is in the midst of this ballet that we meet the celebrated Tyrolienne, so popular nowadays, remarkable for its modulations and for the vocal rhythm which serves as its accompaniment. Before Rossini, no one writing for the stage had thought of using an immediate succession of chords having the character of contrasted tonic harmonies, such as the one that occurs in the thirty-third measure, where the melody outlines an arpeggio within the major triad on B, only to fall back at once into the one on G, the true tonic. This little piece, doubtless written one morning at the breakfast table, has had a truly incredible success, while beauties of an incom-parably higher order have won only very limited approval, although this approval is, to be sure, of quite another sort than that which has welcomed the pretty Tyrolienne so graciously. With some composers, the applause of the crowd is useful but scarcely flattering—for these artists, only the opinion of the discriminating has real value. With others it is just the opposite: only quantity has value, while quality is almost worthless. Until their more frequent dealings with Europeans taught them the value of money, the American Indians pre-ferred a hundred sous to a single gold piece.

After the dances comes the famous scene of the apple. Its style is in general nervous and dramatic. One of Tell's phrases in his dialogue with Gessler seems to us to have real character:

GESSLER: My captive shall he be.
TELL: Let us hope he may be your last.

On the other hand, a movement that seems to us absolutely false in sentiment and expression is that in which Tell, concerned for his son, takes him aside, embraces him, and orders him to leave:

> My heart's dearest treasure,
> Receive my embraces,
> Then depart from me.

Instead of this, it would have been enough to have made him a sign and to have uttered quickly these two words: "Save thyself!" To elaborate upon this idea in an Andante would perhaps have done no harm in an Italian opera, a really Italian one, but in a work like *William Tell*, where reason has been admitted to full civic rights, where not everything is directed towards permitting the singers to shine, such a piece is more than an incongruity—it is an outright nonsense.

The recitative that follows exactly meets the requirements that we have just laid down:

> Rejoin your mother! These my orders:
> That the flame on the mountains now be lighted
> To give to our allies the command to rebel.

This precipitate utterance throws an even more glaring light on the faulty expression that shocked us when this idea was presented before. In compensation, the composer offers us Tell's touching instructions to his little son:

> Move not a muscle, be calm and fearless,
> In prayer bend a suppliant knee!

How admirably the accompaniment of the violoncellos weeps beneath the voice of this father whose heart is breaking as he embraces his boy! The orchestra, almost silent, is heard only in pizzicato chords, each group followed by a rest of half a measure. The bassoons, pianissimo, sustain long plaintive notes. How filled all this is with emotion and anguish—how expressive of the anticipated great event about to be accomplished!

> My son, my son, think of thy mother!
> Patiently she waits for us both.

These last phrases of the melody are irresistibly lifelike; they go straight to the heart.

Let the partisans of popular opinion say what they please. If this sublime inspiration arouses only polite and infrequent applause, there is something about it that is nobler, higher, worthier for a man to take pride in having created, than there is in a graceful Tyrolienne, even though it be applauded by a hundred thousand and sung by the women and children of all Europe. There is a difference between the pretty and the beautiful. To pretend to side with the majority, and to value prettiness at the expense of that which addresses itself to the heart's most intimate sentiments, this is the part of the shrewd businessman, but not that of the artist conscious of his dignity and independence.

The finale of this act includes, in its first section, an admirably energetic passage which is invariably annihilated at the Opéra by the inadequacy of the singer; this is the sudden outburst of the timid Mathilda:

> I claim him as my ward in the name of the sov'reign.
> In indignation a people is watching,
> Take care, take care, he is safe in my arms.

This general indignation is skillfully portrayed, both in the vocal part and in the orchestra; it is as lifelike as Gluck and Spontini. As an accompaniment to the ingeniously modulated melody of the sopranos, the syllabic theme of the men's chorus ("When their pride has misled them") makes an excellent effect. On the other hand, the *stretta* of this chorus consists only of furious cries; to be sure, they are motivated by the text, but they arouse no emotion in the listener, whose ears are needlessly outraged. Here again, it would perhaps have been better to change the wording of the libretto, for it would be difficult if not impossible to set the line, "Cursèd be Gessler's name," except as a savage vociferation having neither melody nor rhythm and paralyzing by its violence all feeling for harmony.

Act 4 reestablishes the individual passions and affords a needed relaxation after the uproar of the preceding scenes. Arnold revisits his father's deserted cottage; his heart filled with a hopeless love and with projects of vengeance, all his senses stirred by the recollections of bloody carnage always before his mind's eye, he breaks down, overcome by the enormity of the affecting contrast. All is calm and silent. Here is peace—and the tomb. And yet an infinity separates him from that breast upon which, at a moment like this, he would so gladly pour out his tears of filial piety, from that heart close to which his own would beat less sadly. Mathilda shall never be his. The situation is poetic, even poignantly melancholy, and it has inspired the musician to write an air which we do not hesitate to pronounce the most beautiful of the entire score. Here the young Melchthal pours out all the sufferings of his soul; here his mournful recollections of the past are painted in the most ravishing of melodies; harmony and modulation are employed only to reinforce the melodic expression, never out of purely musical caprice.

The Allegro with choruses, which follows, is full of spirit and makes a worthy crown for an equally fine scene. At the same time, the piece has only a very indifferent effect upon the public, to judge from the applause with which it is received. For the many it is too refined; delicate shadings like these nearly always escape their attention. Alas, if one could only reduce the public to an assembly of fifty sensible and intelligent persons, how blissful it would be to be an artist!

Since the first performance, the trio accompanied only by the wind instruments has been suppressed, also the piece immediately following it, the prayer sung during the storm. The cut is most inopportune, particularly in view of the prayer, a masterpiece in the picturesque style, whose musical conception is novel enough to have warranted some allowance being made in its favor. Aside from the mise-en-scène, considerations having to do with the decor or the stage machinery were no doubt responsible for the suppression of this interesting part of the score. The thing was accordingly done without hesitation— everyone knows that at the Opéra the directors *support* the music.

From this moment until the final chorus, we shall find nothing but padding. The outbursts of the orchestra while Tell struggles on the lake with the storm, the fragments of recitative interrupted by the chorus—these are things that the musician writes with confidence that no one will listen to them.

The final chorus is another story:

> About us all changes and grows.
> Fresh the air!

This is a beautiful harmonic broadening-out. The *ranz des vaches* floats gracefully above these massive chords and the hymn of Swiss liberty soars upward to heaven, calm and imposing, like the prayer of a just man.

10 Robert Schumann

In contrast to Hector Berlioz, the professional man of letters, Robert Schumann brings to his critical writing romantic idealism and a high purpose. As he tells us himself in his introductory essay, the founding of the *Neue Zeitschrift* in 1834 was a direct outgrowth of his dissatisfaction with the existing state of music and of his desire to bring about a rehabilitation of the poetic principle, "the very thing," as he said later on, "by which we should like to have these pages distinguished from others." The editorial position of the new journal is perhaps most forcefully summed up in Schumann's "speech from the throne" for 1839: "A stern attitude towards foreign trash, benevolence towards aspiring younger artists, enthusiasm for everything masterly that the past has bequeathed." On the whole, these aims are not so very different from those implicit in Berlioz; it is simply that Schumann has less self-interest and less worldly wisdom and that he goes about his task in a more serious way, more humbly and more charitably, if also with greater chauvinism.

"The present is characterized by its parties," Schumann writes in another connection (1836). "Like the political present, one can divide the musical into liberals, middlemen, and reactionaries, or into romanticists, moderns, and classicists. On the right sit the elderly—the contrapuntists, the anti-chromaticists; on the left the youthful—the revolutionaries in their Phrygian caps, the anti-formalists, the genially impudent, among whom the Beethovenians stand out as a special class; in the *Juste Milieu* young and old mingle irresolutely—here are included most of the creations of the day, the offspring which the moment brings forth and then destroys."

In his day, Schumann stood at the very center of the Romantic movement in German music, yet he makes little effort to define its aims and aspirations for us. To him, clearly, these were self-evident: "It is scarcely credible that a distinct romantic school could be formed in music, which is in itself romantic." But in his review of Stephen Heller's Opus 7 (1837) Schumann comes as close as he ever does to a definition and in so doing defines for us also his own personal style. "I am heartily sick of the word 'romanticist,' " he says; "I have not pronounced it ten times in my whole life; and yet—if I wished to confer a brief designation upon our young seer, I should call him one, and what a one! Of that vague, nihilistic disorder behind which some search for romanticism, and of that crass, scribbling materialism which the French neo-romanticists affect, our composer—thank Heaven!—knows nothing; on the contrary, he perceives things naturally, for the most part, and expresses himself clearly and judiciously. Yet on taking up his compositions one senses that there is something more than this lurking in the background—an attractive, individual half-light, more like dawn than dusk, which causes one to see his otherwise clear-cut configurations under an unaccustomed glow. . . . And do not let me overlook the dedication—the coincidence is astonishing. You recall, Eusebius, that we once dedicated something to the Wina of the *Flegeljahre* [by Jean Paul]; the dedication of these impromptus also names one of Jean Paul's constellations—Liane von Froulay [in Jean Paul's *Titan*]. We have in general much in common, an admission that no one should misinterpret—it is too obvious."

FROM *Davidsbündlerblätter*

INTRODUCTORY
(1854)

Near the end of the year 1833 there met in Leipzig, every evening and as though by chance, a number of musicians, chiefly younger men, primarily for social companionship, not less, however, for an exchange of ideas about the art which was for them the meat and drink of life—music. It cannot be said that

TEXT: *Gesammelte Schriften über Musik und Musiker* (Leipzig, 1854); for the essay "New Paths," *Neue Zeitschrift für Musik* 33 (1853): 185–86. Translation by Oliver Strunk. The title "Pages from the League of David" refers to warriors against the Philistines (2 Samuel 5).

musical conditions in Germany were particularly encouraging at the time. On the stage Rossini still ruled, at the piano, with few rivals, Herz and Hünten. And yet only a few years had elapsed since Beethoven, Weber, and Schubert had lived among us. Mendelssohn's star was in the ascendant, to be sure, and marvelous reports were heard of a Pole, one Chopin—but it was not until later that these exerted lasting influence. Then one day an idea flashed across the minds of these young hotheads: Let us not sit idly by; let us attack, that things may become better; let us attack, that the poetic in art may again be held in honor! In this way the first pages of a "New Journal for Music" came into being. But the joy of the solid unanimity of this union of young talents did not continue long. In one of the most cherished comrades, Ludwig Schunke,[1] death claimed a sacrifice. As to the others,[2] some removed from Leipzig altogether for a time. The undertaking was on the point of dissolution. Then one of their number, precisely the musical visionary of the company, one who had until now dreamed away his life more at the piano than among books, decided to take the editing of the publication in hand;[3] he continued to guide it for nearly ten years, to the year 1844. So there arose a series of essays, from which this volume offers a selection. The greater part of the views therein expressed are still his today. What he set down, in hope and fear, about many an artistic phenomenon has in the course of time been substantiated.

Here ought also to be mentioned another league, a more than secret one in that it existed only in the head of its founder—the "Davidsbündler." In order to represent various points of view within the view of art as a whole, it seemed not inappropriate to invent contrasted types of artist, among which Florestan and Eusebius were the most significant, between whom Master Raro stood as intermediary. Like a red thread, this "Davidsbündler" company wound itself through the journal, humorously blending "Wahrheit und Dichtung."[4] Later on, these comrades, not unwelcome to the readers of that time, disappeared entirely from the paper, and from the time when a Peri enticed them into distant climes, nothing further has been heard of their literary efforts.

Should these collected pages, while reflecting a highly agitated time, likewise contribute to divert the attention of those now living to artistic phenomena already nearly submerged by the stream of the present, the aim of their publication will have been fulfilled.

· · · · · ·

1. Talented composer and pianist, friend of Schumann's, coeditor of the *Zeitschrift* during its first year, Schunke died on December 7, 1834, shortly before his twenty-fourth birthday.
2. In addition to Schunke, Schumann's chief collaborators during the first year were Friedrich Wieck and Julius Knorr.
3. During its first year, the *Zeitschrift* described itself as "published by a society of artists and friends of art"; with the first number of the second volume this is changed to read "published under the direction of R. Schumann in association with a number of artists and friends of art."
4. An allusion to the title of Goethe's autobiography, *Aus meinem Leben: Dichtung und Wahrheit*.

AN OPUS TWO[5]
(1831)

Not long ago Eusebius stole quietly in through the door. You know the ironic smile on his pale face with which he seeks to arouse our expectations. I was sitting at the piano with Florestan, who, as you know, is one of those rare men of music who foresee, as it were, all coming, novel, or extraordinary things. None the less there was a surprise in store for him today. With the words "Hats off, gentlemen, a genius!" Eusebius placed a piece of music on the stand. We were not allowed to see the title. I leafed about absentmindedly among the pages; this veiled, silent enjoyment of music has something magical about it. Furthermore, as it seems to me, every composer has his own special way of arranging notes for the eye: Beethoven looks different on paper from Mozart, very much as Jean Paul's prose looks different from Goethe's. In this case, however, it was as though unfamiliar eyes were everywhere gazing out at me strangely—flower-eyes, basilisk-eyes, peacock-eyes, maiden-eyes; here and there things grew clearer—I thought I saw Mozart's "Là ci darem la mano" woven about with a hundred harmonies; Leporello seemed to be actually winking at me, and Don Giovanni flew past me in a white cloak. "Now play it!" Florestan suggested. Eusebius obeyed; huddled in a window alcove, we listened. As though inspired, Eusebius played on, leading past us countless figures from the realest of lives; it was as though the inspiration of the moment lifted his fingers above the usual measure of their capabilities. Florestan's entire approval, except for a blissful smile, consisted, to be sure, in nothing but the remark that the variations might perhaps be by Beethoven or Schubert, had either of them been piano virtuosi—but when he turned to the title page, read nothing more than:

Là ci darem la mano
varié pour le pianoforte par
Frédéric Chopin
Oeuvre 2

and both of us called out in amazement "An opus two!"—and when every face flowed somewhat with more than usual astonishment and, aside from a few exclamations, little was to be distinguished but: "At last, here's something sensible again—Chopin—the name is new to me—who is he?—in any case a genius—isn't that Zerlina laughing there or perhaps even Leporello?"—then, indeed, arose a scene which I prefer not to describe. Excited with wine, Chopin, and talking back and forth, we went off to Master Raro, who laughed a great deal and showed little curiosity about our Opus 2—"for I know you and your newfangled enthusiasm too well—just bring your Chopin here to me some time." We promised it for the next day. Presently Eusebius bid us an

5. This essay was published as early as 1831 in the *Allgemeine musikalische Zeitung*. As the one in which the Davidsbündler make their first appearance, it is given a place here also. [Au.]

indifferent good night; I remained for a while with Master Raro; Florestan, who for some time had had no lodgings, fled through the moonlit alley to my house. I found him in my room at midnight, lying on the sofa, his eyes closed.

"Chopin's variations," he began, as though in a dream, "they are still going around in my head. Surely the whole is dramatic and sufficiently Chopinesque; the introduction, self-contained though it is—can you recall Leporello's leaping thirds?—seems to me to belong least of all to the rest; but the theme—why does he write it in B-flat?—the variations, the final movement, and the Adagio—these are really something—here genius crops up in every measure. Of course, dear Julius, the speaking parts are Don Giovanni, Zerlina, Leporello, and Masetto. In the theme, Zerlina's reply is drawn amorously enough. The first variation might perhaps be called somewhat elegant and coquettish—in it, the Spanish grandee toys aimiably with the peasant maid. This becomes self-evident in the second, which is already much more intimate, comic, and quarrelsome, exactly as though two lovers were chasing each other and laughing more than usual. But in the third—how everything is changed! This is pure moonshine and fairy spell—Masetto watches from afar and curses rather audibly, to be sure, but Don Giovanni is little disturbed. And now the fourth—what is your idea of it? Eusebius played it quite clearly—doesn't it jump about saucily and impudently as it approaches the man, although the Adagio (it seems natural to me that Chopin repeats the first part) is in B-flat minor, than which nothing could be more fitting, for it reproaches the Don, as though moralizing, with his misdeeds. It is bold, surely, and beautiful that Leporello listens, laughs, and mocks from behind the shrubbery, that the oboes and clarinets pour out seductive magic, and that the B-flat major, in full blossom, marks well the moment of the first kiss. Yet all of this is as nothing in comparison with the final movement—is there more wine, Julius?—this is Mozart's whole finale—popping corks and clinking bottles everywhere, in the midst of things Leporello's voice, then the grasping evil spirits in pursuit, the fleeing Don Giovanni—and finally the end, so beautifully soothing, so truly conclusive." Only in Switzerland, Florestan added, had he experienced anything similar to this ending; there, on a fine day, when the evening sun climbs higher and higher to the topmost peak where finally its last beam vanishes, there comes a moment in which one seems to see the white Alp-giants close their eyes. One feels only that one has seen a heavenly vision. "Now Julius, wake up, you too, to new dreams—and go to sleep!"

"Florestan of my heart," I answered, "these private feelings are perhaps praiseworthy, if somewhat subjective; but little as Chopin needs to think of listening to his genius, I still shall also bow my head before such genius, such aspiration, such mastery."

With that we fell asleep.

Julius[6]

6. This essay was Schumann's first published writing.

FLORESTAN'S SHROVE TUESDAY ADDRESS DELIVERED AFTER A PERFORMANCE OF BEETHOVEN'S LAST SYMPHONY
(1835)

Florestan climbed on to the piano and spoke as follows:

Assembled Davidsbündler, that is, youths and men who are to slay the Philistines, musical and otherwise, especially the tallest ones (see the last numbers of the *Comet*[7] for 1833).

I am never overenthusiastic, best of friends! The truth is, I know the symphony better than I know myself. I shall not waste a word on it. After it, anything I could say would be as dull as ditch water, Davidsbündler. I have celebrated regular Ovidian Tristia, have heard anthropological lectures. One can scarcely be fanatical about some things, scarcely paint some satires with one's facial expression, scarcely—as Jean Paul's Giannozzo[8] did—sit low enough in the balloon for men not to believe that one concerns oneself about them, so far, far below do these two-legged creatures, which one calls men, file through the narrow pass, which one may in any case call life. To be sure, I was not at all annoyed by what little I heard. In the main I laughed at Eusebius. A regular clown, he flew impertinently at a fat neighbor who inquired confidentially during the Adagio: "Sir, did not Beethoven also write a battle symphony?" "Yes, that's the 'Pastoral' Symphony," our Euseb replied indifferently. "Quite right, so it is," the fat one expanded, resuming his meditations.

Men must deserve noses, otherwise God would not have provided them. They tolerate much, these audiences, and of this I could cite you magnificent examples; for instance, rascal, when at a concert you were turning the pages of one of Field's nocturnes for me. Unluckily, on one of the most broken-down rattle-boxes that was ever inflicted upon a company of listeners, instead of the pedal I stumbled on the Janissary stop[9]—piano enough, fortunately, so that I could yield to the impulse of the moment and, repeating the stroke softly from time to time, could let the audience believe some sort of march was being played in the distance. Of course Eusebius did his part by spreading the story; the audience, however, outdid themselves in applause.

Any number of similar anecdotes had occurred to me during the Adagio—when the first chord of the Finale broke in. "What is it, Cantor," I said to a trembling fellow next to me, "but a triad with a suspended fifth, somewhat whimsically laid out, in that one does not know which to accept as the bass—

---

7. An "Unterhaltungsblatt" published in Altenburg from 1830 to 1836. In its issue for August 27, 1832, it had printed Schumann's "Reminiscences from Clara Wieck's Last Concerts in Leipzig."
8. Principal character in Jean Paul's "Des Luftschiffers Giannozzo Seebuch," one of the humorous supplements to the second volume of his *Titan* (1801).
9. A pedal producing the effect of bass drum and cymbals or triangle, much favored during the vogue of "Turkish music."

the A of the kettledrum or the F of the bassoons? Just have a look at Türk, Section 19, page 7!"[10] "Sir, you speak very loud and are surely joking." With a small and terrifying voice I whispered in his ear: "Cantor, watch out for storms! The lightning sends ahead no liveried lackeys before it strikes; at the most there is first a storm and after it a thunderbolt. That's just its way." "All the same, such dissonances ought to be prepared." Just at that moment came the second one. "Cantor, the fine trumpet seventh shall excuse you." I was quite exhausted with my restraint—I should have soothed him with a sound blow.

Now you gave me a memorable moment, conductor, when you hit the tempo of the low theme in the basses so squarely on the line that I forgot much of my annoyance at the first movement, in which, despite the modest pretense of the direction "Un poco maestoso," there speaks the full, deliberate stride of godlike majesty.

"What do you suppose Beethoven meant by those basses?" "Sir," I replied gravely enough, "a genius often jests; it seems to be a sort of night watchman's song." Gone was the exquisite moment, once again Satan was set loose. Then I remarked the Beethoven devotees—the way they stood there goggle-eyed, saying: "That's by our Beethoven. That's a German work. In the last movement there's a double fugue. Some reproach him for not excelling in this department, but how he has done it—yes, this is *our* Beethoven." Another choir chimed in with: "It seems as though all forms of poetry are combined in the work: in the first movement the epic, in the second the humorous, in the third the lyric, in the fourth—the blend of them all—the drama." Still another choir really applied itself to praising: "It's a gigantic work, colossal, comparable to the pyramids of Egypt." Still another went in for description: "The symphony tells the story of man's creation: first chaos, then the divine command 'Let there be light,' then the sun rising on the first man, who is delighted with such splendor—in short, it is the whole first chapter of the Pentateuch."

I became more frantic and more quiet. And while they were eagerly following the text and finally applauding, I seized Eusebius by the arm and pulled him down the brightly lighted stairs, smiling faces on either hand.

Below, in the darkness of the street lamps, Eusebius said, as though to himself: "Beethoven—what depths there are in the word, even the deep sonority of the syllables resounding as into an eternity! For this name, it is as though there could be no other characters." "Eusebius," I said with genuine calm, "do you too condescend to praise Beethoven? Like a lion, he would have raised himself up before you and have asked: 'Who, then, are you who presume this?' I do not address myself to you, Eusebius; you mean well—but must a great man then always have a thousand dwarfs in his train? They believe they understand him—who so aspired, who struggled against countless attacks—as they

10. Daniel Gottlob Türk, *Kurze Anweisung zum Generalbaßspielen* (Halle, 1791).

smile and clap their hands. Do those who are not accountable to me for the simplest musical rule have the effrontery to evaluate a master as a whole? Do these, all of whom I put to flight if I drop merely the word 'counterpoint'—do these who perhaps appreciate this and that at second hand and at once call out: 'Oh, this fits our corpus perfectly!'—do these who wish to talk of exceptions to rules they do not know—do these who prize in him, not the measure of his gigantic powers, but precisely the excess—shallow men of the world—wandering sorrows of Werther—overgrown, bragging boys—do these presume to love him, even praise him?"

Davidsbündler, at the moment I can think of no one so entitled but the provincial Silesian nobleman who recently wrote to a music dealer in this fashion:

> Dear sir:
> At last I have my music cabinet nearly in order. You ought to see how splendid it is. Alabaster columns on the inside, a mirror with silk curtains, busts of composers—in short, magnificent! In order, however, to give it a final touch of real elegance I ask you to send me, further, the complete works of Beethoven, *for I like this composer very much.*

What more there is that I should say, I should, in my opinion, scarcely know.

ENTHUSIASTIC LETTERS[11]
(1835)

I. EUSEBIUS TO CHIARA

After each of our musical feasts for the soul there always reappears an angelic face which, down to the roguish line about the chin, more than resembles that of a certain Clara.[12] Why are you not with us, and how may you have thought last night of us Firlenzer, from the "Calm Sea"[13] to the resplendent ending of the Symphony in B-flat major?[14]

Except for a concert itself, I know of nothing finer than the hour before one, during which one hums ethereal melodies to oneself, the finger on the lips, walks up and down discreetly on one's toes, performs whole overtures on the windowpanes. . . . Just then it struck a quarter of. And now, with Florestan, I mounted the polished stairs.

---

11. These letters might also have been called "Wahrheit und Dichtung." They have to do with the first Gewandhaus concerts held under Mendelssohn's direction in October, 1835. [Au.]
     The concerts in question were the first four in the subscription series; their dates were October 4, 11, 22, and 29. They are also covered in more conventional reviews published in the *Allgemeine musikalische Zeitung* for October 14 and 21 and for December 16, with the help of which it is possible to supply certain details passed over in Schumann's account.
12. Quoted from an earlier letter to Clara (*Jugendbriefe* [Leipzig, 1885], p. 266). At the time of the writing of these letters, Clara Wieck was just sixteen.
13. Mendelssohn's overture.
14. Beethoven's Fourth Symphony.

"Seb," said he, "I look forward tonight to many things: first to the whole program itself, for which one thirsts after the dry summer; then to F. Meritis,[15] who for the first time marches into battle with his orchestra; then to the singer Maria,[16] with her vestal voice; finally to the public as a whole, expecting miracles—that public to which, as you know, I usually attach only too little importance." At the word "public" we stood before the old chatelain with his Commendatore face, who had much to do and finally let us in with an expression of annoyance, for as usual Florestan had forgotten his ticket. As I entered the brightly lighted golden hall I may, to judge from my face, have delivered perhaps the following address:

"With gentle tread I make my entrance, for I seem to see welling up here and there the faces of those unique ones to whom is given the fine art of uplifting and delighting hundreds in a single moment. There I see Mozart, stamping his feet to the symphony until a shoe-buckle flies off; there Hummel, the old master, improvising at the piano; there Catalani, pulling off her shawl, for the sound-absorbing carpet has been forgotten; there Weber; there Spohr; and many another. And there I thought also of you, my pure bright Chiara— of how at other times you spied down from your box with the lorgnette that so well becomes you." This train of thought was interrupted by the angry eye of Florestan, who stood, rooted to the spot, in his old corner by the door, and in his angry eye stood something like this:

"Think, Public, of my having you together again at last and of my being able to set you one against another. . . . Long ago, overt ones, I wanted to establish concerts for deaf-mutes which might serve you as a pattern of how to behave at concerts, especially at the finest. . . . Like Tsing-Sing,[17] you were to have been turned to a stone pagoda, had you dared to repeat anything of what you saw in music's magic realm," and so forth. The sudden deathlike silence of the public broke in on my reflections. F. Meritis came forward. A hundred hearts went out to him in that first moment.

Do you remember how, leaving Padua one evening, we went down the Brenta; how the tropical Italian night closed the eyes of one after another? And how, in the morning, a voice suddenly called out: "Ecco, ecco, signori— Venezia!"—and the sea lay spread out before us, calm and stupendous; how on the furthest horizon there sounded up and down a delicate tinkle, as though the little waves were speaking to one another in a dream? Behold—such is the wafting and weaving of the "Calm Sea";[18] one actually grows drowsy from it and is rather thought than thinking. The Beethovenian chorus after Goethe[19] and the accentuated word sound almost raw in contrast to the spider's-web

15. Mendelssohn.
16. Henriette Grabau.
17. A character in Auber's opera *Le Cheval de bronze* (1835).
18. The overture by Mendelssohn.
19. Beethoven's Opus 112.

tone of the violins. Toward the end there occurs a single detached harmony—here perhaps a Nereid fixes the poet with her seductive glance, seeking to draw him under—then for the first time a wave beats higher, the sea grows by degrees more talkative, the sails flutter, the pennant leaps with joy, and now holloa, away, away, away. . . . Which overture of F. Meritis did I prefer, some artless person asked me; at once the tonalities E minor, B minor, and D major[20] entwined themselves as in a triad of the Graces and I could think of no answer better than the best—"Each one!" F. Meritis conducted as though he had composed the overture himself, and though the orchestra played accordingly, I was struck by Florestan's remarking that he himself had played rather in this style when he came from the provinces to Master Raro as an apprentice. "My most fatal crisis," he continued, "was this intermediate state between nature and art; always ardent as was my grasp, I had now to take everything slowly and precisely, for my technique was everywhere found wanting; presently there arose such a stumbling and stiffness that I began to doubt my talent; the crisis, fortunately, did not last long." I for my part was disturbed, in the overture as in the symphony, by the baton,[21] and I agreed with Florestan when he held that, in the symphony, the orchestra should stand there as a republic, acknowledging no superior. At the same time it was a joy to see F. Meritis and the way in which his eye anticipated every nuance in the music's intellectual windings, from the most delicate to the most powerful, and in which, as the most blissful one, he swam ahead of the rest, so different from those conductors on whom one sometimes chances, who threaten with their scepter to beat score, orchestra, and public all in one.

You know how little patience I have with quarrels over tempi and how for me the movement's inner measure is the sole determinant. Thus the relatively fast Allegro that is cold sounds always more sluggish than the relatively slow one that is sanguine. In the orchestra it is also a question of quality—where this is relatively coarse and dense the orchestra can give to the detail and to the whole more emphasis and import; where this is relatively small and fine, as with our Firlenzer, one must help out the lack of resonance with driving tempi. In a word, the Scherzo of the symphony seemed to me too slow; one noticed this quite clearly also in the restlessness with which the orchestra sought to be at rest. Still, what is this to you in Milan—and, strictly speaking, how little it is to me, for I can after all imagine the Scherzo just as I want it whenever I please.

You asked whether Maria would find Firlenz as cordial as it used to be. How can you doubt it? Only she chose an aria which brought her more honor as an artist than applause as a virtuosa.[22] Then a Westphalian music director[23] played

20. *A Midsummer Night's Dream, Fingal's Cave, Calm Sea and Happy Voyage.*
21. Before Mendelssohn, in the days when Matthai was in charge, the orchestral works were performed without a conductor beating time.
22. Weber's inserted aria (1818) "Was sag ich? Schaudern macht mich der Gedanke!" for Cherubini's *Lodoiska* (1791).
23. Otto Gerke.

a violin concerto by Spohr[24]—good enough, but too lean and colorless.

In the choice of pieces, everyone professed to see a change in policy; if formerly, from the very beginning of the Firlenzer concerts, Italian butterflies fluttered about the German oaks, this time these last stood quite alone, as powerful as they were somber. One party sought to read in this a reaction; I take it rather for chance than for intention. All of us know how necessary it is to protect Germany from an invasion by your favorites; let this be done with foresight, however, and more by encouraging the youthful spirits in the Fatherland than by a needless defense against a force which, like a fashion, comes in and goes out.

Just at midnight Florestan came in with Jonathan, a new Davidsbündler, the two of them fencing furiously with one another over the aristocracy of mind and the republic of opinion. At last Florestan has found an opponent who gives him diamonds to crack. Of this mighty one you will hear more later on.

Enough for today. Do not forget to look in the calendar sometimes for August 13, where an Aurora links your name with mine.

Eusebius.

2. To Chiara

The letter carrier coming toward me blossomed out into a flower when I saw the shimmering red "Milano" on your letter. With delight I too recall my first visit to the Scala, just when Rubini was singing there with Méric-Lalande. For Italian music one must listen to in Italian company; German music one can enjoy under any sky.

I was quite right in not reading into the program of the last concert a reactionary intention, for the very next ones brought something Hesperidian. Whereat it was Florestan who amused me most; he finds this actually tiresome, and—out of mere irritation with those Handelians and other fanatics who talk as though they had themselves composed the *Samson* in their nightshirts—does not exactly attack the Hesperidian music, but compares it vaguely with "fruit salad," with "Titian flesh without spirit," and so forth, yet in so comical a tone that you could laugh out loud, did not his eagle eye bear down on you. "As a matter of fact," he said on one occasion, "to be annoyed with Italian things is long since out of fashion, and, in any case, why beat about with a club in this flowery fragrance which flies in and flies out? I should not know which world to choose—one full of nothing but refractory Beethovens or one full of dancing swans of Pesaro. Only two things puzzle me: our fair singers, who after all never know what to sing (excepting everything or nothing)—why do they never chance on something small, say, on a song by Weber, Schubert, Wiedebein; and then our German composers of vocal music, who complain that so little of their work reaches the concert hall—why do they never think of concert pieces, concert arias, concert scenas, and write something of this kind?"

24. No. 11 in G major, Opus 70.

The singer[25] (not Maria), who sang something from *Torvaldo,*[26] began her "Dove son? Chi m'aita?" in such a tremble that I responded inwardly: "In Firlenz, deary; aide-toi et le ciel t'aidera!" Presently, however, she showed her brighter side, the public its well-meant approval. "If only our German song-birds," Florestan interposed, "would not look on themselves as children who think one does not see them when they close their eyes; as it is, they usually hide themselves so stealthily behind their music that one pays the more attention to their faces and thus notices the difference between them and those Italian girls whom I saw singing at one another in the Academy at Milan with eyes rolling so wildly that I feared their artificial passion might burst into flames; this last I exaggerate—still, I should like to read in German eyes something of the dramatic situation, something of the music's joy and grief; beautiful singing from a face of marble makes one doubtful of inner advantage; I mean this in a sort of general way."

Then you ought to have seen Meritis playing the Mendelssohn Concerto in G Minor! Seating himself at the piano as innocently as a child, he now took captive one heart after another, drawing them along behind him in swarms, and, when he set you free, you knew only that you had flown past Grecian isles of the gods and had been set down again in the Firlenzer hall, safe and sound. "You are a very happy master in your art," said Florestan to Meritis when it was over, and both of them were right. Though my Florestan had spoken not a word to me about the concert, I caught him very neatly yesterday. To be precise, I saw him turning over the leaves of a book and noting something down. When he had gone, opposite this passage in his diary—"About some things in this world there is nothing to be said at all—for example, about Mozart's C Major Symphony with the fugue, about many things in Shakespeare, about some things in Beethoven"—I read, written in the margin: "And about Meritis, when he plays the concerto by M."

We were highly delighted with an energetic overture of Weber's,[27] the mother of so many of those little fellows who tag along behind her, ditto with a violin concerto played by young ————,[28] for it does one good to be able to prophesy with conviction of a hard worker that his path will lead to mastery. With things repeated year in and year out—symphonies excepted—I shall not detain you. Your earlier comment on Onslow's Symphony in A[29]—that, having heard it twice, you knew it by heart, bar for bar—is also mine, although I do not know the real reason for this rapid commission to memory. On the one hand I see that the instruments still cling to one another too much and are piled on one another too heterogeneously; on the other hand the melodic

25. Fräulein Weinhold, from Amsterdam.
26. Rossini's *Torvaldo e Dorliska.*
27. Either the Overture to the *Beherrscher der Geister,* played at the third concert on October 22, or that to *Euryanthe,* played at the fourth concert on October 29, probably the former.
28. Wilhelm Uhlrich, who played a concerto by L. W. Maurer.
29. No. 1, Op. 41, played at the fourth concert, on October 29.

threads—the principal and subsidiary ideas—come through so decidedly that, in view of the thick instrumental combination, their very prominence seems to me most strange. The principle ruling here is a mystery to me, and I cannot express it clearly. Perhaps it will stir you to reflection. I feel most at home in the elegant ballroom turmoil of the Minuet, where everything sparkles with pearls and diamonds; in the Trio I see a scene in an adjoining sitting room, into which, through the frequently opened ballroom doors, there penetrates the sound of violins, drowning out words of love. What do you think?

This brings me very conveniently indeed to the A Major Symphony of Beethoven[30] which we heard not long ago. Moderately delighted, we went, late in the evening as it was, to Master Raro. You know Florestan—the way he sits at the piano and, while improvising, speaks, laughs, weeps, gets up, sits down again, and so forth, as though in his sleep. Zilia[31] sat in the bay window, other Davidsbündler here and there in various groups. There was much discussion. "I had to laugh"—thus Florestan began, beginning at the same time the beginning of the symphony—"to laugh at a dried-up notary who discovered in it a battle of Titans, with their effectual destruction in the last movement, but who stole quietly past the Allegretto because it did not fit in with his idea; to laugh in general at those who talk endlessly of the innocence and absolute beauty of music in itself—of course art should conceal, and not repeat, the unfortunate octaves and fifths of life—of course I find, often in certain saintly arias (for example, Marschner's), beauty without truth and, sometimes in Beethoven (but seldom), the latter without the former. But most of all my fingers itch to get at those who maintain that Beethoven, in his symphonies, surrendered always to the grandest sentiments, the sublimest reflections, on God, immortality, and the cosmos, for if that gifted man does point toward heaven with the branches of his flowering crown, he none the less spreads out his roots in his beloved earth. To come to the symphony, the idea that follows is not mine at all, but rather someone's in an old number of the *Cäcilia*[32] (the scene there changed—out of a perhaps exaggerated delicacy toward Beethoven which might well have been spared—to the elegant hall of a count or some such place).

"It is the merriest of weddings, the bride a heavenly child with a rose in her hair—but with one only. I am mistaken if the guests do not gather in the introduction, do not greet one another profusely with inverted commas—very much mistaken if merry flutes do not remind us that the whole village, with its maypoles and their many-colored ribbons, takes joy in Rosa, the bride—very much mistaken if the trembling glance of her pale mother does not seem to ask: 'Dost not know that we must part?' and if Rosa, quite overcome, does not throw herself into her mother's arms, drawing the bridegroom after her with one hand. Now it grows very quiet in the village outside (here Florestan

30. Played at the third concert, on October 22.
31. Clara Wieck.
32. A musical journal published in Mainz by Schott, beginning in 1824.

entered the Allegretto, breaking off pieces here and there); only from time to time a butterfly floats by or a cherry blossom falls. The organ begins, the sun stands at its height, occasional long diagonal beams play through the church with bits of dust, the bells ring diligently, churchgoers gradually take their places, pews are opened and shut, some peasants look closely at their hymn-books, others up into the choir loft, the procession draws nearer—at its head choirboys with lighted tapers and censers, then friends—often turning around to stare at the couple accompanied by the priest—then the parents and friends of the bride, with the assembled youth of the village bringing up the rear. How everything arranges itself, how the priest ascends to the altar, how he addresses, now the bride and now the fortunate one, how he speaks to them of the duties of the bond and of its purposes and of how they may find happi-ness in harmony and love of one another, how he then asks for her 'I do,' which assumes so much forever and forever, and how she pronounces it, firm and sustained—all this prevents my painting the picture further—do as you please with the finale"—thus Florestan broke off, tearing into the end of the Alle-gretto, and it sounded as though the sexton had so slammed the doors shut that the whole church echoed.

Enough. In me, too, Florestan's interpretation has stirred up something, and my alphabet begins to run together. There is much more for me to tell you, but the outdoors calls. Wait out the interval until my next letter with faith in a better beginning.

Eusebius.

DANCE LITERATURE
(1836)

J. C. Kessler:[33] Three Polonaises, Op. 25
Sigismund Thalberg:[34] Twelve Waltzes, Op. 4
Clara Wieck: *Valses romantiques,* Op. 4
Leopold, Edler von Meyer:[35] Salon (Six Waltzes), Op. 4
Franz Schubert: First Waltzes, Op. 9, Bk. I
The same: *Deutsche Tänze,* Op. 33

"And now play, Zilia! I wish to duck myself quite under in the harmonies and only occasionally to poke out my head in order that you may not think me drowned from melancholy; for dance music makes one sad and lax, just as church music, quite the other way, makes one joyful and active—me at least." Thus spake Florestan, as Zilia was already floating through the first Kessler

---

33. Joseph Christoph Kessler, concert pianist and composer for the piano, piano teacher in Lem-berg, Warsaw, Breslau, and Vienna.
34. Sigismund Thalberg, composer for the piano and concert pianist of the first rank, Liszt's chief rival, toured the United States in 1857 together with Vieuxtemps.
35. Pupil of Czerny, concert pianist, toured the United States from 1845 to 1847 and again in 1867 and 1868.

polonaise. "Indeed it would be lovely," he continued, half-listening, half-speaking, "if a dozen lady-Davidsbündler were to make the evening memorable and would embrace each other in a festival of the Graces. Jean Paul has already remarked that girls ought really to dance only with girls (though this would lead, indeed, to there being some weddings fewer); men (I add) ought never to dance at all."

"Should they do so none the less," Eusebius interrupted, "when they come to the trio, he ought to say to his partner-Davidsbündler, 'How simple and how kind you are!' and, in the second part, it would be well if she were to drop her bouquet, to be picked up in flying past and rewarded with a grateful glance."

All this, however, was expressed more in Euseb's bearing and in the music than in anything he actually said. Florestan only tossed his head from time to time, especially at the third polonaise, most brilliant and filled with sounds of horn and violin.

"Now something livelier, and do you play the Thalberg, Euseb; Zilia's fingers are too delicate for it," said Florestan, who soon interrupted to ask that the sections be not repeated, since the waltzes were too transparent—particularly the ninth, which remained on one level, indeed on one measure—"and eternally tonic and dominant, dominant and tonic. Still, it's good enough for those whose ears are in their feet." But, at the end, the one who stood at the foot (a student) called out "Da capo!" in all seriousness, and everyone was obliged to laugh at Florestan's fury at this and at the way he shouted him down, telling him that he might be on his way, that he should interrupt with no further encouragements of this sort or he would silence him with an hour-long trill in thirds, and so forth.

"By a lady, then?" a reviewer might begin, seeing the *Valses romantiques.* "Well, well! Here we shan't need to hunt long for fifths and for the melody!"

Zilia held out four short moonlit harmonies. All listened intently. But on the piano there lay a sprig of roses—Florestan always had vases of flowers in place of the candelabras—and, shaken by the vibration, this had gradually slid down onto the keys. Reaching out for a note in the bass, Zilia struck against this too violently and left off playing, for her finger bled. Florestan asked what the matter was. "Nothing," said Zilia; "as in these waltzes, there is as yet no great pain, only a drop of blood charmed forth by roses." And may she who said this know no other.

A moment later, Florestan plunged into the midst of the brilliant countesses and ambassadresses of the Meyer *salon.* How soothing this is—wealth and beauty, the height of rank and style, with music at the summit; every one speaks and no one listens, for the music drowns all out in waves! "For this," Florestan blurted out, "one really needs an instrument with an extra octave to the right and left, so that one can properly spread out and celebrate." You can have no idea of how Florestan plays this sort of thing and of how he storms away, carrying you along with him. The Davidsbündler, too, were quite worked up, calling in their excitement (musical excitement is insatiable) for "more and more," till Serpentin[36] suggested choosing between the Schubert waltzes and the Chopin boleros. "If, throwing myself at the keyboard from here," Florestan shouted, placing himself in a corner away from the piano, "I can hit the first chord of the last movement of the D Minor Symphony,[37] Schubert wins." He hit it, of course. Zilia played the waltzes by heart.

First waltzes by Franz Schubert. Tiny sprites, ye who hover no higher above the ground than, say, the height of a flower—to be sure, I don't care for the *Sehnsuchtswalzer*, in which a hundred girlish emotions have already bathed, or for the last three either, an aesthetic blemish on the whole for which I can't forgive the author—but the way in which the others turn about these, weaving them in, more or less, with fragrant threads, and the way in which there runs through all of them a so fanciful thoughtlessness that one becomes part of it oneself and believes at the last that one is still playing in the first—this is really first-rate.

In the *Deutsche Tänze*, on the other hand, there dances, to be sure, a whole carnival. "'Twould be fine," Florestan shouted in Fritz Friedrich's[38] ear, "if you would get your magic lantern and follow the masquerade in shadows on the wall." Exit and reenter the latter, jubilant.

The group that follows is one of the most charming. The room dimly lighted—Zilia at the piano, the wounding rose in her hair—Eusebius in his black velvet coat, leaning over her chair—Florestan (ditto), standing on the table and ciceronizing—Serpentin, his legs twined round Walt's[39] neck, sometimes riding back and forth—the painter à la Hamlet, parading his shadow figures through the bull's-eye, some spider-legged ones even running off the wall on to the ceiling. Zilia began, and Florestan may have spoken substantially to this effect, though at much greater length:

"No. 1. In A major. Masks milling about. Kettledrums. Trumpets. The lights go down. Perruquier: 'Everything seems to be going very well.' No. 2. Comic character, scratching himself behind the ears and continually calling out 'Pst, pst!' Exit. No. 3. Harlequin, arms akimbo. Out the door, head over heels. No. 4. Two stiff and elegant masks, dancing and scarcely speaking to one another. No. 5. Slim cavalier, chasing a mask: 'At last I've caught you, lovely zither player!' 'Let me go!' She escapes. No. 6. Hussar at attention, with plume and sabretache. No. 7. Two harvesters, waltzing together blissfully. He, softly: 'Is it thou?' They recognize each other. No. 8. Tenant farmer from the country, getting ready to dance. No. 9. The great doors swing open. Splendid procession of knights and noble ladies. No. 10. Spaniard to an Ursuline: 'Speak at least, since you may not love!' She: 'I would rather not speak, and be understood!' . . ."

But in the midst of the waltz Florestan sprang from the table and out the

---

36. Carl Banck, music critic and composer of songs.
37. See above, p. 104.
38. The deaf painter. [Au.] The painter J. P. Lyser.
39. The pianist Louis Rakemann, who emigrated to America in 1839.

door. One was used to this in him. Zilia, too, soon left off, and the others scattered in one direction and another.

Florestan, you know, has a habit of often breaking off in the very moment when his enjoyment is at its height, perhaps in order to impress it in all its freshness and fullness on the memory. And this time he had his way—for whenever his friends speak to each other of their happiest evenings, they always recall the twenty-eighth of December, 18— . . .

NEW PATHS
(1853)

Years have passed—nearly as many as I devoted to the former editorship of this journal, namely ten—since last I raised my voice within these covers, so rich in memories. Often, despite my intense creative activity, I have felt myself stimulated; many a new and significant talent has appeared; a new musical force has seemed to be announcing itself—as has been made evident by many of the aspiring artists of recent years, even though their productions are chiefly familiar to a limited circle.[40] Following the paths of these chosen ones with the utmost interest, it has seemed to me that, after such a preparation, there would and must suddenly appear some day one man who would be singled out to make articulate in an ideal way the highest expression of our time, one man who would bring us mastery, not as the result of a gradual development, but as Minerva, springing fully armed from the head of Cronus. And he is come, a young creature over whose cradle graces and heroes stood guard. His name is *Johannes Brahms,* and he comes from Hamburg where he has been working in silent obscurity, trained in the most difficult theses of his art by an excellent teacher who sends me enthusiastic reports of him,[41] recommended to me recently by a well-known and respected master. Even outwardly, he bore in his person all the marks that announce to us a chosen man. Seated at the piano, he at once discovered to us wondrous regions. We were drawn into a circle whose magic grew on us more and more. To this was added an altogether inspired style of playing which made of the piano an orchestra of lamenting and exultant voices. There were sonatas—veiled symphonies, rather; lieder, whose poetry one could understand without knowing the words, although a deep vocal melody ran through them all; single piano pieces, in part of a demonic nature, most attractive in form; then sonatas for violin and piano; string quartets—and every work so distinct from any other that each seemed to flow from a different source. And then it seemed as though, roaring along like a river, he united them all as in a waterfall, bearing aloft a peaceful rainbow

40. Here I have in mind Joseph Joachim, Ernst Naumann, Ludwig Norman, Woldemar Bargiel, Theodor Kirchner, Julius Schäffer, Albert Dietrich, not to forget that profoundly thoughtful student of the great in art, the sacred composer C. F. Wisling. As their valiant advance guard I might also mention Niels Wilhelm Gade, C. F. Mangold, Robert Franz, and Stephen Heller. [Au.]
41. Eduard Marxsen, in Hamburg. [Au.]

above the plunging waters below, surrounded at the shore by playful butterflies and borne along by the calls of nightingales.

Later, if he will wave with his magic wand to where massed forces, in the chorus and orchestra, lend their strength, there lie before us still more wondrous glimpses into the secrets of the spirit world. May the highest genius strengthen him for what expectation warrants, for there is also latent in him another genius—that of modesty. His comrades greet him on his first entrance into the world, where there await him wounds, perhaps, but also palms and laurels; we welcome him as a valiant warrior.

In every time, there reigns a secret league of kindred spirits. Tighten the circle, you who belong to it, in order that the truth in art may shine forth more and more brightly, everywhere spreading joy and peace.

R. S.

11   Franz Liszt and Carolyne von Sayn-Wittgenstein

On November 17, 1852, Hector Berlioz's fourteen-year-old *Benvenuto Cellini,* which had not been heard since its dismal failure at the Paris Opéra in 1838 and 1839, was brilliantly revived in Weimar under Franz Liszt's direction. This was neither the first nor the last of Liszt's generous gestures on behalf of his old friend. Years earlier, in Paris, Liszt had been one of Berlioz's most zealous and most effective partisans. In February 1855 he was to arrange a second "Berlioz Week" in Weimar, and at this time the essay on Berlioz's *Harold,* and old project, began to take definite shape. A third series of concerts, in January 1856, led indirectly to the writing and composition of *Les Troyens.*

For some time now, controversy has reigned about the role taken by Liszt in the production of his prose works, as opposed to roles that may have been played by Countess Marie d'Agoult and Princess Carolyne von Sayn-Wittgenstein. Unfortunately, the scholarly debate has been conducted in an oddly polarized manner, one school insisting that Liszt plagiarized the work in its entirety from the two women, the other rescuing the composer from this charge by arguing that neither woman contributed anything beyond secretarial services and ill-advised interference. Although it is clear that each piece of writing must be evaluated individually, the truth in general seems to lie somewhere between the two extremes, in a collaborative effort of some sort.

Carolyne von Sayn-Wittgenstein, a woman of unusually broad education and of intellectual bent, was Liszt's companion during the years he lived in Weimar and his close friend afterward. That it was she who first suggested the essay on Berlioz is clear from the published correspondence, from which, however, it is also clear that Liszt was to provide sketches for her to "develop." The correspondence shows further that Liszt spoke out when "developments" of this kind displeased him, that in the case of the essay on Berlioz he corrected a proof of the first installment, and that the Princess was obliged to consult him before she could cancel a trifling change that he had made in her wording of the title.

FROM *Berlioz and His "Harold" Symphony*
(1855)

[PART 1]

In the realm of ideas there are internal wars, like those of the Athenians, during which everyone is declared traitor to his fatherland who does not publicly take one side or the other and remains an idle spectator of the evil to which the struggle leads. Persuaded of the justice of this procedure, which, if rigorously observed, can only help to put an end to differences and to hasten the victory of those destined for future leadership, we have never concealed our lively and sympathetic admiration for the genius whom we intend to examine today, for the master to whom the art of our time is so decidedly indebted.

All the pros and cons of the noisy quarrel that has sprung up since the appearance of his first works can be reduced to one main point, to suggest which will suffice to show that the consequences inherent in his example go far beyond the pronouncements of those who consider themselves infallible arbitrators in these matters. The blunt antipathies, the accusations of musical high treason, the banishments for life which have been imposed on Berlioz since his first appearance—these have their explanation (why deceive ourselves about it?) in the holy horror, in the pious astonishment which came over musical authorities at the principle implicit in all his works, a principle that can be briefly stated in this form: *The artist may pursue the beautiful outside the rules of the school without fear that, as a result of this, it will elude him.* His opponents may assert that he has abandoned the ways of the old masters; this is easy—who wishes to persuade them of the contrary? His adherents may give themselves the greatest pains to prove that his way is neither always nor yet

TEXT: "Berlioz und seine Haroldsymphonie." *Neue Zeitschrift für Musik* 43 (1855): 25–26, 42–43, 45–46, 49–50, 51–52, 77–79. The essay was published in five installments; the present abridged translation includes the beginning of the first installment, portions of the second and third, and the beginning of the fourth. As printed in 1855, the text is a translation into German, by Richard Pohl, from the French original of Liszt and the Princess Wittgenstein. The later German "translation," by Lina Ramann (*Gesammelte Schriften*, vol. 4 (Leipzig, 1882), 1–102) is simply a fussy revision of the earlier one. Translation by Oliver Strunk.

wholly and completely different from that to which one was formerly used; what do they gain thereby? Both parties remain convinced that Berlioz adheres no less firmly to the creed which we have just pronounced, whether this is demonstrated in fact by one or by one hundred corroborating circumstances. And for the authorities who have arrogated to themselves the privileges of orthodoxy this is a more than sufficient proof of his heresy. Yet since in art no sect maintains a dogma on the basis of revelation and only tradition is authoritative; since music in particular does not, like painting and sculpture, recognize or adhere to an absolute model; the deciding of disputes between orthodox and heresiarchs depends not only on the court of past and present science, but also on the sense for art and for the reasonable in the coming generation. Only after a considerable lapse of time can a final decision be handed down, for what verdict of the present will be acceptable on the one hand to the older generation,[1] which has borne from youth the easy yoke of habit, and on the other hand to the younger generation, who gather belligerently under any banner and love a fight for its own sake? Old and young must then entrust the solution of problems of this sort to a more or less distant future. To this future is alone reserved the complete or partial acceptance of those *violations of certain rules of art and habits of hearing* with which Berlioz is reproached. One point, however, is now already beyond all question. The representatives of the development to come will entertain a quite special respect for works exhibiting such enormous powers of conception and thought and will find themselves obliged to study them intensively, just as even now contemporaries approach them *nolens volens* step by step, their admiration only too often delayed by idle astonishment. Even though these works violate the rules, in that they destroy the hallowed frame which has devolved upon the symphony; even though they offend the ear, in that in the expression of their content they do not remain within the prescribed musical dikes; it will be none the less impossible to ignore them later on as one ignores them now, with the apparent intention of exempting oneself from tribute, from homage, toward a contemporary.

●   ●   ●   ●   ●

[PART 2]

Who has the temerity to deny to our inspired art the supreme power of self-sufficiency? But need making oneself master of a new form mean forever renouncing the hereditary and historically inculcated one? Does one forswear

---

1. "The majority would like to see themselves benefited but do not wish their cherished ways of living disturbed, just as the sick man would gladly regain his health but gives up unwillingly that which has made him sick. . . . When an original work appears, demanding that the listener assimilate its ideas instead of appraising its new spirit in the light of traditional concepts and that he adopt the new concept absolutely essential to new ideas, the majority, in the midst of their fervent longings for the 'new,' shrink from the difficulty and find consolation in the warmed-over old, persuading themselves, wherever possible, that it is new."—Marx, *Die Musik des 19. Jahrhunderts* (2d ed., Leipzig, 1873), pp. 154–55. [Au.]

one's mother tongue when one acquires a new branch of eloquence? Because there are works that demand a simultaneous bringing into play of feeling and thought, shall on this account the pure instrumental style lose its magic for those works that prefer to expend themselves and their entire emotional wealth in music alone without being hindered by a definite object in their freedom of feeling? Would it not amount to a lack of confidence in the vitality of the pure instrumental style were one to anticipate its complete decay simply because there arose at its side a new species, distinct from drama, oratorio, and cantata, but having none the less in common with these the poetic basis?

The dwellers in the antipodes of this new artistic hemisphere will perhaps think to advance a telling argument against it by saying that program music, through its apparent reconciliation of various subspecies, surrenders its own individual character and may not for this reason lay claim to independent existence within the art. They will hold that our art attains its purest expression in instrumental music and that it has in this form arrived at its highest perfection and power, revealed itself in its most kingly majesty, and asserted its direct character most impressively; that music, on the other hand, has from time immemorial taken possession of the word with a view to lending it, through song, the charm and force of its expression and has in consequence always developed in two forms as instrumental and vocal; that these two forms are equally indigenous, equally normal; and that the inventive creator, when he wishes to apply music to definite situations and actual persons, can find sufficient motives in the lyric and dramatic vocal forms; so that there can accordingly be no advantage or necessity for him to cause the peculiar properties of that form of music which exists for its own sake and lives its own life to meet and continue on the same path with the development of that other form which identifies itself with the poetic structure of the drama, with the sung and spoken word.

These objections would be well taken if in art two distinct forms could be *combined,* but not *united.* It is obvious that such a combination may be an unharmonious one, and that the work will then be misshapen and the awkward mixture offensive to good taste. This, however, will be due to a fault of execution, not a basic error. Are not the arts in general, and the several arts in particular, quite as rich in variously formed and dissimilar phenomena as nature is in the vicissitudes of her principal kingdoms and their divisions? Art, like nature, is made up of gradual transitions, which link together the remotest classes and the most dissimilar species and which are necessary and natural, hence also entitled to live.

Just as there are in nature no gaps, just as the human soul consists not alone in contrasts, so between the mountain peaks of art there yawn no steep abysses and in the wondrous chain of its great whole no ring is ever missing. In nature, in the human soul, and in art, the extremes, opposites, and high points are bound one to another by a continuous series of various varieties of *being,* in which modifications bring about differences and at the same time maintain similarities. The human soul, that middle ground between nature and art, finds prospects in nature which correspond to all the shadings and modulations of feeling which it experiences before it rests on the steep and solitary peaks of contradictory passions which it climbs only at rare intervals; these prospects found in nature it carries over into art. Art, like nature, weds related or contradictory forms and impressions corresponding to the affections of the human soul; these often arise from cross currents of diverse impulses which, now uniting, now opposing, bring about a divided condition in the soul which we can call neither pure sorrow nor pure joy, neither perfect love nor thorough egoism, neither complete relaxation nor positive energy, neither extreme satisfaction nor absolute despair, forming through such mixtures of various tonalities a harmony, an individuality, or an artistic species which does not stand entirely on its own feet, yet is at the same time different from any other. Art, regarded generally and in the position it occupies in the history of mankind, would not only be impotent, it would remain incomplete, if, poorer and more dependent than nature, it were unable to offer each movement of the human soul the sympathetic sound, the proper shade of color, the indispensable form. Art and nature are so changeable in their progeny that we can neither define nor predict their boundaries; both comprise a host of heterogeneous or intimately related basic elements; both consist in material, substance, and endlessly diverse forms, each of them in turn conditioned by limits of expansion and force; both exercise through the medium of our senses an influence on our souls that is as real as it is indefinable.

An element, through contact with another, acquires new properties in losing old ones; exercising another influence in an altered environment, it adopts a new name. A change in the relative proportions of the mixture is sufficient to make the resultant phenomenon a new one. The amalgamation of forms distinct in their origins will result, in art as in nature, either in phenomena of quite new beauty or in monstrosities, depending on whether a harmonious *union* or a disagreeable *combination* promotes a homogeneous whole or a distressing absurdity.

The more we persuade ourselves of the diverse unity which governs the All in the midst of which man is situated and of that other unity which rules his very life and history, the more we will recognize the diverse unity which reveals itself in the destiny of art, the more we will seek to rid ourselves of our vicious inclination to carp at and curb it, like gardeners who hem in the vegetation in order to grow hedges in a row or who cripple the healthy tree for the sake of artificial shapes. Never do we find in *living* natural phenomena geometrical or mathematical figures; why do we try to impose them on art, who do we try to subject art to a rectilinear system? Why do we not admire its luxurious, unfettered growth, as we admire the oak, whose gnarled and tangled branches appeal in a more lively way to our imaginations than does the yew, distorted into the shape of a pyramid or mandarin's hat? Why all this desire to stunt and control natural and artistic impulses? Vain effort! The first time the little garden-artist mislays his shears, everything grows as it should and must.

Man stands in inverse relations to art and to nature; nature he rules as its capstone, its final flower, its noblest creature; art he creates as a second nature, so to speak, making of it, in relation to himself, that which he himself is to nature.[2] For all this, he can proceed, in creating art, only according to the laws which nature lays down for him, for it is from nature that he takes the materials for his work, aiming to give them then a life superior to that which, in nature's plan, would fall to their lot. These laws carry with them the ineradicable mark of their origin in the similarity they bear to the laws of nature, and consequently, for all that it is the creature of man, the fruit of his will, the expression of his feeling, the result of his reflection, art has none the less an existence not determined by man's intention, the successive phases of which follow a course independent of his deciding and predicting. It exists and flowers in various ways in conformity with basic conditions whose inner origin remains just as much hidden as does the force which holds the world in its course, and, like the world, it is impelled toward an unpredicted and unpredictable final goal in perpetual transformations that can be made subject to no external power. Assuredly, the scholarly investigator can follow up the traces of its past; he cannot, however, foresee the final purpose toward which future revolutions may direct it. The stars in the heavens come and go and the species inhabiting our earth appear and disappear in accordance with conditions which, in the fruitful and perpetual course of time, bring on and again remove the centuries. Thus it is also with art. The fecundating and life-giving suns of its realm gradually lose their brilliance and warmth, and there appear on its horizon new planets, proud, ardent, and radiant with youth. Whole arts die out, their former life in time recognizable only from the skeletons they leave behind, which, like those of antediluvian races, fill us with astonished surprise; through crossbreeding and blending new and hitherto unknown arts spring up, which, as a result of their expansion and intermingling, will perhaps someday be impelled toward their end, just as in the animal and vegetable kingdoms whole species have been replaced by others. Art, proceeding from man as he himself proceeds, it appears, from nature, man's masterpiece as he himself is nature's masterpiece, provided by man with thought and feeling—art cannot escape the inevitable change common to all that time begets. Coexistent with that of mankind, its life principle, like the life principle of nature, does not remain for long in possession of the same forms, going from one to another in an eternal cycle and driving man to create new forms in the same measure as he leaves faded and antiquated ones behind.

· · · · ·

From this variety in the tempo of artistic development proceeds the difficulty of recognizing it in its portents and precursors. One must have taken a step

2. Compare Richard Wagner, *The Artwork of the Future*, chap. 1, sec.1 (p. 55 above).

forward before one can recognize as such the progress one has made. As long as this progress remains remote, like an anchorage toward which we sail, only a sort of clairvoyance will enable us to assert positively that we are getting ahead as we approach it. We border here so closely on optical illusion that for skeptics, who regard what others take for progress as retrogressive movement, there can be no demonstrations *a priori*. At the same time it would be idle to wish to deny or dispute an upward tendency in the psychological development of the human mind, which, embodying itself in constantly nobler arts and forms, strives after constantly wider radiation, after a brighter light, after an infinite exaltation.[3] And it would be equally idle to consign an art or the least of its forms to the class of immovable objects by seeking to demolish the new forms in which it manifests itself or to destroy the shoots that spring from the seeds of ripened fruit. These can never be stunted; no profane hand can restrain their seasonal impulse.

Strange contradiction! Nothing human stands still; cult, custom, law, government, science, taste, and mode of enjoyment—all change, all are constantly coming and passing away, without rest, without respite; no country is quite like any other, and no century ends in the same atmosphere with which it began; the endeavors, tendencies, improvements, and ideals of each generation plow up the hereditary fields in order to experiment with a new kind of crop. Yet in the midst of all these ferments, in this tempest of time, in this eternal world-rejuvenation, resembling the transformations of nature, if not in majesty then at least in universality, among all the paths of progress is one alone to remain untrodden—among all the manifestations of the human spirit is the development of the purest and most brilliant one to be forbidden, its mobility forever

3. "One cannot reflect on the deeper significance of the three great (so to speak) cardinal arts—plastics, painting, and music—without being constantly reminded of the history of the three great (so to speak) cardinal senses—touch, sight, and hearing. Then quite unsought there come to light most remarkable relations between the evolution of these senses in the animate world of the planets and the evolution of these forces in the history of mankind. Just as touch is the first and altogether most indispensable means by which the living creature orientates itself, so some form of plastics is the first and most essential art of peoples, the earliest to attain to full development. Sight, that miraculous perception of the most delicate light-effects, appears for the first time at a higher level in the animal kingdom, exhibiting, moreover, a certain inconstancy, seating itself now in a single eye, now in thousands of eyes, again on occasion degenerating altogether, even in the highest animal forms. The flowering of painting falls accordingly in mankind's middle period, assuming the most varied forms, coming to the fore and on occasion retreating suddenly into the background. Still later, indeed last of all, hearing develops, merely prefiguring itself in the higher mollusks and only from the fishes on becoming a permanent property of the animal world, seating itself now with greater constancy and symmetry in two organs, no more, no less, a right one and a left one, and from henceforth never again wanting. In similar measure, genuine music appears only in the last centuries; firm in its basic laws, at the same time developing itself and only holding to these as though riding at anchor, capable of the most delicate and most inspired variation, it thus becomes the mystery in which, free from all imitation of the world of actuality, the spiritualized world of feeling is reflected. If those other arts have long since passed the high point in their development, the full flowering of the tonal world falls in most recent times, and here, hidden under a thin shell, there are still latent many secrets, ready assuredly to reveal themselves to the right rhabdomancer."—Carus. [Au.]

held in check? Among all the virtual forces, is it proposed to deny precisely to this force, to the supreme force, the possibility of perfection that spirit inspires in matter, which possibility, an echo of that first command of creation, forms, with its "Become!", a harmonious All from the reorganized elements of an embryonic chaos? Wondrous power, noblest sacred gift of existence! Where else but in art canst thou be found? However man employs himself on any path of life, however he discovers, invents, collects, analyzes, and combines— he *creates* only in the artwork; only here can he out of free will embody feeling and thought in a sensual mold that will preserve and communicate their sense and content. Is art alone, from a given moment on, to remain unaffected by the ebb and flow of its soul, unmoved by the fluctuations of its hopes, unresponsive to all the changing of its dreams, to all the budding and weaving of its ideas? No, certainly not! Art, in general and in particular, sails with mankind down the stream of life, never to mount again to its source. Even when it appears to stand still momentarily, the tides which bear man and his life continue to remain its element. Art moves, strides on, increases and develops, obeying unknown laws, in cycles whose dissimilar return, recurring like the appearance of certain comets, at unpredictable intervals, does not permit the positive assertion that they will not again pass overhead in all their splendor or having passed will not return once more. Only it is not given us to foresee its unawaited reappearance or the undreamed-of glory in which it will then come forward.

●　　●　　●　　●　　●

When the hour of progress strikes for art, the genius is always found in the breach; he fulfills the need of the times, whether it be to bring a discovery from out a misty limbo fully and completely into the light or whether it be to combine single syllables, childishly strung together, into a sonorous word of magical power. It sometimes happens that art blossoms like the plant which gradually unfolds its leaves and that its successive representatives complement one another in equal proportion, so that each master takes only a single step beyond what his teacher has transmitted to him. In such cases, the masses, to whom this slow progress allows ample time, whose *niveau* is only gradually elevated, are enabled to follow the quest for more perfect procedures and higher inspiration. In other cases, the genius leaps ahead of his time and climbs, with one powerful swing, several rungs of the mystic ladder. Then time must elapse until, struggling after him, the general intellectual consciousness attains his point of view; before this happens it is not understood and cannot be judged. In literature, as also in music, this has often been the case. Neither Shakespeare nor Milton, neither Cervantes nor Camoëns, neither Dante nor Tasso, neither Bach nor Mozart, neither Gluck nor Beethoven (to cite only these glorious names) was recognized by his own time in such measure as he was later. In music, which is perpetually in a formative state (and which in our time, developing at a rapid tempo, no sooner accomplishes the ascent of one peak than it begins to climb another), the peculiarity of the genius is that he enriches the art with unused materials as well as with original manipulations of traditional ones, and one can say of music that examples of artists who have, as it were, leaped with both feet into a future time, are here to be found in greatest abundance. How could their anticipation of the style which they recognized as destined for supremacy fail to be offensive to their contemporaries, who had not sufficient strength to tear themselves loose, as they had done, from the comfortable familiarity of traditional forms? Yet, though the crowd turn its back on them, though envious rivals revile them, though pupils desert them, though, depreciated by the stupid and damned by the ignorant, they lead a tortured, hunted life, at death they leave behind their works, like a salutary blessing. These prophetic works transmit their style and their beauty to one after another of those who follow. It often happens that talents little capable of recognizing their significance are the very first to find ways of utilizing certain of their poetic intentions or technical procedures, whose value they estimate according to their lights. These are soon imitated again and thus forced to approach more closely to what was at first misunderstood, until, in the fumbling inherent in such imitations and tentative approaches, there is finally attained the understanding and glorification of the genius who, in his lifetime, demanded recognition in vain. Not until it has become used to admiring works analogous to his, but of lesser value, does the public receive his precious bequest with complete respect and jubilant applause. The old forms, thus made obscure, soon fall into neglect and are finally forgotten by the younger generation that has grown up with the new ones and finds these more acceptable to its poetic ideal. In this way the gap between the genius, gifted with wings, and the public which follows him, snail-like and circumspect, is gradually filled out.

•   •   •   •   •

[PART 3]

The poetic solution of instrumental music contained in the program seems to us rather one of the various steps forward which the art has still to take, a necessary result of the development of our time, than a symptom of its exhaustion and decadence, for we cannot presume that it is now already obliged to resign itself to the subtleties and aberrations of *raffinement* in order that, after having drained all its auxiliary sources and worn out all its means, it may cover up the impotence of its declining years. If hitherto unused forms arise and, through the magic they exert, win acceptance for themselves with thoughtful artists and with the public, in that the former makes use of them while the latter shows its receptivity toward them, it is not easy to demonstrate their advantages and inconveniences in advance so exhaustively that one can strike an average on the basis of which to establish their expectation of longevity and the nature of their future influence. None the less it would be petty and uncharitable to abstain from inquiry into their origin, significance, bearing, and aim in order to treat works of genius with a disdain of which one may later have reason to be ashamed, in order to withhold due recognition to a widening of the field of art, stamping it, on the contrary and without further ado, as the excrescence of a degenerate period.

We shall forgo deriving advantage from a pronouncement of Hegel's if we can be convinced that great minds (those before whose Herculean intellectual labors every head is bowed, quite apart from sympathy for their doctrines) can characterize precisely those forms as desirable which reveal themselves as sickly and contributory to the downfall of art. Hegel appears to foresee the stimulation which the program can give to instrumental music by increasing the number of those understanding and enjoying it when he says, at the end of the chapter on music in his *Aesthetics,* the intuitive correctness of which as a general survey cannot be prejudiced by certain erroneous conceptions, such as its time brought with it:

> The connoisseur, to whom the inner relationships of sounds and instruments are accessible, enjoys in instrumental music its artistic use of harmonies, interwoven melodies, and changing forms; he is wholly absorbed by the music itself and takes a further interest in comparing what he hears with the rules and precepts which he knows in order to appraise and enjoy the accomplishment to the full, though here the ingenuity of the artist in inventing the new can often embarrass even the connoisseur, to whom precisely this or that progression, transition, etc., is unfamiliar. So complete an absorption is seldom the privilege of the amateur, to whom there comes at once a desire to fill out this apparently meaningless outpour of sound and to find intellectual footholds for its progress and, in general, more definite ideas and a more precise content for that which penetrates into his soul. In this respect, music becomes symbolic for him, yet, in his attempts to overtake its meaning, he is confronted by abstruse problems, rapidly rushing by, which do not always lend themselves to solution and which are altogether capable of the most varied interpretations.

We would modify Hegel's opinion only to state it in a more absolute form, for we cannot concede that the *artist* is satisfied with forms that are too dry for the *amateur.* We assert, on the contrary, that the artist, even more insistently than the amateur, must demand emotional content in the formal container. Only when it is filled with the former does the latter have significance for him. The artist and the connoisseur who, in creating and judging, seek only the ingenious construction, the artfully woven pattern, the complex workmanship, the *kaleidoscopic* multiplicity of mathematical calculation and intertwining lines, drive music toward the dead letter and are to be compared with those who look at the luxuriant poetry of India and Persia only from the point of view of grammar and language, who admire only sonority and symmetrical versification, and do not regard the meaning and wealth of thought and image in its expression, its poetic continuity, not to mention the subject which it celebrates or its historical content. We do not deny the usefulness of philological and geological investigations, chemical analyses, grammatical commentaries— but they are the affair of science, not of art. Every art is the delicate blossom which the solid tree of a science bears at the tips of its leafy branches; the roots ought to remain hidden by a concealing coverlet. The necessity and utility of separating the material and substance in which art embodies itself into their component parts with a view to learning to know and to use their properties do not justify the confusing of science and art, of the study of the one with the practice of the other. Man must investigate art and nature; this is however not the goal of his relation to them—it is essentially a preparatory—if likewise important—moment in them. Both are given him primarily for his *enjoyment;* he is to absorb the divine harmonies of nature, to breathe out in art the melodies of his heart and the sighs of his soul. A work which offers only clever manipulation of its materials will always lay claim to the interest of the immediately concerned—of the artist, student, and connoisseur—but, despite this, it will be unable to cross the threshold of the artistic kingdom. Without carrying in itself the divine spark, without being a living poem, it will be ignored by society as though it did not exist at all, and no people will ever accept it as a leaf in the breviary of the cult of the beautiful. It will retain its value only as long as the art remains in a given state; as soon as art moves on to a new horizon and through experience learns improved methods, it will lose all significance save the historic and will be filed away among the archaeological documents of the past. Poetic art works, on the other hand, live for all time and survive all formal revolution, thanks to the indestructible life principle which the human soul has embodied in them.

·   ·   ·   ·   ·

The specifically musical composer, who attaches importance to the consumption of the material alone, is not capable of deriving new forms from it, of breathing into it new strength, for no intellectual necessity urges him—nor does any burning passion, demanding to be revealed, oblige him—to discover new means. To enrich the form, to enlarge it and make it serviceable, is granted, then, precisely to those who make use of it only as one of the means of expression, as one of the languages which they employ in accordance with the dictates of the ideas to be expressed; the formalists can do nothing better or more intelligent than to use, to popularize, to subdivide, and on occasion to rework what the tone poets have won.

The program asks only acknowledgment for the possibility of precise definition of the psychological moment which prompts the composer to create his work and of the thought to which he gives outward form. If it is on the one hand childish, idle, sometimes even mistaken, to outline programs after the event, and thus to dispel the magic, to profane the feeling, and to tear to pieces with words the soul's most delicate web, in an attempt to *explain* the feeling of an instrumental poem which took this shape precisely because its content could not be expressed in words, images, and ideas; so on the other hand the master is also master of his work and can create it under the influence of definite impressions which he wishes to bring to full and complete realization in the listener. The specifically musical symphonist carries his listeners with him into ideal regions, whose shaping and ornamenting he relinquishes to their individual imaginations; in such cases it is extremely dangerous to wish to impose on one's neighbor the same scenes or successions of ideas into which our imagination feels itself transported. The painter-symphonist, however, setting himself the task of reproducing with equal clarity a picture clearly present in his mind, of developing a series of emotional states which are unequivocally and definitely latent in his consciousness—why may he not, through a program, strive to make himself fully intelligible?

•   •   •

If music is not on the decline, if its rapid progress since Palestrina and the brilliant development which has fallen to its lot since the end of the last century are not the preordained limits of its course, then it seems to us probable that the programmatic symphony is destined to gain firm footing in the present art period and to attain an importance comparable to that of the oratorio and cantata—in many respects to realize in a modern sense the meaning of these two species. Since the time when many masters brought the oratorio and cantata style to its highest brilliance, to its final perfection, its successful treatment has become difficult; for other reasons too, whose discussion would here be out of place, the two species no longer arouse the same interest as at the time when Handel animated them with the breath of the winged steed. Oratorio and cantata appear to resemble drama in their impersonation and dialogue. But these are after all external similarities, and close examination reveals at once that undeniable differences of constitution prevail. Conflicts of passions, delineations of characters, unexpected peripetias, and continuous action are in them even more noticeably absent than actual representation; indeed we do not for one moment hesitate to deny a close relation here and are on the contrary persuaded that in this form music approaches rather the antique *epos,* whose essential features it can thus best reproduce. Aside from dialogue, held together by a certain continuity in the action it presents, oratorio and cantata have no more in common with the stage than has the epos; through their leaning toward the descriptive, instrumentation lends them a similar frame. Episode and apostrophe play almost the same role in them, and the effect of the whole is that of the solemn recital of a memorable event, the glory of which falls undivided on the head of a single hero. If we were asked which musical form corresponded most closely to the poetic epos, we should doubt whether better examples could be brought forward than the *Israel, Samson, Judas Maccabaeus, Messiah,* and *Alexander* of Handel, the Passion of Bach, the *Creation* of Haydn, the *St. Paul* and *Elijah* of Mendelssohn.

The program can lend to instrumental music characteristics corresponding almost exactly to the various poetic forms; it can give it the character of the ode, of the dithyramb, of the elegy, in a word, of any form of lyric poetry. If all along it has been expressing the moods proper to these various species, it can by defining its subject draw new and undreamed-of advantages from the approximation of certain ideas, the affinity of certain figures, the separation or combination, juxtaposition or fusion of certain poetic images and perorations. What is more, the program can make feasible for music the equivalent of a kind of poetry unknown to antiquity and owing its existence to a characteristically modern way of feeling—the poem ordinarily written in dialogue form which adapts itself even less readily than the epos to dramatic performance.

• • • • •

Would perhaps the specifically musical symphony be better suited to such subjects? We doubt it. The conflict between its independent style and the one forced on it by the subject would affect us disagreeably, being without evident or intelligible cause. The composer would cease to conduct our imagination into the regions of an ideal common to all mankind and, without definitely announcing the particular path he wishes to choose, would only lead the listener astray. With the help of a program, however, he indicates the direction of his ideas, the point of view from which he grasps a given subject. The function of the program then becomes indispensable, and its entrance into the highest spheres of art appears justified. Surely we have no wish to question the capacity of music to represent characters similar to those the poet princes of our time have drawn. For the rest, we see music arrived at such a point in its relations of dependence on and correspondence with literature, we see at the same time all human feeling and thinking, aim and endeavor, so overwhelmingly directed toward profound inquiry into the sources of our sufferings and errors, we see all other arts, vying one with another in their efforts to satisfy the taste and needs of our time, consumed so specifically by the desire to give expression to this urge, that we consider the introduction of the program into the concert hall to be just as inevitable as the declamatory style is to the opera. Despite all handicaps and setbacks, these two trends will prove their strength in the triumphant course of their development. They are imperative necessities of a moment in our social life, in our ethical training, and as such will sooner or later clear a path for themselves. The custom of providing instrumental pieces with a program has already found such acceptance with the public that musicians cease to struggle against it, regarding it as one of those inevitable facts which politicians call *faits accomplis*. The words of an author previously cited will serve as proof of this.

> Fine instrumental music must reckon with a much smaller number of competent listeners than opera; to enjoy it fully requires genuine artistic insight and a more active and experienced sensitivity. With the large audience, coloring will always pass as expression, for unless it consist of individuals capable of forming an abstract ideal—something not to be expected of a whole auditorium, no matter how select it may be—it will never listen to a symphony, quartet, or other composition of this order without outlining a program for itself during the performance, according to the grandiose, lively, impetuous, serenely soothing, or melancholy character of the music. By means of this trick, listeners identify most concerts of instrumental music

with the expression of certain passionate feelings; they imagine an action differing from those imagined by others as individuals differ among themselves. I speak here of the most cultivated, since for many, frequently for the majority, instrumental music is only a sensual pleasure, if not indeed a tiresome enigma. For them, instrumental music has neither coloring nor expression, and I simply do not know what they look for in it.[4]

Is it not evident from this that it is merely a question of officially recognizing an already existing power with a view to allowing it greater freedom of action and assisting it in the removal of its liabilities, so that henceforward it may work toward its future, toward its fame, not secretly, but in the deliberate repose that comes with an established success?

•　　•　　•　　•　　•

[PART 4]

Through song there have always been *combinations* of music with literary or quasi-literary works; the present time seeks a *union* of the two which promises to become a more intimate one than any that have offered themselves thus far. Music in its masterpieces tends more and more to appropriate the masterpieces of literature. What harm can come to music, at the height to which it has grown since the beginning of the modern era, if it attach itself to a species that has sprung precisely from an undeniably modern way of feeling? Why should music, once so inseparably bound to the tragedy of Sophocles and the ode of Pindar, hesitate to unite itself in a different yet more adequate way with works born of an inspiration unknown to antiquity, to identify itself with such names as Dante and Shakespeare? Rich shafts of ore lie here awaiting the bold miner, but they are guarded by mountain spirits who breathe fire and smoke into the faces of those who approach their entrance and, like Slander, whom Voltaire compares to coals, blacken what they do not burn, threatening those lusting after the treasure with blindness, suffocation, and utter destruction.

To our regret we must admit that a secretly smoldering but irreconcilable quarrel has broken out between *vocational* and *professional* musicians. The latter, like the Pharisees of the Old Law, cling to the letter of the commandment, even at the risk of killing its spirit. They have no understanding of the love revealed in the New Testament, for the thirst after the eternal, the dream of the ideal, the search for the poetically beautiful in every form. They live only in fear, grasp only fear, preach only fear; for them, fear (not precisely the fear of the Lord, however) is the beginning and end of all wisdom; they hang on the language of the law with the pettiness of those whose hearts have not taught them that the fulfillment of the prophecy lies in the abolition of the sacrifice, in the rending of the veil of the temple; their wisdom consists in dogmatic disputes, in sterile and idle speculation on subtleties of the rules. They deny that one may show greater honor to the old masters by seeking out

4. Fétis. [Au].

the germs of artistic development which they embedded in their works than by servilely and thoughtlessly tracing the empty forms whose entire content of air and light they drained themselves in their own day. On the other hand the *vocational* musicians hold that to honor these patriarchs one must regard the forms they used as exhausted and look on imitations of them as mere copies of slight value. They do not hope to glean further harvests from fields sown by giants and believe that they cannot continue the work already begun unless, as the patriarchs did in their time, they create new forms for new ideas, put new wine into new bottles.

To Berlioz and his successes has been opposed from the beginning, like an insurmountable dam, that academic aversion to every art product which, instead of following the beaten path, is formed in accordance with an unaccustomed ideal or called up by incantations foreign to the old rite. But with or without the magisterial permission of the titulary and nontitulary professors—even without that of the illustrious director of the Paris Conservatoire, who visited Berlioz's concerts quite regularly in order, as he put it, "to learn how not to do it"—everyone who would keep up with contemporary art must study the scores of this master, precisely to see what is being done today and "to learn how to do it." And in truth, the so-called classicists themselves are not above making use of overheard and stolen ideas and effects and even, in exceptional cases, of conceding that Berlioz does after all show talent for instrumentation and skill in combining, since he is one of those artists, previously mentioned, who through the wider expression of their feelings and the freer unfolding of their individuality expand and enrich the form and make it serviceable. In the last analysis, however, the hypocrisy of his envious opponents consists in refusing to pay him the tuition they owe and have on their conscience while they publicly tread into the mire everything of his which they are not and never will be capable of imitating and privately pull out all feathers of his which they can use as ornaments themselves. We could name many who rise up against Berlioz, though their best works would be disfigured were one to take from them everything for which they are obliged to him. We repeat, therefore, that unusual treatment of form is not the supreme unpardonable error of which Berlioz is accused; his opponents will indeed concede, perhaps, that he has done art a service in discovering new inflections. What they will never forgive is that form has for him an importance subordinate to idea, that he does not, as they do, cultivate form for form's sake; they will never forgive him for being a thinker and a poet.

Strangely enough, that *union* of music and literature of which we have already spoken, constantly increasing in intimacy, developing itself with surprising rapidity, is gaining firm footing despite the equally lively opposition of *professional* musicians and men of letters. Both parties set themselves against it with the same vigor, with the same obstinacy. The latter, looking askance, see their property being taken over into a sphere where, apart from the value *they* placed on it, it acquires new significance; the former are horrified at a violation of their territory by elements with which they do not know how to deal. The tone poets have hence to contend with a double enmity; they find themselves between two fires. But the strength of their cause compensates for the weakness of their position. Whether one recognizes it or not, the fact remains that both arts, more than ever before, feel themselves mutually attracted and are striving for inner union.

Through the endless variety of its forms, art reproduces the endless variety of constitutions and impressions. There are characters and feelings which can attain full development only in the dramatic; there are others which in no wise tolerate the limitations and restrictions of the stage. Berlioz recognized this. From the church, where it was for so many centuries exclusively domiciled and from whence its masterpieces scarcely reached the outer world, musical art moved by degrees into the theater, setting up there a sort of general headquarters or open house where anyone might exhibit his inspirations in any genre he chose. For a while it would scarcely have entered the head of any musician to regard himself as incapable of composing dramatic works. It seemed as though, on admission to the musical guild or brotherhood, one also acquired and accepted the ability, sanction, and duty to supply a certain number of operas, large or small, romantic or comic, *serie* or *buffe.* All hastened to the contest in this arena, hospitably open to everyone. When the terrain of the boards proved slippery, later on, some crept and others danced on the tightrope; many provided themselves with hammers instead of balancing poles and, when their neighbors struggled to keep their balance, hit them over the head. Some bound golden skates to their feet and with their aid left way behind them a train of poor devils, panting to no avail; certain ones, like messengers of the gods, had at their head and heels the wings given them at birth by genius, by means of which, if they did not precisely make rapid progress, they were able at least to fly on occasion to the summit. And, for all that these last remained, here as elsewhere, very much in the minority, they none the less imposed on their successors so great an obligation to surpass their accomplishment that a moment seems to have arrived which should cause many to ask themselves whether the sense of duty which urges them to join in this turmoil is not a prepossession. Those, indeed, who expect more of fame than a draft to be discounted by the present, more than a gilt-paper crown to be snatched at by fabricators of artificial flowers—let them ask themselves whether they were really born to expend their energies in this field, to course and tourney in these narrow lists; whether their temperament does not impel them toward more ideal regions; whether their abilities might not take a higher flight in a realm governed by fewer constraining laws; whether their freer fantasy might not then discover one of the those Atlantides, blissful isles, or unknown constellations for which all students of the earth and sky are seeking. We for our part are persuaded that not every genius can limit his flight within the narrow confines of the stage and that he who cannot is thus forced to form for himself a new *habitaculum.*

To seek to import a foreign element into instrumental music and to domesticate it there by encroaching upon the independence of feeling through definite subjects offered to the intelligence in advance, by forcing upon a composer a concept to be literally represented or poetically formulated, by directing the attention of the listener, not only to the woven pattern of the music, but also to the ideas communicated by its contours and successions—this seems to many an absurd, if not a sacrilegious undertaking. Small wonder that before Berlioz they cover their heads and let their beards grow—before him who carries this beginning so far that, by symbolizing its presence, he causes the human voice to be heard in the hitherto wholly impersonal symphony; before him who undertakes to impart to the symphony a new interest, to enliven it with an entirely new element; before him who—not content to pour out in the symphony the lament of a common woe, to cause to sound forth in it the hopes of all and to stream forth from its focus the affections and shocks, sorrows and ardors, which pulse in the heart of mankind—takes possession of its powers in order to employ them in the expression of the sufferings and emotions of a specific, exceptional individual! Since the pleasure of listening to orchestral works has always been an altogether subjective one for those who followed the poetic content along with the musical, it seems to many a distortion, a violence done to its character, that the imagination is to be forced to adapt completely outlined pictures to that which is heard, to behold and accept figures in precisely the way the author wills. The hitherto usual effect of pure instrumental music on poetic temperaments may perhaps be compared to that which antique sculpture produces in them; in their eyes, these works also represent passions and forms, generating certain movements of the affections, rather than the specific and particular individuals whose names they bear—names, moreover, which are for the most part again allegorical representations of ideas. For them, Niobe is not this or that woman stricken by this or that misfortune; she is the most exalted expression of supreme suffering. In Polyhymnia they see, not a specific person engaged in specific speech or action, but the visible representation of the beauty, harmony, charm, and magic of that compelling, yet soft and placid persuasion whose eloquence can be concentrated in a single glance. Minerva, for them, is not only the divine, blue-eyed mentor of Ulysses, she is also the noblest symbol of that gift of our spirit which simultaneously judges and divines; who, provided with all the attributes of force, armed with all the weapons of war, is still a friend of peace; who, bearing lance and breast-plate, causes her most beautiful gift, the olive tree, to sprout, promising peace; who, possessor of the terrifying aegis, loses nothing of the kindliness and attraction of her smile, of the slowly sinking cadence of her movements.

12 John Sullivan Dwight

New Englanders in the nineteenth century were well-nigh obsessed with the cultural development and social "progress" of their still artistically young civilization. Boston, with a highly educated population and an atmosphere significantly influenced by idealist philosophy (in its peculiarly American form, transcendentalism), experienced a new kind of dialogue between the transcendent aesthetic and intellectual values of this movement and the older, more acerbic Puritan culture that had marked the city in earlier times.

John Sullivan Dwight (1813–1893), with his genteel background and his degrees from Harvard College and Harvard Divinity School, aptly symbolizes this moment in New England's cultural history. His years spent living in the transcendentalists' utopian community, Brook Farm, deeply impressed him with a sense of connection between aesthetic ideas and social values; thereafter he devoted his life to music criticism, which he saw as a crucial part of the moral education of Boston and of the country in general.

In 1852 he founded *Dwight's Journal of Music: A Paper of Art and Literature,* which appeared under his direction, first weekly and then biweekly, until 1881. It reprinted articles from the major music journals of Europe, carried reports from musical correspondents in other American cities and abroad, kept its readers informed about musical current events, and, most notably, served as the principal vehicle for Dwight's own writing.

Dwight's aesthetic and moral values leap from every page. He was optimistic about the chances that genuine culture would emerge among Americans, despite what he thought of as their excessive utilitarianism and suspicion of "idle" aesthetic activities. All his life he preached that good music education was the only route to this development. He wholeheartedly undertook what was widely considered the obligation of the cultured to suppress "low" and improper music. By the end of his life his tastes were conservative and narrow, but his basically fair-minded nature led him to devote space in many an essay to the fine points of discerning, as he would put it, which music is genuinely Art.

The National Peace Jubilee
(1869)

To-day our columns are entirely occupied with this remarkable project, the dream, the one life purpose, for two years, of Mr. PATRICK S. GILMORE,[1] and

TEXT: *Dwight's Journal of Music* (July 3, 1869): 60–64.

1. Patrick S. Gilmore (1829–1892), Irish bandmaster, composer, and impresario, active in the United States. He was known especially for mounting gigantic concerts.

with its still more remarkable fulfillment in this city on the five days which an Irishman might call the next to "the top of the year," crowning the slope that leads right up to Midsummer, June 15th to 19th inclusive, making the dreamer famous, a popular hero in his way. Indeed we fear such stars as Mendelssohn just now, or Mozart, if they lived among us, would "pale their ineffectual fires" before such Calcine effulgence. The Jubilee has been the all-absorbing topic for the last month. As we have been silent about it during the preparation of the mighty work; and since, with all the extravagances of the plan, it has been pushed forward with such faith and energy that the imagination of the People, the "popular heart," perhaps we should even say the good genius of our People, fired and filled with it, has adopted it and made it its own, transforming it as it were into its own likeness; since it has been crowned with such unique success, we can do no less than gather together what we can of its history, weigh its results from our own point of view, and note the impression it has made on others.

•   •   •   •   •

For ourselves, as our readers know, we came to it sceptically, little disposed to trust or countenance a musical project making such enormous claims, and so unblushingly heralded after the manner of things as uncongenial as possible to the whole sphere of Art. The following letters, which we transfer from the *New York Tribune* of Saturday and Monday last, describe our position candidly, before and since the feast, though not as briefly or concisely as we could have wished. It was due to a very large class of the most sincere, enlightened, earnest friends of music and of culture, who, as far as any public expression was concerned, were entirely silent and unrepresented from the first, to state the way the thing looked to them from the outset, even at the risk of some seeming harshness or unfairness now that the plan is generally counted a success, a great event in some important senses, if not all. As for Mr. Gilmore, he has fairly earned all the reward which a grateful people appear eager to bestow. If the laudations of the newspapers do not turn his head—and so far we know he takes it sanely, modestly and simply—it is infinitely to his credit. So was his behavior during the last days of the Jubilee, in keeping himself and his own peculiar element of "Anvil Choruses," &c., resolutely in the background, rather than spoil the classical programme of the fourth day, or rudely break the fairy spell of the school children's festival.

THE PEACE JUBILEE SUMMED UP

•   •   •   •   •

I. HOW THE PLAN LOOKED AT FIRST, AND HOW IT WAS WORKED UP

At first sight, certainly, the project was vain-glorious. The whole style of the announcement was such as to commend it more to the noisy and spread-eagle class of patriots than to still, thoughtful lovers of their country and of peace; while, in respect to music, its enormous promise, its ambition to achieve "the greatest," to "thrust" greatness upon us by sheer force of numbers, and so eclipse the musical triumphs of the world by saying; "Go to now, let us do ten times the *biggest* thing that ever yet was done"—this, and the extra-musical *effects*, the clap-trap novelties, grotesquely mingled in its programmes, chilled the sympathies of the real, the enlightened, the disinterested music-lovers, who, feeling for the honor and the modesty of Art, two qualities as inseparable in the artistic character as they are in woman, inevitably shrank from such grandiloquent pretension, as much as they inflamed the imagination the igno-rant or only sentimentally and vaguely musical. "Twenty thousand voices!" Why will you have so many, when even the grandest of Handelian Choruses are better-sung by 1,000? And then will "50,000 people" under one roof hear, or let hear, as well as audiences in smaller halls? But it shall be "the Greatest Feast of Sublime and Inspiring Harmony ever heard in any part of the World!" (*sic*). This is calculating greatness upon a mere material scale of numbers; this makes your physical giant a greater man than Shakespeare; this confounds the *grand homme* with the *homme grand.* Shall quantity compete with quality? Shall great in mass be measured against great in kind? We are making musical progress in America; in popular musical education, as well as in the support of high-toned concerts, in some of our cities, we have really something to boast of; but does any one believe that we are yet so musical that we can produce a musical festival as great in quality, in kind, in spirit, as the best of the Old World? To a true musical character, which were the rarer godsend (to *hear,* at least, if not to see): a greatest Jubilee like this, or say some festival at Düssel-dorf, with seven or eight hundred performers, but with Mendelssohn for a conductor, and such an orchestra as only can be found in Germany, and such a programme (not only Handel Oratorios, but *Passion Music* or *Magnificat* of Bach, and, as it was at this last Whitsuntide, with a Joachim to play Beethoven's Concerto, instead of an Ole Bull with "Mother's Prayer"); and above all, with such a *spirit* of sincere, true art and poetry and piety pervading the whole feast, to the exclusion of all heterogeneous nonsense, all flattering of vanities, cater-ing to all tastes and no taste, startling *ad captandum* clap-trap, substitution of *effect* for meaning, to which add decent self-respecting abstinence from the "swell" style of advertisement? Or, not to look so far, compare it with our own best efforts here, with the last Handel and Haydn Festival in Boston Music Hall, where audiences of 3,000 people heard three or four great Oratorios entire, with Choral Symphony of Beethoven, and admirable symphony con-certs besides, all in one week, impressively performed by an orchestra of hardly more than 100 instruments and chorus of 800 voices: was not that, musically, greater?

Mind, we are putting the case as it looked, as it must have looked, to really musical and sensible persons at the outset; as it would certainly have looked to Mendelssohn, had he been living then and here.

The idea and the authorship presented the same aspect. That the projector, master-spirit, brain, and central organizing force of the "greatest musical festival in all the ages" should be, not a Mendelssohn, a Handel, or great musical man of any sort, or hardly one who fellowshipped with artists, but a Gilmore, a clever leader of a local band, an Irishman by birth, but zealous for the land of his adoption, zealous for freedom in a truer than an Irish sense; a man of common education, singularly good natured and, we doubt not, generous; an enthusiast of rather a sentimental type; chiefly known as caterer in music to the popular street taste, dispenser of military and of patriotic airs, exceedingly fond of demonstrations, restless getter up of "monster concerts," in which classical works of genius were pressed into damaging promiscuity with musical *mix pickel* for the million; bountiful in advertising patronage (sure road to favor with the press): one of the glibbest, most sonorous and voluminous in all the wordy ways of "stunning" and sensational announcement:—that such a man should be the breather of the breath of life into the great feast of song to which "all that have life and breath" are summoned; that the grandest conceivable of all musical demonstrations should be in its spirit like unto his spirit; that our whole musical world, with all the musical resources of the nation, should be set revolving round a musician of that stamp, and that at such a bugle's blast all the makers of sweet sounds in all the land should rally to a Jubilee of Peace with him, in his way, was something too much for the common, unsophisticated intellect, musical or not, to take in at once, unless one took it in the nature of a colossal joke. How any sound mind at that time could conceive it possible for a thing so started to succeed as this has done, is inconceivable to this day, after the great success. Now, indeed, the lorgnette is turned round, and, looking through the small instead of the great end, cause and effect may not appear entirely incommensurate.

But Gilmore was in earnest. His "fixed idea" had vital marrow in it, and he knew how to magnetize other efficient people to like earnestness. His great devotion to that fixed idea saw only the shining end, pressed onward gazing steadily into the sun, using for means whatever came most readily to hand—chiefly that cardinal lever of all modern business enterprise, unscrupulous advertising, meant innocently in this case, no doubt, though questionable to squeamish folk like you and me, dear Tribune! And had he not the example of the whole business world to tempt him? And here, too, the swell mob style, the returned Californian digger garb and heavy watch-chain air, with which the thing presented itself, was not particularly inviting to sincere music-lovers, jealous, as we have said, for both the honor and the modesty of art. The finer instincts are the more suspicious of whatever is most loudly advertised. The quiet gentleman we trust, but from the loud-mouthed quack we turn away. Not so, however, with the simple masses; high-spiced advertisement does its perfect work with them. To draw an audience of 50,000, a whole community must by some means or other first become infatuated. Never was such advertising, in editorial even more than business columns, as this same Jubilee has had.

Shrewd dodges, too! Innocent Bostonian, calm and unsuspecting, opens his daily paper one fine morning, and is coolly informed that he—that all musical Boston—is in a great state of excitement about something of which he never heard a hint before! Our neighbor, in *his* (Democratic) newspaper, has read the same; and so through all the party shades of journalism—all agreed for once! Day by day, beginning with mysterious hints, do they the tale unfold foreshadowing the great event. Day by day, in ceaseless round, all vieing with each other, all the newspapers keep lifting corner after corner of the curtain that conceals the miracle too bright for mortal eyes; kindly provide us with smoked glasses too that we may bear the revelation when the great day comes. Count Cagliostro never conjured more adroitly. Biggest, best-drilled orchestra in all creation? That surely was the Press, which unseen fingers played upon, ever one theme with endless variations, as upon the keys of a piano. The whole expression, publicly, was of one side; the advocates of Jubilee, they only had a hearing. And with a *tutti crescendo* of amazing confidence, new wonder upon wonder was proclaimed, not as a thing suggested, but as *fait accompli*, with a: Resolved unanimously, it is to be! No reason to the contrary, no doubt might dare to peep; no uninvaded nook in newspaperdom where any "still, small voice" might seek to be heard. Pence Jubilee had stolen a march upon us in the night and forestalled every channel of communication.

This ringing confidence of the whole Boston Press, this ceaseless roaring deluge of exalting prophesy, was meant to convey the impression to surrounding populations and to distant States that all Boston, with one mind—Boston, famed for music and fine culture—was thoroughly in sympathy with Gilmore, and committed to the project. We were all made ostensibly responsible for the extravagance of the plan, and all the braggadocio with which it was written up. This representation was by no means just or true. There was a vast discrepancy between this newspaper flourish and the private sentiment and conversation in cultivated circles, particularly among those who had the cause of pure musical taste the most at heart; those who, in a sincere and quiet way, it might be, found their best life in the best music. Unconvinced as they were of either the practicability or the desirableness of a musical festival upon so vast a scale, instinctively averse to clap trap, to startlingly "big things," to the whole spirit of the "monster" concert system, mortified, indignant at the boastful attitude in which they found themselves all placed against their will, against their very nature, these were without representation in any public form whatever, except in the exulting taunts of those who had it all their own way. Mr. Gilmore and his early coadjutators doubtless had a host of obstacles to contend with, and it was often up-hill work with them; we honor the faith and perseverance worthy of the Saints, which overcame so signally; but "*these* little ones," who felt, believed another way, and firmly set themselves against the tide, rather than give in ignominiously to what they could not see to be good, had much the harder trial of their faith, their courage, their integrity.

Meanwhile there had been skillful procuring of indorsements of the project;

letters from influential citizens who, not musical themselves, were readily persuaded to a festival of Peace, and not unwilling to have Boston beat the world in the grand scale of its music; letters, too, from prominent musicians who would naturally be the ones to take the lead in practical performance. There was shrewd calculation shown in the order in which individuals were approached, and their adhesion won and published; the prime mover knew his men. Indeed, the thing was worked up with consummate tact; and here lay, probably, the "genius" which has been so freely ascribed to the Projector; for surely the conception, the idea itself, did not require creative imagination, nor invention, until it came to the details of execution, and here, with money, business talent was the one thing needful. And at the critical moment Business stepped in to the rescue; Business, with the money guaranty, with organizing skill, with ready way of rushing its big enterprises through. The application of Dry Goods and Railroad methods saved the whole. The work was well laid out among responsible committees. The word went forth that now the enterprise was on its feet. Conversions became numerous; subscriptions, too; whole business streets were canvassed, and it demanded courage in the unbeliever to say no. The huge Coliseum went up as by magic. The invitation flew abroad to all the singers; 10,000 wanted; New England—Massachusetts, even—was good for nearly the amount, could honor the draft at sight. By choral societies, clubs, choirs, groups who had sung in Conventions, they poured in. Many new societies sprang up for the occasion: musical instruction in the public schools had silently been feeding all these fountains. They came together with enthusiasm; it waxed warmer and brighter with rehearsals; the sense of participating, and feeling like singing particles in the live fragments of the great whole soon to be fused into *one* conscious life, the mutual magnetism, the sense of pride, of progress, of coöperation, while the grand culmination loomed beyond—this was inspiring and uplifting, was a great good in itself, almost enough to offset the brag, the claptrap and the humbug of the earlier stages, even should the consummation fail. As for the grand orchestra (1,000 instruments), it was simply a matter of business and money to bring the elements of that together.

The success of the Jubilee in some shape having become a forgone conclusion, those who now took it in hand to draw the actual working plans soon found it necessary to reduce its scale somewhat to bring it within practicable dimensions. Instead of 20,000 singers, the limit was set at 10,000; the Coliseum, instead of 50,000, was to hold less than 30,000 hearers—say 37,000, counting stage and auditorium together. Large enough, in all conscience. With every such redaction the plan gained in the opinion of really musical persons. One by one many of these gave in, accepted part in the management or in the performance, saying: Since its success is certain, let us try to make it worthy of success; let us mould its character, as far as possible, to some consistency of true artistic end and outline—make it musical in the best sense we can, eliminate some nonsense wholly, keep guns and anvils within reasonable bounds, and give the highest music a fair chance. Hence a considerable modification of the programmes. The 20,000 school children, reduced to 7,000, were to have their own day, sweet and peaceful, set apart, and not be huddled in with the general medley of noisy cannonading choruses and all the boisterous excitement sure to go therewith. The Ninth Symphony was wisely voted quite impracticable. The duration of the Festival, having been increased from three to five days, gave room for two programmes almost exclusively of classical selections. The five programmes as definitely settled were pointed to as miracles of skill and "genius." Yet what was good in them was common, the most familiar choruses of well-known oratorios, &c.; what was uncommon was of questionable taste, as guns and anvils for a sublime occasion. And these incongruous elements were queerly mingled. Which was the ruling element? Which set the key and mainly dominated? Plainly, the pieces which the unmusical many like the best, the national airs, &c., with the anvils. The classical selections had, we must confess, the look of being put in apologetically, in order to conciliate the higher taste. (The "sop to Cerberus" reversed). But we shall see.

II. A Few Notes on the Programmes & Performance

The first day's programme was ceremonial, inaugural, sensational, patriotic. Prayer and addresses, were unheard, while that vast multitude, 12,000 facing 11,000, gazed in wonder on itself, and felt the inspiration of a scene the grandeur and beauty of which were unimaginable before. That spectacle needed no speech, no music even, to make its eloquence sublime and irresistible. That was the secret of the *great* impression throughout all the days: so many beings met and held together there in full sight of each other, and in perfect order. What but music could secure such order? Prayer and speech were brief; but, even could they have been heard, they were superfluous. What fitter prayer than that religious Luther Choral: *"Ein feste Burg,"* which followed? Full, rich, solemn, grand, the chords rolled forth from 10,000 voices, supported by the great orchestra, but even more by that most powerful organ (small, but built for power), which really seemed the backbone of the chorus. We could wish it had been harmonized by Bach, instead of Nicolai, if only that Bach might have had some recognition among the other mighty masters. Two things were proved at once: that there was no increase of loudness at all proportioned to the number of voices; and that, even if the farthest voices reached the ear a fragment of a second later than the nearest, the ear was not aware of it, while many individual imperfections, even false notes, possibly, were swallowed up in the great volume and momentum of the mass. The same held good of the other pieces of plain choral harmony: Keller's "American Hymn," and the concluding "God Save the Queen" (which one of our Psalm Kings, Psalmanazar I., we dare say, has nicknamed "America") sung to "My Country," with all the spread-eagle accompaniments of drums, guns, bells, &c. The Mozart "Gloria" was a good selection for a day of Peace, and, though it moved unsteadily, yet by its animation and its clear intention made most hearers deaf to faults. Wagner's

Tannhäuser Overture did not prove a fortunate selection for that great orchestra, nor had it any special fitness for the occasion, except as a piece of stirring effect music. In few parts of the vast space could much of it be heard; the violins and brass told well; the reeds, intrusted with the theme at times, were lost. The Overture to "Tell" fared somewhat better, at least in the spirited finale, though the opening, so beautiful with violoncellos (60 of them,) was dumb show to all but the nearest. One envied the singers their places round the rim of the great seething instrumental maelstrom, looking down into it as well as hearing. The "Ave Maria" solo, built by Gounod upon a prelude of Bach, was notable for the rich *obligato* unison of the 200 violins (though all there was of Bach about it, the arpeggio modulation, complete in itself, and used by Gounod for accompaniment, was covered up so as to be imperceptible), and for the clearness with which Mme. Rosa's[2] voice penetrated the whole space, although it sounded far off and in miniature, as if heard through the wrong end of an opera glass. In the *Inflammatus* her triumph was more signal, while the great choral climaxes look like the grander summits in the memory of mountain scenery. The rest was sensational: "Star-Spangled Banner," glorified by such broad treatment, with artillery and bells beside—a signal, as it were, to all the world outside that Jubilee had reached its highest moment— and with the melody so divided between deeper and higher voices as to overcome the difficulty for average singers of its great compass. That indeed was thrilling! March from "The Prophet," by full band of one thousand—business enough for all their throats of brass. And Verdi's "Anvil Chorus," causing wildest excitement—not precisely a legitimate effect of music, not the kind of excitement or emotion which musical people seek; fatal to that mood and temper of an audience in which music as such can be felt. Such effects are *extra* musical; the spectacle, the hundred scarlet firemen, &c., had much to do with it. Besides, the hundred anvils had a queer and toy-like sound, jingle of sleigh bells rather than the honest Vulcan *ring.* This was Mr. Gilmore's day, and he conducted all the patriotic pieces, including the opening Choral, in which he realized a good *pianissimo,* one of the finest effects of a vast multiple of voices. Mr. Eichberg[3] conducted in the *Tannhäuser* overture, and "Coronation March;" Mr. Zerrahn[4] in the solos and the *Gloria.*

The second was a great day of excitement. Added to the *éclat* of the Festival, now in full tide of success, was the visit of the President rather disturbing the conditions precedent for the "Grand Classical Programme," which had been much relied on for the conversion or conviction of the musically cultivated. The crowd was enormous—double that of the day before; curiosity, hero-worship, swelling heart of patriotism, doubtless drew more than music did. Of course

2. Euphrosyne Parepa-Rosa (1836–1874), Scottish soprano who toured extensively in the United States.
3. Julius Eichberg (1824–1893), German-American violinist, composer, and teacher.
4. Carl Zerrahn (1829–1909), flutist and conductor of many ensembles including the Handel and Haydn Society and the Harvard Musical Association orchestra.

not the best sort of audience either to hear or let hear. Well, the selections were all excellent; though we would except, perhaps, the opening Festival Overture by Nicolai on Luther's Choral. The plain Choral, to our mind, was grander, than with that orchestral counterpoint and trivial episodical theme between the stanzas; not being great work in that kind, like Bach's, it weakens the impression. Of three Handel Choruses, "See the conquering hero" was the most effective; "And the Glory of the Lord," was taken so slow as to make it hard to sing—a necessity, real or fancied, in conducting so vast a multitude through any labyrinthine movement. We were surprised that we could hear Miss Phillipps's[5] voice so well; there is a weight in her rich tones that carries far and quietly pervades. The piece, one of the best for her, and one of her best efforts, Mozart's *"Non piu di fiori,"* was too good for the crowd, not heard by some on account of restless noise, and not appreciated by the majority. Such a crowd contributes nothing on its own part to music, does not truly listen, but waits to be smitten and carried away. "He watching over Israel," the gentle, softly swelling chorus from *Elijah,* strange to say, proved one of the most successful of all the choruses that week; like a broad Amazon the stream moved steadily and evenly within bounds, and the round, full, smooth quality of the collective tone is something memorable. "Let the bright Seraphim" was just the perfect selection for Parepa-Rosa in that place, and was the chiefest triumph of her voice. With Arbuckle's[6] trumpet obligato (one longs for the real crackling old-fashioned *trumpet* though) it made great effect, by no means so great as it would be in a smaller hall; but the half-musical, which is by far the larger part of any such great audience, always need the *personal element* to interest them in music, and go the full half-way to meet a solo. The intermission was of course filled with the Hero-President. Then came Part II., the great Schubert Symphony in C, Mr. Zerrahn's capital selection for his grand orchestra; great hopes had been placed on that, for what symphonic work can bear such magnified presentment, if not that work? Alas! the Tantalus cup was rudely snatched away. The Symphony was to be sacrificed; the other element, fasting from native noise and anvils and free swing of hurrah boys, had grown irrepressible. To the brave President all music is alike, they say, and how easy for some one of the irrepressibles to prompt him to express a wish for good Spread-Eagle Scream with anvils! So into the programme, unannounced, and right before the Symphony, were thrust bodily "Star Spangled Banner" and "Anvil Chorus," once and again, until the building shook with thunder of applause; all mood for finer music was destroyed, all fine conditions broken up, Prospero Schubert's wand tossed under feet. The Symphony was killed ! knocked on the head by anvils! The wand, however, was picked up and waved for form's sake. But it had grown late; people were weary, restless, moving about, or starting homeward, talking aloud, in no mood to listen or let others hear; so the first move-

5. Adelaide Phillipps (1833–1882) English singer and actress, student of Manuel Garcia.
6. Matthew Arbuckle (1828–1883), Scottish-American bandmaster and cornetist.

ment and the Scherzo were omitted; the beautiful Andante (of the "heavenly length") was scarcely heard, and never did the impetuous sublime finale, with the thunder thumps of double basses (think of 70 or 80 of them!) sound so feebly. Were we right in the suspicion that the "classical" programmes were apologetic, meant to be like the "off nights" in a theatre, a compliment to musical taste, while the substantial meal was for the fire-eaters, the sensationalists who go forth "seeking a sign?" Good Mr. Zerrahn's best opportunity was frustrated; he could not try the effect of monster orchestra on this the chosen symphony. How much more satisfactory it may have been in the rehearsal, we do not know. Poor chance after this for Haydn choruses: "The Marvelous Work," and "The Heavens are telling;" for, sing as they might to an audience preoccupied, it still went: "The *anvils* are telling." The selected trio of a dozen solo singers on each part was very pleasing when it could be heard; but there was much floundering in the great chorus, and what was most "telling," as was just said, was retrospective and subjective: the chords those hammers set to vibrating were still undamped.

Third day, like the last, but more so. I was not there, and should have had to be dragged there after that fatigue. It was the 17th of June—of course, the chief day in the anvil calendar. That should have been the President's day; so the two kinds could have been kept distinct, one day for music and one day for glory.

Fourth day, Friday, best of all. The one really *musical* occasion, when the programme, choice in itself, was preserved in its purity. I had the fortune to sit very near the stage, and found it by far the best place for hearing. Even the orchestra became appreciable. Mr. Eichberg led Weber's "Jubilee" Overture, which perhaps went best of all the orchestral pieces in the festival. Mr. Zerrahn led all the rest. The glorious old C minor Symphony of Beethoven, the one of all others the best known among us, and most sure of close attention, was cut short, needlessly, as there was time enough, and the vast audience was calm; the chance at last seemed offered. But no, the experience of Wednesday had unnerved the valor and faith for Symphonies in that place; there was not courage left to risk it. So the first movement ("Fate knocking at 'he door") was left out; so, too, was the Scherzo—the curiosity to hear 80 double basses execute their scramble went ungratified; and, though the glorious March Finale sounded very well (and the Andante, too), yet robbed of its prelude, out of which it grows so marvelously, it lost half its effect, while the return of the three-four Scherzo rhythm in the middle of the march was meaningless. This was the only misdemeanor of the concert. Miss Philipps sang that large and simple aria of Handel, *"Lascia,"* &c., in her noblest style, and with incredible effect for that vast place. The ten thousand singers had grown more at home in their work, more blended and assimilated by common effort and enthusiasm, now burning at something like white heat, and almost everything went better than before with them. Best of all, the grave and solid chorals from St. Paul— that with the startling trumpet interlude, "Sleepers, awake," especially. It is the solid, ponderous swing of the great mass of sound in plain, long chords like these, sound equally diffused and oceanic, yet, like the wide waste of waters, smooth and unobtrusive, that dwells in the mind as the best, the true effect of choral force so multiplied. Yet all must own that that more rapid graphic, difficult, exciting chorus of Mendelssohn, the great Rain chorus from "Elijah" was, on the whole, the choral achievement of the whole Festival, which most signally rewarded effort. It was electrifying. Zerrahn, wisely, would not risk a repetition. The down rush through the scale of those two hundred violins was a thing to thank God for, like the rain. The Haydn chorus, the "Inflammatus," this time with eight choice soprani for the solo, the Prayer from "Moses," and the Mozart *Gloria* again, made good impression, though faults might be found had one the impression present. The *Gloria* past, the Handel *Hallelujah* alone remains, and we await it strong in the peace and security of a pure musical communion so far unbroken. But think not that "the other element" has all this time been sitting quite so patiently. Creditable it was, indeed, to musical taste and culture here, that the vast audience had not shrunk perceptibly before a programme altogether classical; but think not that *all* those 20,000 people came there without some inward assurance that the Anvil Chorus would appear and take its throne, as matter of course, by divine right of its own, divine right of disorder! Loud was the clamor for it. Fortunately, the means and men for it were absent: or rather, thanks and all honor to Mr. Gilmore, who modestly yielded the command that day, and absolutely refused to have the programme interrupted. Yet the *Hallelujah* suffered after the confusion; singers had grown weary, nervous too, perhaps, and the effect of the great chorus, even with all those means was not so overwhelming as it has been on more ordinary occasions. It was on the whole a noble concert, heartily enjoyed by all so placed that they could listen, and a comparison of this with Wednesday's concert gives a capital illustration of a great point in the art of programme-making—the importance, namely, of keeping incongruous elements distinct.

It was on Saturday morning, the School Children's day, that we were touched and made to *feel* for once. The charming scene, the innocent, pure spirit of the whole, the fresh, sweet, silvery voices of the 7,000 children, admirably true and blended in three-part song and unison, their own expressions of delight, their waving of handkerchiefs, and silvery shouts of applause, the kaleidoscopic unity of movement in their physical and vocal gymnastic exercises, all combined to make an exquisite impression. It was good to be there. It meant much for the future and for culture. It was not an art occasion, to be sure, and did not pretend to be. It was unique, a side of the Festival entirely by itself; the most genuine and sincere of all, and, in many respects, the most interesting. The beauty of it was that it did not pretend or strive to be anything but just what it was. But when the exercises came to measured breathing, then to the first utterance of a pure tone, swelling and dying away with the most beautiful *crescendo* and *diminuendo* that we ever heard, and finally to the blended tones of the Trichord, purity itself, like the white ray of "holy light" divided by the prism, we were fain to call that just the most exquisite moment of the whole week's Festival. Simple, but divine; impersonal, but alive; without conscious meaning, but implying all! And, after such an illustration as the whole Jubilee had given of the musical resources of our people, was it not worth the while to see the nursery where the seeds thereof are sown?

III. The Net Results

As an *occasion,* of a new kind, of unexampled magnitude (unless in semi-barbarous times or Oriental countries)—whatever may have been musically—the Jubilee was a success. All acknowledge it, not without joy, even though at times it may come over some of us again in the character it wore from the first, as a strange overshadowing apparition, a vast work of willfulness, which had intrinsically, ideally, no right to be. As a man eminent in letters and in public life remarked to me yesterday, the amount of it is this: "A ridiculous plan redeemed by a magnificent success." Its friends had a perfect right to be wild over it. Many an unbeliever has been wholly or in great part converted, or at least reconciled to it. It has become a splendid Fact, which has to be accepted. If the projector and his fellow architects were wrong, attempting the impossible, in many points of view the undesirable, they "builded better than they knew." It seems as if—the ball once set in motion, or, rather, the vigorous first twist once given at the heart and centre of the revolving and soon formidably expanding maelstrom—as the dream and the intense will of one, magnetizing a few, then many, passed by degrees into a popular movement, assuming almost national dimensions, until the very air was full of it—soon every particle and feature of it, as it were, underwent "a sea change" in the tempering, transforming, vitalizing, and idealizing element of the new, best life and genius of a great, free People; having adopted it almost before they knew it, and hardly knowing what it was, they meant that it should be American in some sense which they could be proud of, and that the biggest gathering and musical array in human history, in spite of its extravagances, should still denote us truly, and be an earnest to the world of what an ambition for the true glory of a great nation, what a sleepless ideal of an ever higher type of Citizenship and of Society, what an energy and wealth of means, what a zeal for culture, what a principle of order and deep love of harmony are in us, spite of our diversities and the wide space over which we spread. And so it came to pass. And New England, Boston was the place for it. We need not attempt to show what has been so universally acknowledged, that such a feast could have succeeded nowhere else but here.

Musically, the Jubilee had its chief triumphs in precisely those selections which were the least purely musical, of no account as Art, no interest to earnest music-lovers. The parts that were addressed to these were certainly not great successes, and yet more successful than they for the most part had anticipated.

Reasons *a priori* were against great success, and the results do not disprove
their soundness.

Consider, in the first place, the mingling of incongruous, internecine elements in the programmes, as we have seen; an incongruity involved in the
mixed motives of the plan. There lay the knot of the difficulty: the project was
ambiguous; music needs a simple *motive*. To fire the imaginations of 50,000
people and bring them all together, something other than good music had to
be held up to them; a pure feast of high Art could not do it, nor could the
genius of high Art do otherwise than run away and hide its face from such
publicity as that. On the other hand, when it came to the ambitious promise of
combining all the vocal and orchestral resources of the land, conductors of
high standing, artists schooled in Philharmonic concerts, accustomed to the
interpretation of the great masters, how could *their* coöperation be had without
giving them fit work to do, making the occasion worthy of them? You can have
them for Mozart, Beethoven, and Schubert, but not for Anvil Choruses and
"Yankee Doodle" only. The pride of their profession, and what there is select,
superior in it, has to be respected. They must appear to work for Art, else will
they come? Now, the question was not simply of a Musical Festival, but also of
a Peace Jubilee. Doubtless, in Mr. Gilmore's mind, the desire to display the
musical resources of the land combined in one collective effort found sincere
opportunity in the return of Peace. Monster Concerts were his passion; Peace
and Country, also, were no strangers to his heart. Glorious and sublime it
seemed to him to make the two ends meet; what an electric chain of sparks,
brightness unspeakable, shot through his brain at the bringing of those two
poles together! Then, again, as the circle widened, less ideal motives came in:
the Jubilee would give Boston "such an advertisement as it never had;" trade
would flow to us, &c., (though many burnt their fingers). These motives were
most openly avowed, and the appeal to hundreds of subscribers was mainly put
upon these grounds. All very well; but not for Music. Symphonies were promised to conciliate the musical; guns and anvils, national airs, &c., to draw the
million and make no huge a project practicable. We have seen how the two got
on together; how the anvils killed the Symphony, and how hard was abstinence
from anvils when a classical programme was for once allowed its course.—
There could not be a better illustration of the law in programme-making, to
which we have alluded: that elements incongruous be kept apart, as damaging,
if not destructive, to each other. Each piece for its effect is much dependent
on what goes before and after; sensational pieces, sure to be encored, rob all
that follow of all fair chance for attention or effect. It is the art of picture-
hanging as applied to music. We are far from saying that all the good things
were lost: not a few of them were highly enjoyable to thousands favorably
placed, some of the noble choruses, no doubt, to all. One cheering sign, too,
could be read in all this, in the mere indication, spite of imperfect realization,
of so many good things: it showed how strong and deeply seated, how wide-

spread the love of the highest kinds of music has become in our community, since it was found essential to conciliate it and defer to it so largely in these programmes.

•   •   •   •   •

But I must hasten to a close. Whether the Festival considered musically, were very good or not, it musically *did* good. At any rate to all those singers and performers. It was a great experience for them. It has given them a new impulse, a new consciousness of strength, a new taste of the joy of unity of effort, a new love of cooperation, and a deeper sense of the divine significance and power of music than they ever had. It has caused hundreds of choral societies to spring into existence for the time being, many of which will certainly prove permanent; and their first bond of union has been the practice of *good* music, of master-works of Handel, Haydn, Mozart, Mendelssohn, which, having tasted once in such deep draughts, they will not readily abandon for weak trash. Education must come out of it. It has *planted,* well and widely, for the future.

Was it not good to be there, too, as listener, as looker-on, as sympathetic part and parcel of it? Who would willingly have been left out of such a grand occasion? The greatest assemblage of human beings under one roof ever known! A scene so overwhelming, so sublime, so beautiful from every point of view! An almost boundless sea of live humanity; and all so cheerful, all so happy, full of kindness, rejoicing in the sense of Country and of Brotherhood! Tens on tens of thousands, yet such admirable *Order!* Could any object, any influence but Music, hold such countless restless atoms in such order?

Finally, in a still wider way it has done good. It has given to tens of thousands of all classes (save, unfortunately, the poorest), who were there to hear, and, through them, to thousands more, to whole communities, a new belief in Music: a new conviction of its social worth; above all, of its importance as a pervading, educational and fusing element in our whole democratic life; a heavenly influence which shall go far to correct the crudities, tone down, subdue and harmonize the loud, self-asserting individualities, relieve the glaring and forthputting egotism of our too boisterous and boastful nationality. Thousands now have faith in Music, who never did have much before; thousands for the first time respect it as a high and holy influence, who very likely looked upon it as at the best an innocent, if not a dissipating, idle pleasure. Public opinion, henceforth, will count it among the essentials of that "liberal education," which is the birthright of a free American, and no longer as a superfluous refinement of an over-delicate and fashionable few. We shall no longer have to plead against such odds to claim, that Music have her permanent, her honored seat among the "humanities" of learning and of general culture. We begin to see how Music is to teach a people manners, mutual deference, and, without outward cold authority, without appeal to fear, but freely and divinely from within, inspire the instinct of respect, of fond and childlike reverence for something still above us, be we where we may,—and this is real Self-respect. So far as the Jubilee has wrought this conversion among unbelieving or indifferent thousands, it has done incalculable good; and if, for this alone, we cannot be too grateful to the men who (whatever our mistrust of motives and of methods once) have given us a great experience.

Boston, June 25, 1869

IV

MUSICAL MEANING AND EXPRESSION

13 E. T. A. Hoffmann

A standard-bearer of German romanticism, E. T. A. Hoffmann was born in 1776 in Königsberg and died in 1822 in Berlin. His talents were manifold: he was a poet, a critic, a composer, a theater manager, a draftsman, and a public servant. Best remembered for his fantastic novels, Hoffmann was deeply devoted to music and for some time made music his profession. Among his works for the stage the most important is the opera *Undine* (1813–14). Hoffmann was one of the fathers of modern musical journalism and in this field opened the way to Robert Schumann and Richard Wagner. His literary works testify to the deeply musical nature of his poetic inspiration. In turn, Hoffmann's poetic visions have inspired musical works of the most disparate character. Schumann's *Kreisleriana,* Jacques Offenbach's *Les Contes d'Hoffmann,* Ferruccio Busoni's *Die Brautwahl* are cases in point.

Beethoven's Instrumental Music

(1813)

When we speak of music as an independent art, should we not always restrict our meaning to instrumental music, which, scorning every aid, every admixture of another art (the art of poetry), gives pure expression to music's specific nature, recognizable in this form alone? It is the most romantic of all the arts—one might almost say, the only genuinely romantic one—for its sole subject is the infinite. The lyre of Orpheus opened the portals of Orcus—music discloses to man an unknown realm, a world that has nothing in common with the external sensual world that surrounds him, a world in which he leaves behind him all definite feelings to surrender himself to an inexpressible longing.

Have you even so much as suspected this specific nature, you miserable composers of instrumental music, you who have laboriously strained yourselves to represent definite emotions, even definite events? How can it ever have occurred to you to treat after the fashion of the plastic arts the art diametrically opposed to plastic? Your sunrises, your tempests, your *Batailles des trois Empereurs,*[1] and the rest, these, after all, were surely quite laughable aberrations, and they have been punished as they well deserved by being wholly forgotten.

TEXT: "Beethovens Instrumental-Musik." *Sämtliche Werke,* ed. C. G. von Maassen, vol. 1 (Munich and Leipzig, 1908) pp. 55–58, 60–61, 62–64. As published in 1814 among the "Kreisleriana" of the *Fantasiestücke in Callot's Manier* (and earlier, anonymously, in the *Zeitung für die elegante Welt* for December 1813), this essay combines and condenses two reviews published anonymously in the *Allgemeine musikalische Zeitung* (Leipzig) for July 1810 and March 1813. Translation by Oliver Strunk.

1. Perhaps Hoffmann is thinking of Louis Jadin's "La grande bataille d'Austerlitz," published in an arrangement for the piano by Kühnel of Leipzig in 1807 or earlier.

In song, where poetry, by means of words, suggests definite emotions, the magic power of music acts as does the wondrous elixir of the wise, a few drops of which make any drink more palatable and more lordly. Every passion—love, hatred, anger, despair, and so forth, just as the opera gives them to us—is clothed by music with the purple luster of romanticism, and even what we have undergone in life guides us out of life into the realm of the infinite.

As strong as this is music's magic, and, growing stronger and stronger, it had to break each chain that bound it to another art.

That gifted composers have raised instrumental music to its present high estate is due, we may be sure, less to the more readily handled means of expression (the greater perfection of the instruments, the greater virtuosity of the players) than to the more profound, more intimate recognition of music's specific nature.

Mozart and Haydn, the creators of our present instrumental music, were the first to show us the art in its full glory; the man who then looked on it with all his love and penetrated its innermost being is—Beethoven! The instrumental compositions of these three masters breathe a similar romantic spirit—this is due to their similar intimate understanding of the specific nature of the art; in the character of their compositions there is none the less a marked difference.

In Haydn's writing there prevails the expression of a serene and childlike personality. His symphonies lead us into vast green woodlands, into a merry, gaily colored throng of happy mortals. Youths and maidens float past in a circling dance; laughing children, peering out from behind the trees, from behind the rose bushes, pelt one another playfully with flowers. A life of love, of bliss like that before the Fall, of eternal youth; no sorrow, no suffering, only a sweet melancholy yearning for the beloved object that floats along, far away, in the glow of the sunset and comes no nearer and does not disappear—nor does night fall while it is there, for it is itself the sunset in which hill and valley are aglow.

Mozart leads us into the heart of the spirit realm. Fear takes us in its grasp, but without torturing us, so that it is more an intimation of the infinite. Love and melancholy call to us with lovely spirit voices; night comes on with a bright purple luster, and with inexpressible longing we follow those figures which, waving us familiarly into their train, soar through the clouds in eternal dances of the spheres.[2]

Thus Beethoven's instrumental music opens up to us also the realm of the monstrous and the immeasurable. Burning flashes of light shoot through the deep night of this realm, and we become aware of giant shadows that surge back and forth, driving us into narrower and narrower confines until they destroy *us*—but not the pain of that endless longing in which each joy that has climbed aloft in jubilant song sinks back and is swallowed up, and it is only in this pain, which consumes love, hope, and happiness but does not destroy

---

2. Mozart's Symphony in E-flat Major, known as the "Swan Song." [Au.]

them, which seeks to burst our breasts with a many-voiced consonance of all the passions, that we live on, enchanted beholders of the supernatural!

Romantic taste is rare, romantic talent still rarer, and this is doubtless why there are so few to strike that lyre whose sound discloses the wondrous realm of the romantic.

Haydn grasps romantically what is human in human life; he is more commensurable, more comprehensible for the majority.

Mozart calls rather for the superhuman, the wondrous element that abides in inner being.

Beethoven's music sets in motion the lever of fear, of awe, of horror, of suffering, and wakens just that infinite longing which is the essence of romanticism. He is accordingly a completely romantic composer, and is not this perhaps the reason why he has less success with vocal music, which excludes the character of indefinite longing, merely representing emotions defined by words as emotions experienced in the realm of the infinite?

The musical rabble is oppressed by Beethoven's powerful genius; it seeks in vain to oppose it. But knowing critics, looking about them with a superior air, assure us that we may take their word for it as men of great intellect and deep insight that, while the excellent Beethoven can scarcely be denied a very fertile and lively imagination, he does not know how to bridle it! Thus, they say, he no longer bothers at all to select or to shape his ideas, but, following the so-called daemonic method, he dashes everything off exactly as his ardently active imagination dictates it to him. Yet how does the matter stand if it is *your* feeble observation alone that the deep inner continuity of Beethoven's every composition eludes? If it is *your* fault alone that you do not understand the master's language as the initiated understand it, that the portals of the innermost sanctuary remain closed to you? The truth is that, as regards self-possession, Beethoven stands quite on a par with Haydn and Mozart and that, separating his ego from the inner realm of harmony, he rules over it as an absolute monarch. In Shakespeare, our knights of the aesthetic measuring rod have often bewailed the utter lack of inner unity and inner continuity, although for those who look more deeply there springs forth, issuing from a single bud, a beautiful tree, with leaves, flowers, and fruit; thus, with Beethoven, it is only after a searching investigation of his instrumental music that the high self-possession inseparable from true genius and nourished by the study of the art stands revealed.

Can there be any work of Beethoven's that confirms all this to a higher degree than his indescribably profound, magnificent symphony in C minor? How this wonderful composition, in a climax that climbs on and on, leads the listener imperiously forward into the spirit world of the infinite! . . . No doubt the whole rushes like an ingenious rhapsody past many a man, but the soul of each thoughtful listener is assuredly stirred, deeply and intimately, by a feeling that is none other than that unutterable portentous longing, and until the final chord—indeed, even in the moments that follow it—he will be powerless to step out of that wondrous spirit realm where grief and joy embrace him in the form of sound. The internal structure of the movements, their execution, their instrumentation, the way in which they follow one another—everything contributes to a single end; above all, it is the intimate interrelationship among the themes that engenders that unity which alone has the power to hold the listener firmly in a single mood. This relationship is sometimes clear to the listener when he overhears it in the connecting of two movements or discovers it in the fundamental bass they have in common; a deeper relationship which does not reveal itself in this way speaks at other times only from mind to mind, and it is precisely this relationship that prevails between sections of the two Allegros and the Minuet and which imperiously proclaims the self-possession of the master's genius.

How deeply thy magnificent compositions for the piano have impressed themselves upon my soul, thou sublime master; how shallow and insignificant now all seems to me that is not thine, or by the gifted Mozart or that mighty genius, Sebastian Bach! With what joy I received thy seventieth work, the two glorious trios, for I knew full well that after a little practice I should soon hear them in truly splendid style. And in truth, this evening things went so well with me that even now, like a man who wanders in the mazes of a fantastic park, woven about with all manner of exotic trees and plants and marvelous flowers, and who is drawn further and further in, I am powerless to find my way out of the marvelous turns and windings of thy trios. The lovely siren voices of these movements of thine, resplendent in their many-hued variety, lure me on and on. The gifted lady who indeed honored me, Capellmeister Kreisler,[3] by playing today the first trio in such splendid style, the gifted lady before whose piano I still sit and write, has made me realize quite clearly that only what the mind produces calls for respect and that all else is out of place.

Just now I have repeated at the piano from memory certain striking transitions from the two trios.

•   •   •   •   •

How well the master has understood the specific character of the instrument and fostered it in the way best suited to it!

A simple but fruitful theme, songlike, susceptible to the most varied contrapuntal treatments, curtailments, and so forth, forms the basis of each movement; all remaining subsidiary themes and figures are intimately related to the main idea in such a way that the details all interweave, arranging themselves among the instruments in highest unity. Such is the structure of the whole, yet in this artful structure there alternate in restless flight the most marvelous pictures in which joy and grief, melancholy and ecstasy, come side by side or intermingled to the fore. Strange figures begin a merry dance, now floating off

3. The eccentric, half-mad musician from whose literary remains Hoffmann pretends to have taken his "Kreisleriana." Schumann borrows the title of his Opus 16 from these sketches of Hoffmann's (published in two groups as a part of his *Fantasiestücke in Callot's Manier*).

into a point of light, now splitting apart, flashing and sparkling, evading and pursuing one another in various combinations, and at the center of the spirit realm thus disclosed the intoxicated soul gives ear to the unfamiliar language and understands the most mysterious premonitions that have stirred it.

That composer alone has truly mastered the secrets of harmony who knows how, by their means, to work upon the human soul; for him, numerical proportions, which to the dull grammarian are no more than cold, lifeless problems in arithmetic, become magical compounds from which to conjure up a magic world.

Despite the good nature that prevails, especially in the first trio, not even excepting the melancholy Largo, Beethoven's genius is in the last analysis serious and solemn. It is as though the master thought that, in speaking of deep mysterious things—even when the spirit, intimately familiar with them, feels itself joyously and gladly uplifted—one may not use an ordinary language, only a sublime and glorious one; the dance of the priests of Isis can be only an exultant hymn. Where instrumental music is to produce its effect simply through itself as music and is by no means to serve a definite dramatic purpose, it must avoid all trivial facetiousness, all frivolous *lazzi* [gags]. A deep temperament seeks, for the intimations of that joy which, an import from an unknown land, more glorious and more beautiful than here in our constricted world, enkindles an inner, blissful life within our breasts, a higher expression than can be given to it by mere words, proper only to our circumscribed earthly air. This seriousness, in all of Beethoven's works for instruments and for the piano, is in itself enough to forbid all those breakneck passages up and down for the two hands which fill our piano music in the latest style, all the queer leaps, the farcical capriccios, the notes towering high above the staff on their five- and six-line scaffolds.

On the side of mere digital dexterity, Beethoven's compositions for the piano really present no special difficulty, for every player must be presumed to have in his fingers the few runs, triplet figures, and whatever else is called for; nevertheless, their performance is on the whole quite difficult. Many a so-called virtuoso condemns this music, objecting that it is "very difficult" and into the bargain "very ungrateful."

Now, as regards difficulty, the correct and fitting performance of a work of Beethoven's asks nothing more than that one should understand him, that one should enter deeply into his being, that—conscious of one's own consecration—one should boldly dare to step into the circle of the magical phenomena that his powerful spell has evoked. He who is not conscious of this consecration, who regards sacred Music as a mere game, as a mere entertainment for an idle hour, as a momentary stimulus for dull ears, or as a means of self-ostentation—let him leave Beethoven's music alone. Only to such a man, moreover, does the objection "most ungrateful" apply. The true artist lives only in the work that he has understood as the composer meant it and that he then performs. He is above putting his own personality forward in any way, and all his endeavors are directed toward a single end—that all the wonderful enchanting pictures and apparitions that the composer has sealed into his work with magic power may be called into active life, shining in a thousand colors, and that they may surround mankind in luminous sparkling circles and, enkindling its imagination, its innermost soul, may bear it in rapid flight into the faraway spirit realm of sound.[4]

4. Hoffmann's essay was brought to Beethoven's attention in February or March 1820 by someone who wrote, during a conversation with him: "In the *Fantasiestücke* of Hoffmann there is much talk about you. Hoffmann used to be the music-director in Bromberg; now he is a state counsellor. They give operas by him in Berlin." On the strength of this, evidently, Beethoven wrote the following letter to Hoffman on March 23, 1820:

> Through Herr ———, I seize this opportunity of approaching a man of your intellectual attainments. You have even written about my humble self, and our Herr ——— showed me in his album some lines of yours about me. I must assume, then, that you take a certain interest in me. Permit me to say that, from a man like yourself, gifted with such distinguished qualities, this is very gratifying to me. I wish you the best of everything and remain, sir.
>
> Your devoted and respectful
> Beethoven

14 Marc André Souchay and Felix Mendelssohn

Instrumental music of the Romantic period has long inspired curiosity and controversy as to the possible meanings and references it might hold. Many pieces seem virtually to invite such speculation with suggestive poetic titles or other programmatic glimmers, and many contemporary commentators felt free to explicate compositions in apparently extramusical terms. Mendelssohn's famous *Songs without Words* would surely be ripe for poetic interpretation— why "songs," otherwise?—were it not for a well-known 1842 letter in which the composer seems to reject summarily any such possibility.*

Mendelssohn's explanation of his discomfort is interesting for his assertion that music's import, far from being too vague, is rather too *definite* for verbal translation. But even more fascinating is his corollary and surprisingly modernist

---

* Current scholarship suggests, however, that his attitude was rather more nuanced. See R. Larry Todd, " 'Gerade das Lied wie es dasteht': On Text and Meaning in Mendelssohn's *Lieder ohne Worte*," in *Musical Humanism and Its Legacy: Essays in Honor of Claude Palisca*, ed. Nancy Kovaleff Baker and Barbara Russano Hanning [Stuyvesant, N.Y.: Pendragon Press, 1992], pp. 355–79; and especially John Michael Cooper, "Words without Songs? Of Texts, Titles, and Mendelssohn's *Lieder ohne Worte*," in *Musik als Text: Bericht über den 19. Kongress der Gesellschaft für Musikforschung, Freiburg im Breisgau 1993*, ed. Hermann Danuser [forthcoming].

insistence that words themselves are too ambiguous for accurate communication to be taken for granted.

Until now, it has not been known exactly what question about his *Songs* Mendelssohn was answering in his famous letter. We are pleased to include that query here for the first time, unearthed in the Bodleian Library by John Michael Cooper. Marc André Souchay, Jr. (1796–1868) was a distant cousin of Cécile Jeanrenaud, Mendelssohn's wife; his devoted attachment to Mendelssohn's music is evident in his heartfelt efforts to make their meaning his own.

An Exchange of Letters
(1842)

Most noble sir,

Please do not think badly of me if my great enthusiasm for your compositions finally wins over my sense of propriety, and I dare to burden you with some few lines from my pen.

Even some time ago I would not have denied myself the joy of asking you, noble sir, for advice and opinions concerning certain circumstances; but I was always prevented from doing so by a sense of modesty, for I feared that it might be understood as mere audacity and impudence. But recently the great hospitality demonstrated by you, noble sir, toward Messrs. Heiß and Lieber, whose acquaintance I made here in Kassel, has emboldened me to set my long-standing wish down in words, since perhaps I too might succeed in receiving a few kind words from you, noble sir, in response.

First of all, I must give you my warmest thanks for the kindness you showed to me through my father last winter. According to your advice, I came to Kassel to receive instruction in theory from Court Chamber-musician Hauptmann; in him I found not only an outstanding teacher, but also an equally fatherly friend. I shall never forget the half-year I spent with him, nor the extraordinary kindness with which he always received me. [But] even more than for his fine instruction and friendship I am indebted to him for his openness, for it is at his suggestion that I have decided (partly from lack of talent, partly because of my poor health) not to continue my *study* of music. He was able, through his frank, well-intentioned judgments, to help me more than did years of pretending from my dear father and other friends. Although it is with heavy heart that I have now given up this study, in which most of the happiness in my life seemed to reside, music will still continue to bring to me the most beautiful of

TEXT: Music Division, Bodleian Library, Oxford: MS. M. Deneke Mendelssohn c. 42, No. 69 (incoming correspondence, "Mendelssohn Green Books") and MS. M. Deneke Mendelssohn c. 32, fols. 56–57; the latter is the most authoritative source of Mendelssohn's letter available since the original, in private hands, is inaccessible. Transcriptions and translations by John Michael Cooper. We are grateful to Peter Ward Jones of the Bodleian Library for permission to publish the translations here.

times and the noblest and most sublime joy; and even under present circumstances it can bring me only the greatest joy to have dedicated myself completely to music for some time, for because of it I am now in a position to bring pleasure and enjoyment to myself as a dilettante.

The most wonderful piano pieces that I know have for years been your *Songs without Words*. Even when I was still a child, I found in them such distinctive feeling and penetrating emotion that they became my favorite of all piano pieces. But this deep feeling, which emerged long ago, has become ever greater, and now that I have formulated for myself a definite idea for each of these masterful works—now they give me twice the pleasure; my earlier love and fondness for them have become complete enthusiasm.

Of course, I have often been laughed at for my fantastic ideas, even by people whom I had to acknowledge and honor as practicing musicians—for example, my current teacher here, the Court Chamber-musician Deichert, who will hear nothing of ideas, but only of notes! But that cannot be correct; I cannot imagine that there is no poem behind these masterful paintings. I beg you, noble sir, not to take it as arrogance if I dare to share my opinion openly with you, but rather to seek the reason for my daring in my extraordinary veneration for you and in my eagerness. I believe it would not be incorrect to say that the various meanings of the songs could perhaps be the following: *Vol. 1:* no. 1, resignation; no. 2, melancholy; no. 3, scene of a *par-force* hunt[1], no. 4, praise of the goodness of God; no. 6, Venetian gondolier-song. *Vol. 2:* no. 1, depiction of a devout and thankful person who has been sought after; no. 2, hunting scene; no. 4, strong desire to go out into the world; no. 5, lullaby; no. 6, Venetian gondolier-song. *Vol. 3:* no. 1, boundless but unrequited love, which therefore often turns into longing, pain, sadness, and despair, but always becomes peaceful again; no. 2, anxious expectation (alternating longing, anxiety, and pain); no. 3, love song; no. 4, contentment; no. 5, despair; no. 6, duet. *Vol. 4:* no. 2, longing; no. 3, despair; no. 5, warlike folk-song.

For the pieces left out I have thus far been unable to formulate any ideas. That many of the songs can be interpreted in very different ways, and that the style of performance always depends upon the interpretation, is certain. The judgment of Herr Hilf, who so often heard these pieces played by you yourself in Leipzig, made me very happy: he said that I play them in pretty much the same fashion as you. I think that these pieces, which are after all supposed to be songs, must be performed like songs for singing, and that, especially in some emotional ones, one does not need to hold to a strict tempo as with other compositions—indeed, often, should not, for the emotion would fade into apathy.

You would make me unspeakably happy with a few words concerning these

---

1. Originally, a royal hunt, at which the attendance of the king's retainers was required; later, an organized hunting party.

ideas—I would never forget your goodness and humility in doing so, honorable
Doctor, and even if my entire point of view is wrong I would be proud to have
received a correction from you. . . .

Your most obedient servant,
M. A. Souchay
of Lübeck
Kassel, October 12, 1842 . . .

. . . There is so much talk about music, and so little is said. I believe that
words are not at all up to it, and if I should find that they were adequate I
would stop making music altogether. People usually complain that music is so
ambiguous, and what they are supposed to think when they hear it is so unclear,
while words are understood by everyone. But for me it is exactly the opposite—
and not just with entire discourses, but also with individual words; these, too,
seem to be so ambiguous, so indefinite, in comparison with good music, which
fills one's soul with a thousand better things than words. What the music I
love expresses to me are thoughts not too *indefinite* for words, but rather too
definite.

Thus, I find in all attempts to put these thoughts into words something correct, but also always something insufficient, something not universal; and this
is also how I feel about your suggestions. This is not your fault, but rather the
fault of the words, which simply cannot do any better. So if you ask me what I
was thinking of, I will say: just the song as it stands there. And if I happen to
have had a specific word or specific words in mind for one or another of these
songs, I can never divulge them to anyone, because the same word means one
thing to one person and something else to another, because only the song can
say the same thing, can arouse the same feelings in one person as in another—
a feeling which is not, however, expressed by the same words.

Resignation, melancholy, praise of God, a *par-force* hunt: one person does
not think of these in the same way as someone else. What for one person is
resignation is melancholy for another; to a third person, neither suggests anything truly vivid. Indeed, if one were by nature an enthusiastic hunter, for him
the *par-force* hunt and the praise of God could come down pretty much to the
same thing, and for the latter the sound of horns would truly be the proper
way to praise God. We [on the other hand] would hear nothing but the *par-
force* hunt, and if we were to debate with him about it we would get absolutely
nowhere. The words remain ambiguous, but we both understand the music
properly.

Will you accept this as my answer to your question? It is at any rate the
only one I know how to give—though these, too, are nothing but ambiguous
words. . . .

Felix Mendelssohn Bartholdy
Berlin, October 15, 1842

15 Eduard Hanslick

Eduard Hanslick (1825–1904) enjoyed a successful career as a music critic, one of the first to make a profession of it, after a brief stint as a civil servant. Hanslick spent most of his life in Vienna, at the heart of musical current events. Through his regular criticism, he gradually became known as a supporter of Brahms and a polemicist against the Wagnerian school of modern music. His best known piece of writing is surely his brief treatise, *Vom Musikalisch-Schönen (On the Musically Beautiful)*, which was first published in 1854 and went through ten editions within its author's lifetime.

For a brief and quite clearly written book, *On the Musically Beautiful* has given rise to a surprisingly extensive literature of debate. In some quarters, Hanslick is best known for opinions he did not hold; he is often accused, for instance, of advocating a heartless formalism, as though music were a kind of audible calculus.

Not so. Hanslick argued that music is a primarily sensuous art, one of "specifically musical" beauty rather than of conceptual, quasi-literary content. While he made it his principal business to discredit the then-current notion that the primary function of music is to represent emotion, he does not deny that music frequently arouses feelings, nor even that we can aptly characterize much music by analogy with our emotional life. But he wants us to understand that those feelings come, through technical means, from particular patterns within the music and not by some alchemy directly from the soul of the composer. "The artist is inscrutable," he tells us, "but the artwork is not."

Hanslick's goal, therefore, is a scientific musical aesthetics, and another nuance often overlooked is his insistence upon the specificity of this topic. He distinguishes clearly between art-historical questions and aesthetic ones; far from forbidding "intentional" or "contextual" investigations for their own sake, he simply insists that their findings are not relevant to an aesthetic evaluation of the work at hand.

FROM *Vom Musikalisch-Schönen*
(1891)

So far we have proceeded negatively and have sought merely to refute the erroneous assumption that the beauty of music has its being in the representa-

TEXT: *On the Musically Beautiful: A Contribution towards the Revision of the Aesthetics of Music,* trans. and ed. Geoffrey Payzant [from the eighth edition (1891) of *Vom Musikalisch-Schönen*] (Indianapolis: Hackett, 1986), chap. 3, pp. 32–35, 38–44. Used by permission. Editorial notes are Payzant's.

tion of feeling. To that sketch, we now have to fill in the positive content. This we shall do by answering the question: What kind of beauty is the beauty of a musical composition?

It is a specifically musical kind of beauty. By this we understand a beauty that is self-contained and in no need of content from outside itself, that consists simply and solely of tones and their artistic combination.

• • • • •

Nothing could be more misguided and prevalent than the view which distinguishes between beautiful music which possesses ideal content and beautiful music which does not. This view has a much too narrow conception of the beautiful in music, representing both the elaborately constructed form and the ideal content with which the form is filled as self-subsistent. Consequently this view divides all compositions into two categories, the full and the empty, like champagne bottles. Musical champagne, however, has the peculiarity that it grows along with the bottle.

One particular musical conception is, taken by itself, witty; another is banal. A particular final cadence is impressive; change two notes, and it becomes insipid. Quite rightly we describe a musical theme as majestic, graceful, tender, dull, hackneyed, but all these expressions describe the musical character of the passage. To characterize this musical expressiveness of a motive, we often choose terms from the vocabulary of our emotional life: arrogant, peevish, tender, spirited, yearning. We can also take our descriptions from other realms of appearance, however, and speak of fragrant, vernal, hazy, chilly music. Feelings are thus, for the description of musical characteristics, only one source among others which offer similarities. We may use such epithets to describe music (indeed we cannot do without them), provided we never lose sight of the fact that we are using them only figuratively and take care not to say such things as "This music portrays arrogance," etc.

Detailed examination of all the musical determinations of a theme convinces us, however, that, despite the inscrutableness of the ultimate ontological grounds, there is a multitude of proximate causes with which the ideal expression of a piece of music is in precise correlation. Each individual musical element (i.e., each interval, tone-color, chord, rhythmic figure, etc) has its own characteristic physiognomy, its specific mode of action. The artist is inscrutable, but the artwork is not.

One and the same melody will not sound the same when accompanied by a triad as when accompanied by a chord of the sixth. A melodic interval of a seventh is wholly unlike a sixth. The accompanying rhythm of a motive, whether loud or soft, on whatever kind of musical instrument, modifies the motive's specific coloration. In brief, each individual factor in a musical passage necessarily contributes to its taking on its own unique ideal expression and having its effect upon the listener in this way and no other. What makes

Halévy's music bizarre and Auber's charming, what brings about the peculiarities by which we at once recognize Mendelssohn and Spohr, can be traced to purely musical factors without reference to the obscurities of the feelings.

Why Mendelssohn's numerous six-five chords and narrow diatonic themes, Spohr's chromaticisms and enharmonic relations, Auber's short, bipartite rhythms, etc., produce just these specific, unequivocal impressions: These questions, of course, neither psychology nor physiology can answer.

If, however, we are asking about proximate causes (and this is a matter of importance especially in connection with the arts), the powerful effect of a theme comes not from the supposed augmentation of anguish in the composer but from this or that augmented interval, not from the trembling of his soul but from the drumstrokes, not from his yearning but from the chromaticism. The correlation of the two we shall not ignore; on the contrary, we shall soon examine it more closely. We should keep in mind, however, that scientific examination of the effect of a theme can only be done with those aforementioned invariable and objective data, never with the supposed state of mind which the composer externalizes by means of them. If we want to reason from that state of mind directly to the effects of the work or to explain the latter in terms of the former, we might perhaps arrive at a correct conclusion but will have omitted the most important thing, the middle term of the syllogism, namely, the music itself.

The proficient composer possesses a working knowledge, be it more by instinct or by deliberation, of the character of every musical element. Nevertheless, a theoretical knowledge of these characters, from their most elaborate constructions to the least discriminable element, is required for scientific explanation of the various musical effects and impressions. The particular feature by which a melody has its power over us is not merely some kind of obscure miracle of which we can have no more than an inkling. It is rather the inevitable result of musical factors which are at work in the melody as a particular combination of those factors. Tight or broad rhythm, diatonic or chromatic progression, each has its characteristic feature and its own kind of appeal. That is why a trained musician, from a printed account of an unfamiliar composition, will get a much better idea of it if he reads, for example, that diminished sevenths and tremolos predominate, than from the most poetical description of the emotional crisis through which the reviewer went as a result of listening to it.

Investigation of the nature of each separate musical element and its connection with a specific impression (just of the facts of the matter, not of the ultimate principles) and finally the reduction of these detailed observations to general laws: that would be the philosophical foundation of music for which so many authors are yearning (without, incidentally, telling us what they really understand by the expression "philosophical foundation of music"). The psychological and physical effect of each chord, each rhythm, each interval, however, is by no means explained by saying that this is red, the other green, this is hope, the other discontent, but only by subsuming the particular musical qualities under general aesthetical categories and these in turn under a supreme principle. If, in the former manner, the separate factors were explained in their isolation, it would then have to be shown how they determine and modify each other in their various combinations. Most musically learned people have granted to harmony and contrapuntal accompaniment the preeminent position as the ideal content of a composition. In making this claim, however, they have proceeded much too superficially and atomistically. Some people have settled upon melody as the prompting of genius, as the vehicle for sensuousness and feeling (the Italians are famous for this); harmony has been cast opposite melody in the role of vehicle for the genuine content, being learnable and the product of deliberation. It is curious the way people keep going along with such a superficial way of looking at things. There is basic truth in both claims, but neither at this level of generality nor in isolation do they carry weight. The mind is a unity, and so is the musical creation of an artist. A theme emerges fully armed with its melody and its harmony, together, out of the head of the composer. Neither the principle of subordination nor that of opposition applies to the essence of the relation of harmony to melody. Both can in one place pursue their own lines of development and in another place readily subordinate one to the other. In either case, the highest degree of ideal beauty can be achieved. Is it perhaps the (very sketchy) harmony in the principal themes of Beethoven's "Coriolanus" overture and Mendelssohn's "Hebrides" which confers upon them the expression of brooding melancholy? Would Rossini's "Oh, Matilda" or a Neapolitan folksong achieve more spirit if a basso continuo or a complicated chord sequence replaced the sparse harmonic background? Each melody must be thought up along with its own particular harmony, with its own rhythm and sonority. The ideal content is due only to the conjunction of them all; mutilation of any one part damages also the expression of the remainder. That melody or harmony or rhythm should be able to predominate is to the advantage of all, and to consider on the one hand all genius to be in chords, and on the other all triviality to be in the lack of them, is sheer pedantry. The camellia blooms without scent; the lily, without color; the rose delights us with both color and scent. These qualities cannot be transferred from one to another, yet each of the blossoms is beautiful.

So the "philosophical foundation of music" would have to try first of all to find out which necessary ideal determinants are connected with each musical element, and in what manner they are connected. The double requirement of a strictly scientific framework and the most elaborate casuistics makes the task a very formidable but not quite insurmountable one: to strive for the ideal of an "exact" science of music after the model of chemistry or of physiology.

•   •   •   •   •

It is only recently that people have begun looking at artworks in relation to the ideas and events of the times which produced them. In all likelihood this undeniable connection also applies to music. Being a manifestation of the human mind, it must, of course, also stand in interrelation with the other activities of mind: with contemporaneous productions of the literary and visual arts, the poetic, social, scientific conditions of its time, and ultimately with the individual experiences and convictions of the composer. The examination and demonstration of this interrelation are therefore warranted with regard to individual composers and works, and they are truly profitable. Yet we must always keep in mind that drawing such a parallel between artistic matters and special historical circumstances is an art-historical and not at all an aesthetical procedure. While the connection between art history and aesthetics seems necessary from the methodological point of view, yet each of these two sciences must preserve unadulterated its own unique essence in the face of unavoidable confusion of one with the other. The historian, interpreting an artistic phenomenon in its wider context, might see in Spontini the expression of the French Empire period, in Rossini the political restoration. The aesthetician, however, has to limit himself exclusively to the works of these men, to inquire what in these works is beautiful and why. Aesthetical inquiry does not and should not know anything about the personal circumstances and historical background of the composer; it hears and believes only what the artwork itself has to say. It will accordingly discover in Beethoven's symphonies (the identity and biography of the composer being unknown) turbulence, striving, unappeasable longing, vigorous defiance; but that the composer had republican sympathies, was unmarried and becoming deaf, and all the other features which the art historian digs up as illuminating it will by no means glean from the works and may not be used for the evaluation of them. To compare differences in world view between Bach, Mozart, and Haydn and then go back to the differences between their compositions may count as a very attractive and meritorious exercise, yet it is infinitely complicated and will be the more prone to fallacies, the stricter the causal connection it seeks to establish. The danger of exaggeration as a result of accepting this principle is extraordinarily great. We can all too easily interpret the most incidental contemporary influence as a matter of inherent necessity and interpret the perpetually untranslatable language of music any way we like. It is purely on account of quick-witted delivery that the same paradox spoken by a clever person sounds like wisdom but, spoken by a simple person, sounds like nonsense.

Even Hegel, in discussing music, often misled in that he tacitly confused his predominantly art-historical point of view with the purely aesthetical and identified in music certainties which music itself never possessed. Of course there is a connection between the character of every piece of music and that of its author, but for the aesthetician this is not open to view. The idea of necessary connection between all phenomena can in its actual application be exaggerated to the point of caricature. Nowadays it takes real heroism to declare, in opposition to this pleasantly stimulating and ingeniously represented trend, that historical comprehension and aesthetical judgment are two different things.[1] It is objectively certain, first, that the variety of impressions of the various works and schools is based upon crucially dissimilar arrangements of the musical elements, and second, that what rightly pleases in a composition, be it the strictest fugue of Bach or the dreamiest nocturne of Chopin, is *musically* beautiful.

Even less than with the classical can the musically beautiful be equated with the architectonic, which includes the musically beautiful as one of its branches. The rigid grandeur of superimposed towering figurations, the elaborate entwining of many voices, of which none is free and independent, because all of them are—these have their own ageless rightness. Yet those marvellously sombre vocal pyramids of the old Italians and Netherlanders are just one small part of the realm of the musically beautiful, just as are the many exquisitely wrought saltcellars and silver candelabra of the venerable Sebastian Bach.

Many aestheticians consider that musical enjoyment can be adequately explained in terms of regularity and symmetry. But no beauty, least of all musical beauty, has ever consisted entirely in these. The most insipid theme can be constructed with perfect symmetry. *Symmetry* is merely a relational concept; it leaves open the question: What is it, then, that appears symmetrical? Orderly structure may be detected among the trivial, shabby fragments of even the most pathetic compositions. The musical sense of the word demands always new symmetrical creations.[2]

Most recently Oersted has expounded this Platonic view in connection with

---

1. If we mention in this connection *Musikalischen Charakterköpfe* by [W. H.] Riehl [Stuttgart and Tübingen, 1853], it is with grateful acknowledgment of this brilliant and stimulating book. [Au.]
2. I permit myself to quote here from my book *Die Moderne Oper* by way of illustration.

   The well-known saying that the "truly beautiful" can never lose its charm, even after a long time, is for music little more than a pretty figure of speech. (And anyway, who is to be the judge of what is "truly beautiful"?) Music is like nature, which every autumn lets a whole world of flowers fall into decay, out of which arise new flowerings. All music is the work of humans, product of a particular individuality, time, culture, and is for this reason permeated with mortal elements of various life-expectancies. Among the great musical forms, opera is the most complex and conventional and therefore the most transitory. It may be saddening that even the most excellent and brilliant new operas (such as those of Spohr and Spontini) are already beginning to disappear from the theatres. But reality is indefeasible, and the process cannot be halted by blaming the evil spirit of the time, as people have always done. Time is itself a spirit, and it produces its own embodiment. In contrast to the study place of the silent score-reader, the operatic stage is the forum for the actual demands of the public. The stage symbolizes the life of drama, and the struggle for its possession is drama's struggle for existence. In this struggle, a trifling work quite frequently overcomes its betters if it conveys to us the breath of our time, the heartbeat of our sentiments and desires. The public, like the artist, has a legitimate inclination toward the new in music, and criticism which has admiration only for the old and not also the courage to recognize the new undermines artistic production. We must renounce our belief in the deathlessness of the beautiful. Has not every age proclaimed with the same misguided confidence the imperishability of its best operas? Yet Adam Hiller declared in Leipzig that if ever the operas of Hasse ceased to delight, general anarchy must ensue. And yet Schubart, the music-aesthetician from Hohenasperg, assured us concerning Jomelli that it unthinkable that this composer could ever fall into oblivion. And who today ever heard of Hasse and Jomelli? (Preface.) [Au.]

music by means of the example of the circle, for which he claims positive beauty.[3] We may suppose that he had no firsthand experience of such an atrocity as an entirely circular composition.

Perhaps more out of caution than from need, we may add in conclusion that the musically beautiful has nothing to do with mathematics. This notion, which laymen (sensitive authors among them) cherish concerning the role of mathematics in music, is a remarkably vague one. Not content that the vibrations of tones, the spacing of intervals, and consonances and dissonances can be traced back to mathematical proportions, they are also convinced that the beauty of a musical work is based on number. The study of harmony and counterpoint is considered a kind of cabala which teaches compositional calculus.

Even though mathematics provides an indispensable key for the investigation of the physical aspects of musical art, its importance with regard to completed musical works ought not to be overrated. In a musical composition, be it the most beautiful or the ugliest, nothing at all is mathematically worked out. The creations of the imagination are not sums. All monochord experiments, acoustic figures, proportions of intervals, and the like, are irrelevant: The domain of aesthetics begins where these elementary relationships, however important, have left off. Mathematics merely puts in order the rudimentary material for artistic treatment and operates secretly in the simplest relations. Musical thought comes to light without it, however. I confess that I do not understand it when Oersted asks: "Would the lifetime of several mathematicians be enough to calculate all the beauties of a Mozart symphony?"[4] What is there that should or can be calculated? Perhaps the ratio of the vibrations of each tone with those of the next or the lengths of individual phrases or sections with relation to each other? What makes a piece of music a work of art and raises it above the level of physical experiment is something spontaneous, spiritual, and therefore incalculable. In the musical artwork, mathematics has just as small or great a share as in the productions of the other arts. For ultimately mathematics must also guide the hand of the painter and sculptor; mathematics is involved in the measures of verses, in the structures of the architect, and in the figures of the dancer. In every precise study, the application of mathematics, as a function of reason, must find a place. Only we must not grant it an actual, positive, creative power, as so many musicians and aesthetical conservatives would cheerfully have it. Mathematics is in a way like the production of

Eduard Hanslick, *Die Moderne Oper* (Berlin, 1875), pp. vi–viii. Regarding Hiller on Hasse: perhaps Hanslick refers to a review of the latter by the former in *Wöchentliche Nachrichten und Anmerkungen die Musik betreffend* (14 April 1767), p. 326. Regarding Schubart on Jomelli: C. F. D. Schubart, *Ideen zu einer Ästhetik der Tonkunst* (reprint ed. Leipzig: Reclam, 1977), p. 68.

3. H. C. Oersted, trans. K. L. Kannegießer, *Neue Beiträge zu dem Geist in der Natur* (Leipzig, 1850), pp. 17–21; trans. L. & J. B. Horner, *The Soul in Nature* (London, 1852), pp. 334–41.

4. *Geist in der Natur,* vol. 3, German by Kannegießer, p. 32. [Au.] Oersted, *Geist,* p. 32; *Soul,* p. 347.

feelings in the listener: It occurs in all the arts, but only in the case of music is a big fuss made about it.

Likewise some people have frequently drawn a parallel between speech and music and have tried to lay down the laws of the former as the laws of the latter. The kinship of song with speech is close enough that one might go along with the similarity of physiological conditions or with their common characteristics as revealing the inner self through the human voice. The analogical relationships are so striking that there is no need for us to go into the matter here. So we would just grant explicitly that, wherever music actually deals just with the subjective revealing of an inner longing, the laws governing speech will in fact to some extent be decisive for song.

That the person who gets into a rage raises the pitch of his voice, while the voice of a speaker who is recovering his composure descends; that sentences of particular gravity will be spoken slowly, and casual ones quickly: These and their like the composer of songs, particularly of dramatic songs, ignores at his peril. However, some people have not been content with these limited analogies but consider music itself to be a kind of language (though more unspecific or more refined), and now they want to abstract the laws of its beauty from the nature of language and trace back every attribute and effect of music to its affinity with language. We take the view that, where the specifics of an art are concerned, their differences with regard to respective domains are more important than their similarities. Such analogies are often enticing but are not at all appropriate to the actual essence of music. Undistracted by them, aesthetical research must push unrelentingly on to the point where language and music part irreconcilably. Only from this point will the art of music be able to germinate truly fruitful aesthetical principles. The essential difference is that in speech the sound[5] is only a sign, that is, a means to an end which is entirely distinct from that means, while in music the sound is an object, i.e., it appears to us as an end in itself. The autonomous beauty of tone-forms in music and the absolute supremacy of thought over sound as merely a means of expression in spoken language are so exclusively opposed that a combination of the two is a logical impossibility.

The essential center of gravity thus lies entirely differently in language and music, and around these centers all other characteristics arrange themselves. All specifically musical laws will hinge upon the autonomous meaning and beauty of the tones, and all linguistic laws upon the correct adaptation of sound to the requirements of expression.

The most harmful and confused views have arisen from the attempt to understand music as a kind of language; we see the practical consequences every day. Above all, it must seem appropriate to composers of not much creative power to regard autonomous musical beauty (which to them is inaccessi-

5. In this sentence *sound* translates the German word *Ton,* here used in its general, nonmusical sense.

ble) as a false, materialistic principle and to opt for the programmatic significance of music. Quite apart from Richard Wagner's operas, we often come across interruptions in the melodic flow of even the most insignificant instrumental pieces, due to disconnected cadences, recitatives, and the like. These startle the hearer and behave as if they signify something special, but in fact they signify nothing but ugliness. Some people have taken to praising modern compositions which keep breaking up the overall rhythm and developing inexplicable bumps and heaped-up contrasts. Thus they would have music strive to burst forth from its narrow limits and elevate itself to speech. To us this kind of commendation has always seemed equivocal. The limits of music are by no means narrow, but they are very precisely drawn. Music can never be "elevated" to the level of speech (strictly speaking, from the musical standpoint, one must say "lowered"), since music obviously would have to be an elevated kind of speech.[6]

6. It will not have gone unnoticed that one of the most original and magnificent works of all time has, by virtue of its splendor, contributed to the well-beloved fiction of modern music criticism about "the craving of music's inner self for the definiteness of verbal speech" and "the casting aside of the fetters of the harmonic proportions in sound." We refer to Beethoven's Ninth Symphony. It is one of those spiritual watersheds which interpose themselves insuperably between opposing currents of conviction.

For some musicians, the grandeur of "intention," the spiritual significance of the abstract purpose, comes ahead of everything else. Such musicians place the Ninth Symphony at the summit of all music, while the few who, clinging to the unfashionable view of beauty, struggle on behalf of purely aesthetical claims, are a bit restrained in their admiration. As may be guessed, the problem is mainly with the Finale, since, concerning the sublime (though not flawless) beauty of the first three movements, little disagreement will arise among attentive and competent listeners. In this last movement, we have never been able to see more than the vast shadow of a titanic body. That from lonely despair a soul is brought in joy to reconciliation is a thought whose immensity a person could understand perfectly while yet finding the music of the last movement (for all its brilliance) unbeautiful. We know all too well the universal disapprobation which attaches to so heterodox a view. One of the most gifted and versatile of German scholars, who in the "A. Allgemeine Zeitung" (1853) undertook to challenge the formal analysis of the Ninth Symphony, acknowledged for this reason the comical necessity of identifying himself in the title as a "numbskull." He directed attention to the aesthetical monstrosity involved in having a multimovement instrumental work end with a chorus and compared Beethoven to a sculptor who carved the legs, torso, and arms of a figure out of colorless marble and then colored the head. Presumably at the entry of the human voices every sensitive listener must be overcome by the same discomfort, "since here the work shifts its center of gravity with a jolt, and thereby threatens to knock the listener down." Almost a decade later, to our delight, the "numbskull" was unmasked and turned out to be David Strauss. ["Musikalische Briefe von einem beschränkten Kopfe." *Allgemeine Zeitung* (Augsburg), No. 217 (August 15, 1853), pp. 3465–66. Reprinted in D. F. Strauss, *Kleine Schriften* (Leipzig, 1862), p. 418.]

On the other hand, the estimable Dr. Becher, who may here be considered the representative of a whole school of thought, said, concerning the fourth movement, in an essay about the Ninth Symphony published in 1843: "With regard to originality of form, as well as magnificence of composition and the bold sweep of individual conceptions, it is a product of Beethoven's genius not at all to be compared with any other existing musical work." He declares that for him this movement, "with Shakespeare's *King Lear* and perhaps a dozen other manifestations of the human spirit, towers in its immense poetical power above those other artistic peaks like a Dhaulāgiri among the Himalayas." Like almost all his kindred spirits, Becher gives a detailed account of the meaning of the "content" of each of the four movements and their deep symbolism,

Even our singers forget this, who in deeply moving passages bellow words, indeed phrases, as if speaking them, and believe they have thereby demonstrated the highest degree of intensification of music. They fail to notice that the transition from singing to speaking is always a descent, so that the highest normal tone in speech sounds even deeper than the deepest sung tone of the same voice. Just as bad as these practical consequences, indeed worse, because they cannot be experimentally refuted, are theories which would foist upon music the laws of development and construction of speech, as had been attempted in earlier times by Rousseau and Rameau and more recently by the disciples of R. Wagner. The true heart of music, the formal beauty which gratifies in itself, would thereby be pierced through, and the chimera of "meaning" pursued. An aesthetics of musical art must therefore take as its most important task to set forth unrelentingly the basic distinction between the essence of music and that of language and in all deductions hold fast to the principle that, where the specifically musical is concerned, the analogy with language does not apply.

---

but of the music, he has nothing to say [A. J. Becher, "Filharmonische Akademie" (review). *Sonntagsblätter* No. 13 (1843), pp. 297, 295. See Geoffrey Payzant, "Eduard Hanslick and the 'Geistreich' Dr. Alfred Julius Becher," *The Music Review* 44 (1983): 104–15.]. This is utterly characteristic of a whole school of music criticism which, in reply to the question of whether the music is beautiful or not, prefers to sidestep into a solemn disquisition about some great thing the music is supposed to mean. [Au.]

16 Edmund Gurney

Edmund Gurney (1847–1888) was a passionate lover of music born, however, without sufficient talent to make it his profession. His education at Trinity College, Cambridge, was followed by abortive attempts at careers in both medicine and law. Ultimately, he devoted his life to the psychological investigation of music and other phenomena and to parapsychological studies.

In *The Power of Sound,* Gurney explores the origins and nature of music in ways characteristic of his time and place. He enters into scientific dialogue with the likes of James Sully, Herbert Spencer, and Charles Darwin, as well as several continental contemporaries interested in similar questions. Like Eduard Hanslick, Gurney argues that music's power is not referential or representational, but he parts company with his Viennese predecessor in his insistence that it *is* primarily a matter of emotion. This assertion is not romantic, however, but is made within the new scientific spirit of the late nineteenth century. Like his colleagues in science, Gurney is searching not only for a scientific basis of judgment and criticism, but for the evolutionary foundation of the emotions as well.

Along with its evident commitment to evolutionary ideas, Gurney's book also partakes of the efforts to turn the new discipline of psychology away from philosophical speculation and make it an empirical science. For a long time the discipline found itself limited to the experimental method known as introspection, or the examination of the experimenter's own responses. As Gurney notes, "such descriptions . . . can only be arrived at by considerable attention to one's own sensations: I can but hope that as they represent my own experience truly, however inadequately, others may find them to correspond in some degree with theirs."

FROM *The Power of Sound*
(1880)

MUSIC AS IMPRESSIVE AND MUSIC AS EXPRESSIVE

We now pass on to quite a new branch of our enquiry. So far we have been considering Music almost entirely as a means of *im*pression, as a presentation of impressive (or, as too often happens, unimpressive) phenomena. We have now to distinguish this aspect of it from another, its aspect as a means of *ex*pression, of creating in us a consciousness of images, or of ideas, or of feelings, which are known to us in regions outside Music, and which therefore Music, so far as it summons them up within us, may be fairly said to *express*. The chief difficulty in getting a clear view of this part of the subject lies in the vagueness and looseness of thought which is apt to run in the track of general and abstract terms: and this being so, I can only make my argument clear by insisting on the clear separation of the sets of conceptions which come under the heads of *im*pression and *ex*pression respectively, or at any rate may be justifiably so classified after due definition.

The distinction is made very simple by considering that expression involves *two* things, one of which is expressed by the other. The expression may take the form of imitation, as when an appearance or a movement of anything is purposely suggested by some aspect or movement given to something else. Or the thing expressed may be an idea, as when a fine idea is expressed by a metaphor; or a feeling, as when suffering is expressed by tears; or a quality, as when pride is expressed by a person's face or demeanour. As regards expression of qualities, some preliminary explanation is necessary. When a quality is so permanent and general and familiar an attribute of anything that our idea of the thing comprises the quality, the latter does not seem separable enough for us to conceive of it as expressed; and thus we should not naturally say that a tree expressed greenness, or a dark night darkness, or a church-steeple height. In a word, a thing is expressive of *occasional* attributes, not of the essential

TEXT: *The Power of Sound* (London, 1880), chap. 14, pp. 312–18, 347–48.

attributes of its class. There is a doubtful region where such phrases might be used even of very general qualities with reference to some special idea in the speaker's mind: thus a Platonist might say that the face of nature expressed beauty, conceiving of beauty as a single principle, which is one thing; capable of manifesting itself in this or that form, which is another thing: but we should not, in an ordinary way, say that a flower expresses beauty, or a lion strength, but that the flower *is* beautiful and the lion strong. So with respect to musical forms or motions; they are so familiarly conceived as aiming at being beautiful and vigorous, such qualities are so identified with our idea of their function, that we do not naturally think of them as *expressing* beauty and vigour. So with qualities identified with the most general effects of impressive sound on the organism; we do not conceive of any sounds, musical or non-musical, as expressing soothingness or excitingness. But we do not quarrel with the description of music as having a romantic or passionate or sentimental expression, even though the analogy of the effect to modes of feeling known outside Music may be of the dimmest and most intangible kind; and when some more special and distinctive quality appears, such as agitation or melancholy, when a particular feeling in ourselves is identified with a particular character in a particular bit of music, then we say without hesitation that such a particular bit *expresses* the quality or feeling.[1]

It is true that there is a very important method of using words like *expressive* in relation to Music, in the absence of particular describable qualities or particular suggestions of any sort; a usage which has been more than once adopted in this book, and which it seems to me impossible to forego. Thus we often call music which stirs us more *expressive* than music which does not; and we call great music *significant,* or talk of its *import,* in contrast to poor music, which seems meaningless and insignificant; without being able, or dreaming we are able, to connect these general terms with anything *expressed* or *signified.* This usage was explained, at the end of the sixth chapter, as due to the inevitable association of music with utterance, and of utterance with something external to itself which is to be expressed,[2] as our ideas are external to the sounds in

1. The necessary connection of quality and feeling should be noted: for there being no personality in music, the qualities it can be in itself expressive of must be identified with some affection of ourselves. Thus we should not say that quick or slow music expressed such impersonal qualities as speed or slowness, but possibly hilarity or solemnity. Music may present even decided qualities which are not suggestive of any special and occasional mode of feeling in ourselves. Thus a melody may be *simple,* but as it does not make us feel simple, and as we have no definite mode of feeling identified with the contemplation of so general a quality, we should not naturally say that it *expressed* simplicity; unless there were some simplicity external to it, in some words or person associated with it. The feeling in ourselves need not necessarily be the *same* as the quality attributed to the music: the special feeling corresponding to melancholy music is melancholy, but the special feeling corresponding to capricious or humorous music is not capriciousness or humorousness, but surprise or amusement: clearly, however, this mode of feeling is sufficiently identified with the contemplation of the quality. [Au.]
2. Quite apart from the notion of such a something to be expressed, our habitual projection either of the composer's or of the performer's or of some imaginary personality behind the music we

which we utter them. But even those who take the transcendental view that something *is* so expressed or signified by all beautiful music—whether the something be the 'Will of the World,' as Schopenhauer taught, or any other supposed' fundamental reality to which our present conceptions are inadequate—may still perfectly well accept the following proposition: that there is a difference between music which is expressive in the sense of definitely suggesting or inspiring images, ideas, qualities, or feelings belonging to the region of the *known* outside music, and music which is *not* so expressive, and in reference to which terms of expression and significance, however intuitive and habitual, could only be logically pressed by taking them in a quite peculiar sense, and postulating an *unknown* something behind phenomena, which the phenomena are held to reveal or signify, or, according to Schopenhauer, to 'objectify.'

The distinction as thus stated does not altogether coincide with that conveyed by the words *expressive* and *impressive;* since there is nothing to prevent music which is *ex*pressive in the former and tangible sense from being also *im*pressive by its beauty. As the true distinction involved in the words is between two different *aspects* of Music, both of these may naturally be presented by the same specimen; and indeed we shall find that no music is really expressive in any valuable way which does not also impress us as having the essential character of musical beauty; an unpleasing tune may be lugubrious but not melancholy. But the great point, which is often strangely ignored and for the sake of which the distinction has been thus pedantically emphasised, is that *ex*pressiveness of the literal and tangible sort is either *absent or only slightly present*[3] in an immense amount of *im*pressive music; that to suggest describable images, qualities, or feelings, known in connection with other experiences, however frequent a characteristic of Music, makes up no inseparable or essential part of its function; and that this is not a matter of opinion, or of theory as to what should be, but of definite everyday fact.

The immense importance of this truth, and of its relation to the facts of

---

hear may naturally lead to such phrases as that some one expresses himself or expresses his personality or expresses his soul in the music; in the same sense, *e.g.,* as a theist may hold the Creator to express himself in the beauties of Nature: such a use need not at all confuse the distinction in the text. The word expression, again, in such a general phrase as 'playing with expression' does not mean the signification of any thought or feeling external to the music, but merely the making the utmost, the literal squeezing out, of all the beauty which is there *in* the music. [Au.]

3. It is hard to word this so as to obviate all possible objections. In modern music it may perhaps be the case, more often than not, that some one out of the category of descriptive adjectives may seem at any rate more appropriate than most others: words like energetic, peaceful, solemn, and so on, may be made to cover an immense amount of ground. But the qualities may be said to be slightly expressed if they excite no special remark; if one's impression, if it runs at all into words, is far more vividly 'how beautiful,' or 'how indescribable, how utterly a musical experience,' than 'how extraordinarily solemn,' or 'how exceptionally peaceful.' [Au.]

expression, will further appear when expression has been separately considered; but this independent impressiveness is so entirely at the foundation of the argument that it will be best to start by briefly recalling its root and groundwork. We found these, it will be remembered, in the fusion and sublimation of those strongest elementary passions and emotions which, according to Mr. Darwin's view[4] were associated with the primeval exercise of the musical faculty, the primeval habit of following tones and rhythm with pleasure; and in the light of generally admitted principles of hereditary association, we found no extraordinary difficulty in connecting what are now some of the most profound stirrings of our emotional nature with those crude elements which were yet the most profound emotional stirrings possible to our progenitors. In this connection it is well worth noting that at every stage which comes under our observation, Music seems capable of stirring up the strongest excitement that a being who musically typifies that stage can experience. This enjoyment to the utmost of the best that can be got is exemplified equally in the case of singing-birds, and of the gibbon, moved with rapture at his own performance of the chromatic scale, and of the savage repeating over for hours his few monotonous strains and maddened by the rhythmic beat of the drum, and of the ancient Greek spellbound by performances for the like of which we should probably tell a street-performer to pass on, and of a circle of Arabs sobbing and laughing by turns in ecstasies of passion at the sound of their native melodies, and of the English child to whom some simple tune of Mozart's reveals the unguessed springs of musical feeling, or of the adult in his loftiest communings with the most inspired utterances of Beethoven.[5] And it is all-important to observe that these emotional experiences are essentially connected, throughout the whole long course of development, with the distinctly *melodic* principle, with the presentation of a succession of single sound-units; such series being exemplified in the percussive drummings of the spider and in the song of the gibbon, as well as in the distinguishable lines of tune indispensable to the emotional character of modern composition. So that our general theory entirely bears out the view which in the fifth chapter was deduced from simple musical experi-

4. The comments of Darwin to which Gurney refers are principally found in *The Expression of the Emotions in Men and Animals* (1872), although there are also occasional references to musical sound as an aspect of sexual selection in *The Descent of Man* (1871). Darwin's observations, in their turn, often respond to the ideas of Herbert Spencer in "The Origin and Function of Music" (1858).

5. What is said here may be connected with what was said in the tenth chapter as to the rapid obsolescence of music. The newer and apparently more original kinds of Ideal Motion often make older music seem tame and trite. But it would certainly be most unfair to think of comparing, as regards amount of enjoyment, our own musical experiences with those of a person in the middle of the last century, by comparing the pleasure *we* derive from Beethoven with that which *we* derive from, *e.g.*, the earlier works of Haydn. Evidence entirely confirms what *a priori* we might have guessed, that that earlier music stirred its hearers to the very depths, in a manner which we can only realise by recalling some of the strains which have had a similar effect on ourselves in childhood. [Au.]

ence, that the ground for the essential effects of the art must be sought, not in any considerations connected with large or elaborate structure, or with rich complexity of parts, or splendid masses of tone, but in the facts of mere note-after-note melodic motion.

And while the theory, in its invocation of the strongest of all primitive passions, as germs for the marvellously sublimated emotions of developed Music, seems not only adequate but unique in its adequacy to account generally for the power of those emotions, it further connects itself in the most remarkable manner with that more special peculiarity of independent impressiveness which is now under review; with the fact which attentive examination of musical experience more and more brings home to us, that Music is perpetually felt as strongly emotional while defying all attempts to analyse the experience or to define it even in the most general way in terms of definite emotions. If we press close, so to speak, and try to force our feelings into declaring themselves in definite terms, a score of them may seem pent up and mingled together and shooting across each other—triumph and tenderness, surprise and certainty, yearning and fulfilment; but all the while the essential magic seems to lie at an infinite distance behind them all, and the presentation to be not a subjective jumble but a perfectly distinct object, productive (in a thousand minds it may be at once) of a perfectly distinct though unique and undefinable affection. This is precisely what is explained, if we trace the strong undefinable affection to a gradual fusion and transfiguration of such overmastering and pervading passions as the ardours and desires of primitive loves; and it is in reference to these passions of all others, both through their own possessing nature and from the extreme antiquity which they permit us to assign to their associative influence, that a theory of fusion and transfiguration in connection with a special range of phenomena seems possible and plausible. The problem is indeed a staggering one, by what alchemy abstract forms of sound, however unique and definite and however enhanced in effect by the watching of their evolution moment by moment, are capable of transformation into phenomena charged with feeling, and yet in whose most characteristic impressiveness separate feelings seem as fused and lost as the colours in a ray of white light: but at any rate the suggested theory of association is less oppressive to the speculative mind than the everyday facts of musical experience would be in the absence of such a far-reaching explanation of them.

The more serious difficulty, we found, came later. When we merely ask why are melodic forms emotionally impressive, and why are they emotionally impressive after a fashion which defies analysis or description, the association-theory comes to our assistance. But the further question, why one melodic form is felt as emotionally impressive and another not, reveals in a moment how much any such general theory leaves unaccounted for; and our further examination of melodic forms showed that the faculty of discernment, the faculty in which the cognisance of them is wholly vested, is one whose nature and action have to be accepted as unique and ultimate facts, and whose judgments are absolute, unreasoning, and unquestionable.[6] It is not necessary to repeat what has been said in the preceding chapters as to this extraordinary and independent faculty of co-ordinating a series of time- and pitch-relations into forms or notions, and of deriving various degrees of satisfaction or dissatisfaction from the proportions so progressively contemplated; nor as to the somewhat difficult but still warrantable supposition that the *satisfactory* action of the faculty, the concentration of it on such proportions as give it adequate scope and exercise, is the only mode whereby the flood-gates of emotion from the associational region are opened, and the perception of the form transfused and transfigured; the transfusion *ipso facto* preventing our knowing what the mere perception, the simple musical impression as it might be if the informing associational elements were non-existent, would in itself amount to.

But we now come to the consideration of certain points in musical forms and in the exercise of the musical faculty which are new; these being specially connected with Music in its *expressive* aspect. As long as Music is regarded only as a means of *impression,* as productive of a sort of emotion which, however definite and crude may have been its unfused and undeveloped germs, has been for ages so differentiated as to convey no suggestion of its origin, and is unknown outside the region of musical phenomena—as long as the forms, however various and individual to the musical sense, still present a musical character undistinguished and unpervaded by any particular definable feeling of joy, gloom, triumph, pathos, &c.—no examination of their structure from outside (as we abundantly saw in the seventh and following chapters) throws the slightest light on that musical character and its varieties: no rules can be framed which will not be so general as to include the bad as well as the good. The exercise of the musical faculty on such and such a form is found pleasurable and emotional, its exercise on such and such another is found neutral, or unsatisfactory and irritating; and that is all: a mode of perception which is unique defies illustration, and on this ground the only answer to the questions which present themselves is the showing why they are unanswerable. But when we come to the *expressive* aspect of Music, to the definite suggestion or portrayal of certain special and describable things known outside Music, whether images of objects or ideas or qualities or feelings, we should naturally expect to be able to trace in some degree the connection of any special suggestion or shade of character with some special point or points in the musical form and the process by which we follow it: and we have now to examine the various modes in which such connections may present themselves. None of them, it will now be evident, can be held accountable for any musical *beauty* which may be present: a tune is no more constituted beautiful by an expression, *e.g.,* of mournfulness or of capriciousness than a face is. The impressiveness which we call beauty resides in the unique musical experience whose nature and

---

6. Absolute and unquestionable, not of course as final or competent judgments of merit or anything else, but in reference to the power of a particular bit of music to affect a particular individual at a particular time. [Au.]

history have just been summarised: but in proportion as the beauty assumes a special and definable character or aspect, it does so in virtue of features in the musical form which are also special and definable.

It will be convenient to consider first the expression of qualities and feelings; the suggestion by music of objects and ideas being of a much more external and accidental kind. In our ordinary experience the natural mode in which qualities and feelings are expressed otherwise than by speech[7] is of course physical movement of some kind; thus human beings express confidence and good spirits by rapid and decisive movements, solemnity by measured movements, agitation by spasmodic movements, and so on. Now the Ideal Motion of Music gives us an aspect of physical movement ready made; the aspect, namely, of pace and rhythm; which can be presented without any sound at all by movements in space, and the correspondence of which with movements in space we perpetually exemplify in our own persons, as we follow and in any way keep time with Music. Moreover the Ideal Motion regarded in its completeness, without such particular reference to the rhythmic element, will be found to present certain faint affinities to external movement and gesture. But while it is naturally in motion that we should look for the signs of definite emotional states, or, as we commonly say, the *expression* of such states, in Music there are three other features connected with expression, two of which belong especially to the tone- or pitch-element apart from peculiarities of motion; the use, namely, of the major or the minor 'mode,' and of occasional noticeable harmonies; the other being *timbre* or sound-colour.

·   ·   ·   ·   ·

In conclusion, I can imagine that a reader who has given assent to the various propositions and arguments which have been presented in this chapter, may still feel that, after all, there is a sense in which Music may be truly considered a reflection of the inner life. I am far from denying that such is the case: the error is in not seeing that so far as the idea has any sort of generality of application, the reflection itself must be of the most general and indefinite kind; very different from the definable expression, with its dubious and fragmentary appearances, which we have been discussing. Characters far too wide to be regarded, without absurdity, as what the pieces were written to express, or as what their merit and individuality consist in their expressing, may still make a sort of undefined human atmosphere under which the distinct musical forms are revealed and the distinct musical impressions received. Moreover, if the following and realising of music be regarded as itself *one complete domain* of inner life, we may then perceive that it is large and various enough, full enough

7. The relation of Music to Speech will be discussed in succeeding chapters, with results which will supplement without otherwise affecting the arguments in the present chapter. The emotional elements which music may gain by association with definite words and scenes will also be subsequently treated of; and certain extensions of the senses in which Music can be considered expressive will present themselves in connection with Song and Opera. [Au.]

of change and crisis and contrast, of expectation, memory, and comparison, of general forms of perception which have been employed in other connections by the same mind, for the course of musical experience, as felt under these most abstract aspects and relations, to present a dim affinity to the external course of emotional life. In this way we may feel, at the end of a musical movement, that we have been living an engrossing piece of life which, in the variety and relations of its parts, has certain qualities belonging to any series of full and changing emotions: and this feeling may impress us with much more of reality than any attempted ranking of the several parts and phases of the music under particular heads of expression. It is easy to distinguish general affinities of this kind from anything referable to the more definite categories. Such qualities, *e.g.*, as evenness and continuity, or interruptedness and variability, of musical movement, may suffice to suggest a sort of kinship between musical and other trains of feeling, while far too abstract to define or guarantee the character of the pieces where they occur, and able equally to cover the most various content: the slowness and sustainedness of an *adagio* movement, for instance, often described as typical of a peaceful flow of consciousness, we have found to be as compatible with the undefinable stirrings of musical passion as with the definable expression of calm. Another instance of abstract relationship, equally remote from definite suggestion and expression, may be found in the faint analogy of mingling currents of music to that mingling of various strains of feeling and idea which is so frequent a feature of our ordinary life: it would be absurd in the vast majority of such cases to attempt to represent each musical current as typifying some distinguishable train of known feeling, so that here the quality common to the musical and the extra-musical experience seems so abstract as to be little more than harmonious concomitance of several elements in each: yet this mere parallelism of complexity seems enough to open up in Music faint tracts of association with extra-musical life. A similar affinity has been attributed to the predominance of a single melodic theme in relation to its accompaniment; where the mere relation may possibly suggest our general experience of prominent strains of feeling as standing out from the general stream of consciousness, whose other elements make for it a sort of dimly-felt background.

And Music condenses a very large amount of inner life, of the sort of experience which might lend itself to such general associations, into a very brief space of actual time. The successions of intensity and relaxation, the expectation perpetually bred and perpetually satisfied, the constant direction of the motion to new points, and constant evolution of part from part, comprise an immense amount of alternations of posture and of active adjustment of the will. We may perhaps even extend the suggestions of the last paragraph so far as to imagine that this ever-changing adjustment of the will, subtle and swift in Music beyond all sort of parallel, may project on the mind faint intangible images of extra-musical impulse and endeavour; and that the ease and spontaneity of the motions, the certainty with which a thing known or dimly divined as about to happen *does* happen, creating a half-illusion that the notes are obeying the controlling force of one's own desire, may similarly open up vague channels of association with other moments of satisfaction and attainment. But these affinities are at any rate of the most absolutely general kind; and whatever their importance may be, they seem to me to lie in a region where thought and language struggle in vain to penetrate.

V

MUSIC THEORY AND PEDAGOGY

17 Adolf Bernhard Marx

FROM *The Theory of Musical Composition*
(1868)

SONATA FORM

The loose concatenation of various themes and transitions appeared as a character trait of the rondo forms. In the rondo, at first only one theme, the main theme, was important enough to be repeated; it thus stood as the single fixed part of the whole, and for precisely that reason it always had to be brought back in essentially the same manner and in the same key. Thus it provided an element of constancy; but at the same time, the frequent returns to the same point kept the modulations from developing more freely and energetically, limiting them almost exclusively to the spaces between main and subsidiary themes.

The fourth, and especially the fifth, rondo forms went beyond this confining cycle. Because they combine main and subsidiary themes into a more unified whole, especially in the third part, where they bring them back (with the closing theme, if there is one) closely bound together by the main key, one recognizes in these forms another, and higher, orientation: the *separate* themes no longer matter in *isolation;* rather, the intimate union of individual themes in a whole—the *whole* in its inner *unity*—becomes the main concern. In such a

TEXT: *Die Lehre von der musikalischen Komposition,* 4th ed. (Leipzig, 1868), vol. 3 *(Die angewandte Kompositionslehre),* bk. 6 *(Die Komposition für selbständige Instrumente),* pp. 201–2, 220–26, 228–32, 244–51. Translation and notes by Scott Burnham. Throughout, references to musical examples given elsewhere in the book are omitted from the text.

Immediately preceding the excerpted discussion, Marx surveys the rondo forms, presenting them as an evolving series crowned by the sonata form. For Marx, the distinguishing feature of this family of forms is the motion-oriented alternation of thematic utterance *(Satz)* and transitional passage *(Gang)*. Marx represents the rondo forms schematically as follows (MT: main theme [*Hauptsatz*] ST: subsidiary theme [*Seitensatz*] CT: closing theme [*Schlusssatz*] Tr: transition [*Gang*]);

First Rondo Form	MT Tr MT
Second Rondo Form	MT ST (Tr) MT
Third Rondo Form	MT ST1 Tr MT ST2 Tr MT
Fourth Rondo Form	MT ST1 Tr MT ST2 Tr MT ST1
Fifth Rondo Form	MT ST1 Tr CT ST2 Tr MT ST1 Tr CT

Satz is a wonderfully flexible term that Marx uses to refer to any closed structure, from the level of a phrase to that of an entire movement. Its diametrical opposite is *Gang,* an open-ended, often transitional, passage. In the present translation *Satz* is usually rendered "theme," as this is the level on which Marx most frequently uses the word. *Gang* is rendered "transition."

whole the isolated theme begins to lose its fixity; no longer there merely for itself, it need not hold to its place, self-contained: it now moves (at least the first subsidiary theme moves) from its original spot to another position (from the dominant or relative key to the main key), and it does so for the sake of the whole, which now wants to close with greater unity and with more material in the main key.

·   ·   ·   ·   ·

The *sonata form*[1] completes what the fourth and fifth rondo forms have begun. Generally speaking, it does this in a twofold manner. First, it gives up the foreign element (the second subsidiary theme) that the fifth rondo form still maintains between the first and third parts, and keeps only those two parts themselves, now more unified internally. This results in the *small sonata form*, or *sonatina form.* Next, it forms a new second, or middle, part—one unified with the first part and indeed made from the same material. This results in *sonata form proper.*[2]

Both forms, or rather, both manners of the one sonata form are used for fast as well as slow movements. We will study it first in fast movements, since it is here, where motion from one section to another predominates along with the liveliness of the sections themselves, that the nature of the form is most clearly revealed.[3]

·   ·   ·   ·   ·

SECTION THREE: SONATA FORM

It immediately becomes apparent that sonatina form is one of those transitional configurations that are certainly justified and necessary both intrinsically and in the sequence of all art forms, but in which a distinct formal concept has not yet reached full ripeness.

The sonatina strove beyond the rondo forms to a more intimate unity of content; but it achieved this by sacrificing a section of the content of those earlier forms—the second subsidiary theme—with a consequent lessening of significance. And, then again, it was inclined to insert a transitional or bridge passage in place of the omitted part; this proves that the rejected second part

1. As is well known, *sonata* means ... a musical work for one (or two) instruments, made by joining several separate movements together, for instance, Allegro, Adagio, Scherzo, and Finale. Lacking another name already in currency, however, we designate with the name *sonata form* the wholly determinate form of a single movement. The name "allegro" or "allegro form," which is used now and again, is unsuitable because the sonata form is frequently used for slow movements as well. [Au.]

2. Marx's temporal language ("first" the sonatina form, "next" sonata form) in this paragraph and elsewhere reflects his understanding of sonata as a teleologically emerging realization of the spirit of form.

3. Sections One and Two, on sonatina form, are omitted here. Marx presents the small form first in order, as he says, to prepare the ground for the study of the larger.

had its own justification. But what is inserted in its place cannot truly replace it; thus this form is good only for cursory constructions.

This observation leads directly to sonata form itself and its essential character trait: sonata form cannot dispense with a *middle section;* it must assume a *three-part* form. But this middle, or second, part may not introduce *foreign* material—a second subsidiary theme—as in the rondo forms, for this would disrupt the unity whose complete attainment is in fact the task of the sonata. Consequently, the second part[4] of sonata form must hold to the content of the first part, either *exclusively,* or at least *primarily.*

Thus the main features of the new form are arranged as follows:

Part 1	Part 2	Part 3
MT ST Tr CT	———	MT ST Tr CT

One recognizes immediately that the first and last parts, broadly speaking, are familiar from the fifth rondo form and the sonatina form; only the middle part is essentially new.

Before turning to this new part, the most important object of this stage of our study, we note several considerations that follow from our view of the form so far.

First. Let us imagine a piece of music that persists in its main and subsidiary themes through *three* parts: we must acknowledge a deeper meaning in such persistent content than was the case with sonatina form. Or, in other words, the composer must be more compelled by these themes, he must feel predisposed to work with them more intently. Thus themes that are indeed well suited for that slighter form appear too inconsequential for the higher sonata form.

Second. The mere act of repeating a theme already reveals the inclination to grasp it as if it were a possession. Thus in the rondo forms the main theme especially served as a mainstay of the whole, to which one returned to repeat it again and again. A higher interest is manifest in the sonata form. No longer satisfied to bring back such a theme as if it were a dead possession, it enlivens

---

4. According to customary usage, *only two parts* are recognized in those pieces written in sonata form. The first part, which is usually repeated and is conspicuously isolated by the repeat sign, is treated as such; everything else, that is *the second and third parts together,* are treated as a single second part—this is often the case with the fifth rondo form also. But the distinction between the second and third parts, as we already know, is so essential that we cannot ignore it without distorting our perception of the form and losing sight of its rationale. In fact, this has been recognized before now, for within the so-called second part (the combined second and third parts) the return of the main theme and everything after it has been called the *reprise,* while that which precedes the reprise was called the *working-through (Durcharbeitung).* This would indeed mean *three* parts with an essential distinction of the third from the second! Yet the names seem less than exact (the third part is in no way a mere reprise or repetition, and working-through takes place in all sections and, moreover, in many other art forms as well), and this practice—an impediment to study—lumps together in the second part things that then only have to be differentiated again. [Au.]

it instead, lets it undergo variation and be repeated in different manners and with different destinations: it transforms the theme into *an Other,* which is nonetheless recognized as the offspring of the first theme and which stands in for it. The rondo cannot entertain essential alterations of its themes, but only peripheral changes (whereas the sonata form can embrace these as well).

In these transformations, obviously, lies the power to stimulate a more varied and intensified interest in the theme. Thus it is possible, in this larger form, to elevate a theme that is in itself of little significance to the status of a worthy and satisfying subject. Indeed, the power of the form and of the composer not infrequently shows itself to great advantage precisely with those beginnings that appear less important at first blush—although it seems *inartistic* to search out such a theme deliberately, just to show off one's talent, and *negligent* to take up the first good idea that comes along and go to work on it without feeling called to it or excited about it. One of the most successful examples of this sort is offered by the first movement of Beethoven's G major sonata, Op. 31. The main theme, spilling over with ingenious humor, has this as its germ:

Were this to stand for itself, alone and unvaried, one could certainly deem it full of energy but not of significance. Yet under its stimulus the spirit of the artist rings upon it the most ingenious changes, in wonderful succession; they take hold of us ever more profoundly, finally offering even milder harmonies to our unexpectedly moved souls. To assume that the master chose his theme for such a play of technical facility would be to award him paltry praise befitting a schoolboy. There was no question of technique here: for the artist there is no technique. What the artistic spirit seizes becomes its own—under the sway of fervent love it becomes a precious and living witness to that spirit. This process can be recognized and demonstrated with this Beethovenian theme, as with every artwork, and every artist knows it. Technique—outward skill or, worse, vainglorious play—has nothing to do with such artistic love.

Third. That light and capricious, even superficial, manner in which the sonatina form jumps from the half cadence of its main theme into the subsidiary theme and its key center can no longer suffice in the higher sonata form, where the whole is thoroughly permeated and informed by the urge for a unified, powerful sense of forward and progressive motion. A real transition is now necessary, one that will lead us unequivocally from the realm of the main theme into that of the subsidiary theme, and then establish it firmly.

To this end, and in accordance with long recognized precepts, there is a modulation *in the First Part* from the main theme and its key to the dominant of the dominant, and from there back to the dominant. In minor-key movements, as also has long been known, the modulation ordinarily goes not to the dominant but to the relative major.

From these easily settled points we now turn to the most important one, the construction of the second part, which demands separate consideration.

SECTION FOUR: THE SECOND PART OF SONATA FORM

As has already been established, the second part of a sonata form contains in essence no new content. As a consequence it must concern itself principally with the content of the first part—that is, with the main theme, with the subsidiary theme, and even with the closing theme—and specifically, it may deal with only one theme, with two, or even with all of them. But this involvement is in no way just a matter of repetition, as in the handling of the main theme in the rondo. Rather, the recurring themes are *chosen, ordered and connected,* and *varied,* in ways suitable to each different stage of the composition.

Thus it is clear that the second part manifests itself primarily as the locus of variety and motion, and once again we see the original antithesis, the fundamental law of all musical structure now revealed in the three parts of the sonata form: *rest—motion—rest.* The impulse for greater variety in the ordering and disposition of the material lies in the character of the second (or motion-oriented) part. Its general task is as follows: to lead, with material selected from the first part, from the conclusion of the first part to the pedal point on the dominant of the main key, and then to the entrance of the third part. But variety is chiefly found in the linkage *(Anknüpfung),* the way one leads on from the first part, and then in the carrying-through *(Durchführung)*[5] of content that is wholly or at least primarily borrowed from the first part.

It would hardly be possible or necessary to enumerate, much less to begin sketching out, all the typical and unusual procedures that may be used in the

---

5. This term tries to capture both the sense of leading-through and the sense of carrying out, or executing; both senses were implied in the term *Durchführung* before it simply became the equivalent of our musico-formal designation "development."

second part of sonata form; we must limit ourselves to the most important, those which illustrate the main tendencies.[6]

•   •   •   •   •

If we look back for a moment to the rondo forms, we see that it is the first gesture of the second part that most unequivocally distinguishes the sonata form from them and is the mark of the sonata form's characteristic energy and heightened unity. Here too the main theme appears for a second time, as it does in the third and fourth rondo forms, and it will appear again, perhaps unaltered, in the third part. But it has become something else, and not just in peripheral aspects of accompaniment but indeed in its essential features (even in mode).[7] We may indeed deem these changes essential, for, as has been shown, they are called for by the very conditions under which the main theme is constrained to reappear. It was already determined that the main theme has to avoid its initial key here as assiduously as it had to maintain it in the rondo forms; the principle of motion, of progress, was thereby elevated over the subordinate principle of stability that was manifest in the rondo forms.

•   •   •   •   •

It is hoped that these examples—only a few of countless possible ones—will suffice here too to open the door to progress for the student who has gone thus far with us. Here, as always, it is *of utmost importance* that he convince himself that there are inexhaustible ways and means available to the experienced; then that he make them all his own through reflection, steadfast work, and study of the masters (this latter, however, only when he has mastered these lessons to the point of fluency in his own works, so that he will never imitate but always create by his own power); and last, that he ensure, through uninterrupted attention to a work once begun and undisturbed submersion in its atmosphere and ideas, the completion of the work in a unified fashion true to its initial impetus.

•   •   •   •   •

SECTION SEVEN: SUPPLEMENTARY REMARKS ON THE WORKING OUT OF THE SECOND PART

Since the manner of introducing the second part forms an integral whole with the way the rest of it is realized, we have treated its further continuation

---

6. Here and in the next two sections (not included), Marx discusses, with many homemade musical examples, different ways of beginning the second part: with an immediate return to the main theme (sec. IV), with an entirely new theme (sec. V), with a closing theme that refers back to the main theme or an independent closing theme, or with a "transition-like" introduction (sec. VI).

7. Having considered above which tonalities are suitable for use when starting the second part with the main theme, Marx concludes that, since one cannot use the dominant or the tonic, the tonic minor or the relative minor of the dominant would work best.

simultaneously with the various ways of beginning it, in accordance with the practical bent and method of this entire book. But we had to direct our attention primarily to the introduction, covering the rest in the shortest and simplest way, in order to attain an overview of the second part and to do so repeatedly, even if the full range of its possible configurations could not be illustrated.

Under these circumstances several supplementary hints on the working out of the second part are now called for, which will require but few words.

1. To begin with, it goes without saying that all the important features of the second part that we have demonstrated may appear in greater profusion and at greater length than shown in this textbook, where for the sake of space the tersest exposition—only enough to shed some light—must have priority over a richer and more extensive treatment.

In particular, the transitions and pedal points will usually need further realization. It is hoped that our examples will suffice, since by now it should be clear that nothing is easier than the continuation of a transitional passage or a pedal point once it has been initiated; how much farther one ought to go must be decided in accordance with the particular tendency of each case.

The only general advice we can give is that one would do well—if particular considerations of content and mood do not demand otherwise—to give a certain proportion or equipoise to the various sections, such that the second part is *approximately* as long as the first, the returning main or subsidiary theme groups *approximately* match the preceding or subsequent transitional material, and so forth. This balanced structure expresses the evenhanded and sympathetic scrutiny that the composer should extend to all the sections of his creation, and it calls forth the pleasant feeling of a just and secure control in the listener as well, even if the latter is not equipped to keep tally of such things and is perhaps not even entirely aware of the whole organism that so pleases and benefits him. But the urge to achieve such proportion must never degenerate into an anxious *tallying* and *counting* of measures, above all during composition; this would be the death of any artistic impulse. Even back in [our discussion of] song form, a much more limited and easily surveyable territory, we moved beyond exact proportion to a general sense of proportion, and became convinced that the former was not necessary to achieve the pleasant and rational effect of the latter. If we allowed ourselves even there to answer four bars with five or six, and so forth, then a few bars more or less matter still less here, in compositions so much larger and more complex.

2. We know already from our treatment of polyphony that transitions and themes can be formed or continued polyphonically as well as homophonically. Thus it is obvious that in the sonata form as well, and particularly in the carrying-through of preexisting themes and transitional motives that forms the second part, one can make extensive use of polyphony. As is well known, polyphony enables us to give a whole new meaning to a theme, especially by means of the types of inversion, to gain an entirely new perspective on a famil-

iar theme, and to lend the whole, even in the midst of all these configural changes, a unity and solidity hardly possible in larger realizations except through the use of polyphonic techniques. . . .

3. Thus it follows that one can even make use of fugue in carrying out the second part. It is clear, however, that no actual, freestanding fugue can occur here but merely the use of fugal technique for some part of the section.

Neither the main nor the subsidiary themes can serve as the subject of the fugue; it must be formed from motives taken from these themes, usually from their beginnings. In most cases the choice would have to fall on the main theme, since, for reasons already known, it tends to have the most energetic and thus most promising configuration for fugal working-out *(Fugenarbeit)*. But we can form no rule from this; very often the subsidiary theme is better suited for the construction of a fugue subject, or better fits the mood of the composition as the second part progresses.

•   •   •   •   •

4. Finally, one must mention that sometimes the second part not only begins with the continuation of the closing theme but is exclusively dedicated to the carrying-through *(Durchführung)* of this theme. This occurs whenever the closing theme is the most compelling to the composer, and the main and subsidiary themes are less in need of any further working through because of their makeup—if, for example, they contain a much-repeated germinal theme and therefore their original appearance itself provided sufficient variety. . . . Anyone who understands in general how to develop a theme . . . will be indifferent as to whether the theme to be developed was originally a closing theme or some other.

However, one must regard this situation as exceptional, since it places the center of gravity on a secondary theme instead of on one of the primary (main or subsidiary) ones.

SECTION EIGHT: THE THIRD PART OF SONATA FORM

Concerning the formation of the third part of sonata form there is little to add to what was said in the section on the fifth rondo form, since the third part is essentially shaped just like the third part of that rondo form. It begins with the main theme repeated in its entirety, even altered at some especially suitable point, and perhaps—especially if the second part dealt more with the subsidiary or closing themes—further realized.

The subsidiary theme follows the main theme, as we know, and of course in the main key; touching on the keys of the subdominant and dominant serves to make the main key's establishment here all the more decisive. The allusion to the first of these keys can be easily dispatched, or even completely omitted, if this key was heavily stressed in the second part. This modulation is fashioned differently according to the particular circumstances of each individual piece.

In most cases it takes place within the main theme, by leading it onward as a transition.

At times, when the main theme is firmly closed, a special transitional passage or a chain of phrases *(Satzkette)* will be appended, and the modulation to the subdominant is achieved just as the modulation to the dominant of the dominant was in the first part.

Sometimes it may seem appropriate to introduce the subsidiary theme simply at first, but then to modulate with it to the subdominant and from there through the dominant back again to the main key. . . . At other times, this spot can be used—like a kind of supplement to the second part—for another working out of the main theme or its motives, if the main theme seems especially momentous or fertile, or if it has not been treated in the second part.

• • • • •

Finally, the closing theme, too, or the transition that precedes it, can be expanded or an extension may be added that brings the main theme to the fore once again. All such expansions do not belong to the essence of the form and are not necessary, so they can easily become a nuisance. One must surely weigh every single case to determine whether there is a call for such enlargements, whether the themes need and are worthy of more frequent treatment—and whether such reiterations in the third part are sufficiently important to justify their presence.

18 Hermann Helmholtz

Hermann Helmholtz (1821–1894) was one of the greatest scientists of the nineteenth century, a polymath whose talents encompassed mathematics, optics, electrodynamics, physiology, and even meteorology. In the scientific world he is best remembered for a famous lecture in 1847 in which he formulated the law of the conservation of energy. Fortunately for the world of music, his was an empiricism heavily tinged with his own love of the aesthetic, and musical acoustics occupied his attention for a time. We are fortunate as well that Alexander J. Ellis, an English scientist of equal distinction in the field of acoustics, undertook to translate Helmholtz's great book on the subject.

Helmholtz was determined to refute romantic "Nature philosophy" and the vestiges of "vital force" theory in contemporary biology, to free scientific investigation from its remaining metaphysical fetters. He argued that all natural phenomena could be explained empirically, including beauty's effects on us. In his optics studies and in *On the Sensations of Tone* (first published in 1863), he searched for the scientific basis of these effects and investigated the reliability of the senses—highly complex and often imperfect in design—as conduits of information from the external world.

His search for the physical scientific basis of musical phenomena is not unusual for his time, in which the empirical spirit reigned. Nonetheless, Helmholtz never attempted to attribute the full experience of music to nature—as simpler minds were determined to do—but acknowledged the preeminent role of artistic invention and human creativity even in the structure of scales and tuning systems. The following excerpt is taken from the very end of the book; Helmholtz's ruminations on "the wonders of great works of art" provide an especially interesting conclusion to a treatise on physiological acoustics.

FROM *On the Sensations of Tone*
(1877)

ESTHETICAL RELATIONS

•　•　•　•　•

In the last part of my book, I have endeavoured to shew that the construction of scales and of harmonic tissue is a product of artistic invention, and by no means furnished by the natural formation or natural function of our ear, as it has been hitherto most generally asserted. Of course the laws of the natural function of our ear play a great and influential part in this result; these laws are, as it were, the building stones with which the edifice of our musical system has been erected, and the necessity of accurately understanding the nature of these materials in order to understand the construction of the edifice itself, has been clearly shewn by the course of our investigations upon this very subject. But just as people with differently directed tastes can erect extremely different kinds of buildings with the same stones, so also the history of music shews us that the same properties of the human ear could serve as the foundation of very different musical systems. Consequently it seems to me that we cannot doubt, that not merely the composition of perfect musical works of art, but even the construction of our system of scales, keys, chords, in short of all that is usually comprehended in a treatise on Thorough Bass, is the work of artistic invention, and hence must be subject to the laws of artistic beauty. In point of fact, mankind has been at work on the diatonic system for more than 2500 years since the days of Terpander and Pythagoras, and in many cases we are still able to determine that the progressive changes made in the tonal system have been due to the most distinguished composers themselves, partly through

TEXT: *On the Sensations of Tone as a Physiological Basis for the Theory of Music*, translated by Alexander J. Ellis from the fourth (1877) edition of *Lehre von dem Tonempfindungen;* second English edition, 1885, pp. 365–71.

their own independent inventions, and partly through the sanction which they gave to the inventions of others, by employing them artistically.

The esthetic analysis of complete musical works of art, and the comprehension of the reasons of their beauty, encounter apparently invincible obstacles at almost every point. But in the field of elementary musical art we have now gained so much insight into its internal connection that we are able to bring the results of our investigations to bear on the views which have been formed and in modern times nearly universally accepted respecting the cause and character of artistic beauty in general. It is, in fact, not difficult to discover a close connection and agreement between them; nay, there are probably fewer examples more suitable than the theory of musical scales and harmony, to illustrate the darkest and most difficult points of general esthetics. Hence I feel that I should not be justified in passing over these considerations, more especially as they are closely connected with the theory of sensual perception, and hence with physiology in general.

No doubt is now entertained that beauty is subject to laws and rules dependent on the nature of human intelligence. The difficulty consists in the fact that these laws and rules, on whose fulfilment beauty depends and by which it must be judged, are not consciously present to the mind, either of the artist who creates the work, or the observer who contemplates it. Art works with design, but the work of art ought to have the appearance of being undesigned, and must be judged on that ground. Art creates as imagination pictures, regularly without conscious law, designedly without conscious aim. A work, known and acknowledged as the product of mere intelligence, will never be accepted as a work of art, however perfect be its adaptation to its end. Whenever we see that conscious reflection has acted in the arrangement of the whole, we find it poor.

> Man fühlt die Absicht, und man wird verstimmt.
> (We feel the purpose, and it jars upon us.)[1]

And yet we require every work of art to be reasonable, and we shew this by subjecting it to a critical examination, and by seeking to enhance our enjoyment and our interest in it by tracing out the suitability, connection, and equilibrium of all its separate parts. The more we succeed in making the harmony and beauty of all its peculiarities clear and distinct, the richer we find it, and we even regard as the principal characteristic of a great work of art that deeper thought, reiterated observation, and continued reflection shew us more and more clearly the reasonableness of all its individual parts. Our endeavour to comprehend the beauty of such a work by critical examination, in which we partly succeed, shews that we assume a certain adaptation to reason in works of art, which may possibly rise to a conscious understanding, although such understanding is neither necessary for the invention nor for the enjoyment of the beautiful. For what is esthetically beautiful is recognised by the immediate

---

1. Actually, *So fühlt man Absicht und man ist verstimmt.* Goethe, *Torquato Tasso*, Act 2, scene 1.

judgment of a cultivated taste, which declares it pleasing or displeasing, without any comparison whatever with law or conception.

But that we do not accept delight in the beautiful as something individual, but rather hold it to be in regular accordance with the nature of mind in general, appears by our expecting and requiring from every other healthy human intellect the same homage that we ourselves pay to what we call beautiful. At most we allow that national or individual peculiarities of taste incline to this or that artistic ideal, and are most easily moved by it, precisely in the same way that a certain amount of education and practice in the contemplation of fine works of art is undeniably necessary for penetration into their deeper meaning.

The principal difficulty in pursuing this object, is to understand how regularity can be apprehended by intuition without being consciously felt to exist. And this unconsciousness of regularity is not a mere accident in the effect of the beautiful on our mind, which may indifferently exist or not; it is, on the contrary, most clearly, prominently, and essentially important. For through apprehending everywhere traces of regularity, connection, and order, without being able to grasp the law and plan of the whole, there arises in our mind a feeling that the work of art which we are contemplating is the product of a design which far exceeds anything we can conceive at the moment, and which hence partakes of the character of the illimitable. Remembering the poet's words:

> Du gleichst dem Geist, den du begreifst
> (Thou'rt like the spirit thou conceivest),[2]

we feel that those intellectual powers which were at work in the artist, are far above our conscious mental action, and that were it even possible at all, infinite time, meditation, and labour would have been necessary to attain by conscious thought that degree of order, connection, and equilibrium of all parts and all internal relations, which the artist has accomplished under the sole guidance of tact and taste, and which we have in turn to appreciate and comprehend by our own tact and taste, long before we begin a critical analysis of the work.

It is clear that all high appreciation of the artist and his work reposes essentially on this feeling. In the first we honour a genius, a spark of divine creative fire, which far transcends the limits of our intelligent and conscious forecast. And yet the artist is a man as we are, in whom work the same mental powers as in ourselves, only in their own peculiar direction, purer, brighter, steadier; and by the greater or less readiness and completeness with which we grasp the artist's language we measure our own share of those powers which produced the wonder.

Herein is manifestly the cause of that moral elevation and feeling of ecstatic satisfaction which is called forth by thorough absorption in genuine and lofty works of art. We learn from them to feel that even in the obscure depths of a healthy and harmoniously developed human mind, which are at least for the

2. Goethe, *Faust*, Pt 1, l. 511.

present inaccessible to analysis by conscious thought, there slumbers a germ of order that is capable of rich intellectual cultivation, and we learn to recognise and admire in the work of art, though draughted in unimportant material, the picture of a similar arrangement of the universe, governed by law and reason in all its parts. The contemplation of a real work of art awakens our confidence in the originally healthy nature of the human mind, when uncribbed, unharassed, unobscured, and unfalsified.

But for all this it is an essential condition that the whole extent of the regularity and design of a work of art should *not* be apprehended consciously. It is precisely from that part of its regular subjection to reason, which escapes our conscious apprehension, that a work of art exalts and delights us, and that the chief effects of the artistically beautiful proceed, *not* from the part which we are able fully to analyse.

If we now apply these considerations to the system of musical tones and harmony, we see of course that these are objects belonging to an entirely subordinate and elementary domain, but nevertheless they, too, are slowly matured inventions of the artistic taste of musicians, and consequently they, too, must be governed by the general rules of artistic beauty. Precisely because we are here still treading the lower walks of art, and are not dealing with the expression of deep psychological problems, we are able to discover a comparatively simple and transparent solution of that fundamental enigma of esthetics.

The whole of the last part of this book has explained how musicians gradually discovered the relationships between tones and chords, and how the invention of harmonic music rendered these relationships closer, and clearer, and richer. We have been able to deduce the whole system of rules which constitute Thorough Bass, from an endeavour to introduce a clearly sensible connection into the series of tones which form a piece of music.

A feeling for the melodic relationship of consecutive tones, was first developed, commencing with Octave and Fifth and advancing to the Third. We have taken pains to prove that this feeling of relationship was founded on the perception of identical partial tones in the corresponding compound tones. Now these partial tones are of course present in the sensations excited in our auditory apparatus, and yet they are not generally the subject of conscious perception as independent sensations. The conscious perception of everyday life is limited to the apprehension of the tone compounded of these partials, as a whole, just as we apprehend the taste of a very compound dish as a whole, without clearly feeling how much of it is due to the salt, or the pepper, or other spices and condiments. A critical examination of our auditory sensations as such was required before we could discover the existence of upper partial tones. Hence the real reason of the melodic relationship of two tones (with the exception of a few more or less clearly expressed conjectures, as, for example, by Rameau and d'Alembert) remained so long undiscovered, or at least was not in any respect clearly and definitely formulated. I believe that I have been able to furnish the required explanation, and hence clearly to exhibit the whole connection of the phenomena. The esthetic problem is thus referred to the common property of all sensual perceptions, namely, the apprehension of compound aggregates of sensations as sensible symbols of simple external objects, without analysing them. In our usual observations on external nature our attention is so thoroughly engaged by external objects that we are entirely unpractised in taking for the subjects of conscious observation, any properties of our sensations themselves, which we do not already know as the sensible expression of some individual external object or event.

After musicians had long been content with the melodic relationship of tones, they began in the middle ages to make use of harmonic relationship as shewn in consonance. The effects of various combinations of tones also depend partly on the identity or difference of two of their different partial tones, but they likewise partly depend on their combinational tones. Whereas, however, in melodic relationship the equality of the upper partial tones can only be perceived by *remembering* the preceding compound tone, in harmonic relationship it is determined by *immediate sensation,* by the presence or absence of beats. Hence in harmonic combinations of tone, tonal relationship is felt with that greater liveliness due to a present sensation as compared with the recollection of a past sensation. The wealth of clearly perceptible relations grows with the number of tones combined. Beats are easy to recognise as such when they occur slowly; but those which characterise dissonances are, almost without exception, very rapid, and are partly covered by sustained tones which do not beat, so that a careful comparison of slower and quicker beats is necessary to gain the conviction that the essence of dissonance consists precisely in rapid beats. Slow beats do not create the feeling of dissonance, which does not arise till the rapidity of the beats confuses the ear and makes it unable to distinguish them. In this case also the ear feels the difference between the undisturbed combination of sound in the case of two consonant tones, and the disturbed rough combination resulting from a dissonance. But, as a general rule, the hearer is then perfectly unconscious of the cause to which the disturbance and roughness are due.

The development of harmony gave rise to a much richer opening out of musical art than was previously possible, because the far clearer characterisation of related combinations of tones by means of chords and chordal sequences, allowed of the use of much more distant relationships than were previously available, by modulating into different keys. In this way the means of expression greatly increased as well as the rapidity of the melodic and harmonic transitions which could now be introduced without destroying the musical connection.

As the independent significance of chords came to be appreciated in the fifteenth and sixteenth centuries, a feeling arose for the relationship of chords to one another and to the tonic chord, in accordance with the same law which had long ago unconsciously regulated the relationship of compound tones. The relationship of compound tones depended on the identity of two or more partial tones, that of chords on the identity of two or more notes. For the musician, of course, the law of the relationship of chords and keys is much more intelligible than that of compound tones. He readily hears the identical tones, or sees them in the notes before him. But the unprejudiced and uninstructed hearer is as little conscious of the reason of the connection of a clear and agreeable series of fluent chords, as he is of the reason of a well-connected melody. He is startled by a false cadence and feels its unexpectedness, but is not at all necessarily conscious of the reason of its unexpectedness.

Then, again, we have seen that the reason why a chord in music appears to be the chord of a determinate root, depends as before upon the analysis of a compound tone into its partial tones, that is, as before upon those elements of a sensation which cannot readily become subjects of conscious perception. This relation between chords is of great importance, both in the relation of the tonic chord to the tonic tone, and in the sequence of chords.

The recognition of these resemblances between compound tones and between chords, reminds us of other exactly analogous circumstances which we must have often experienced. We recognise the resemblance between the faces of two near relations, without being at all able to say in what the resemblance consists, especially when age and sex are different, and the coarser outlines of the features consequently present striking differences. And yet notwithstanding these differences—notwithstanding that we are unable to fix upon a single point in the two countenances which is absolutely alike—the resemblance is often so extraordinarily striking and convincing, that we have not a moment's doubt about it. Precisely the same thing occurs in recognising the relationship between two compound tones.

Again, we are often able to assert with perfect certainty, that a passage not previously heard is due to a particular author or composer whose other works we know. Occasionally, but by no means always, individual mannerisms in verbal or musical phrases determine our judgment, but as a rule we are mostly unable to fix upon the exact points of resemblance between the new piece and the known works of the author or composer.

The analogy of these different cases may be even carried farther. When a father and daughter are strikingly alike in some well-marked feature, as the nose or forehead, we observe it at once, and think no more about it. But if the resemblance is so enigmatically concealed that we cannot detect it, we are fascinated, and cannot help continuing to compare their countenances. And if a painter drew two such heads having, say, a somewhat different expression of character combined with a predominant and striking, though indefinable, resemblance, we should undoubtedly value it as one of the principal beauties of his painting. Our admiration would certainly not be due merely to his technical skill; we should rather look upon his painting as evidencing an unusually delicate feeling for the significance of the human countenance, and find in this the artistic justification of his work.

Now the case is similar for musical intervals. The resemblance of an Octave to its root is so great and striking that the dullest ear perceives it; the Octave seems to be almost a pure repetition of the root, as it, in fact, merely repeats a part of the compound tone of its root, without adding anything new. Hence the esthetical effect of an Octave is that of a perfectly simple, but little attractive interval. The most attractive of the intervals, melodically and harmonically, are clearly the Thirds and Sixths,—the intervals which lie at the very boundary of those that the ear can grasp. The major Third and the major Sixth cannot be properly appreciated unless the first five partial tones are audible. These are present in good musical qualities of tone. The minor Third and the minor Sixth are for the most part justifiable only as inversions of the former intervals. The more complicated intervals in the scale cease to have any direct or easily intelligible relationship. They have no longer the charm of the Thirds.

Moreover, it is by no means a merely external indifferent regularity which the employment of diatonic scales, founded on the relationship of compound tones, has introduced into the tonal material of music, as, for instance, rhythm introduced some such external arrangement into the words of poetry. I have shewn, on the contrary, in Chapter XIV., that this construction of the scale furnished a means of measuring the intervals of their tones, so that the equality of two intervals lying in different sections of the scale would be recognised by immediate sensation. Thus the melodic step of a Fifth is always characterised by having the second partial tone of the second note identical with the third of the first. This produces a definiteness and certainty in the measurement of intervals for our sensation, such as might be looked for in vain in the system of colours, otherwise so similar, or in the estimation of mere differences of intensity in our various sensual perceptions.

Upon this reposes also the characteristic resemblance between the relations of the musical scale and of space, a resemblance which appears to me of vital importance for the peculiar effects of music. It is an essential character of space that at every position within it like bodies can be placed, and like motions can occur. Everything that is possible to happen in one part of space is equally possible in every other part of space and is perceived by us in precisely the same way. This is the case also with the musical scale. Every melodic phrase, every chord, which can be executed at any pitch, can be also executed at any other pitch in such a way that we immediately perceive the characteristic marks of their similarity. On the other hand, also, different voices, executing the same or different melodic phrases, can move at the same time within the compass of the scale, like two bodies in space, and, provided they are consonant in the accented parts of bars, without creating any musical disturbances. Such a close analogy consequently exists in all essential relations between the musical scale and space, that even alteration of pitch has a readily recognised and unmistakable resemblance to motion in space, and is often metaphorically termed the ascending or descending *motion* or *progression* of a part. Hence, again, it becomes possible for motion in music to imitate the peculiar characteristics of motive forces in space, that is, to form an image of the various impulses and forces which lie at the root of motion. And on this, as I believe, essentially depends the power of music to picture emotion.

It is not my intention to deny that music in its initial state and simplest forms may have been originally an artistic imitation of the instinctive modulations of the voice that correspond to various conditions of the feelings. But I cannot think that this is opposed to the above explanation; for a great part of the natural means of vocal expression may be reduced to such facts as the following: its rhythm and accentuation are an immediate expression of the rapidity or force of the corresponding psychical motives—all effort drives the voice up—a desire to make a pleasant impression on another mind leads to selecting a softer, pleasanter quality of tone—and so forth. An endeavour to imitate the involuntary modulations of the voice and make its recitation richer and more expressive, may therefore very possibly have led our ancestors to the discovery of the first means of musical expression, just as the imitation of weeping, shouting, or sobbing, and other musical delineations may play a part in even cultivated music, (as in operas), although such modifications of the voice are not confined to the action of free mental motives, but embrace really mechanical and even involuntary muscular contractions. But it is quite clear that every completely developed melody goes far beyond an imitation of nature, even if we include the cases of the most varied alteration of voice under the influence of passion. Nay, the very fact that music introduces progression by fixed degrees both in rhythm and in the scale, renders even an approximatively correct representation of nature simply impossible, for most of the passionate affections of the voice are characterised by a gliding transition in pitch. The imitation of nature is thus rendered as imperfect as the imitation of a picture by embroidery on a canvas with separate little squares for each shade of colour. Music, too, departed still further from nature when it introduced the greater compass, the mobility, and the strange qualities of tone belonging to musical instruments, by which the field of attainable musical effects has become so much wider than it was or could be when the human voice alone was employed.

Hence though it is probably correct to say that mankind, in historical development, first learned the means of musical expression from the human voice, it can hardly be denied that these same means of expressing melodic progression act, in artistically developed music, without the slightest reference to the application made of them in the modulations of the human voice, and have a more general significance than any that can be attributed to innate instinctive cries. That this is the case appears above all in the modern development of instrumental music, which possesses an effective power and artistic justification that need not be gainsaid, although we may not yet be able to explain it in all its details.

.   .   .

Here I close my work. It appears to me that I have carried it as far as the physiological properties of the sensation of hearing exercise a direct influence on the construction of a musical system, that is, as far as the work especially belongs to natural philosophy. For even if I could not avoid mixing up esthetic problems with physical, the former were comparatively simple, and the latter much more complicated. This relation would necessarily become inverted if I attempted to proceed further into the esthetics of music, and to enter on the theory of rhythm, forms of composition, and means of musical expression. In all these fields the properties of sensual perception would of course have an influence at times, but only in a very subordinate degree. The real difficulty would lie in the development of the psychical motives which here assert themselves. Certainly this is the point where the more interesting part of musical esthetics begins, the aim being to explain the wonders of great works of art, and to learn the utterances and actions of the various affections of the mind. But, however alluring such an aim may be, I prefer leaving others to carry out such investigations, in which I should feel myself too much of an amateur, while I myself remain on the safe ground of natural philosophy, in which I am at home.

19 Amy Fay

Amy Fay was a celebrated American concert pianist as well as a lecturer and teacher. She lived for a time in each of three major musical centers, Boston, Chicago, and New York, and became active in organizations to promote women's participation, such as the Amateur Music Club and the New York Women's Philharmonic Society (which she also served as president).

Fay was born in Louisiana in 1844. At the age of twenty-five she traveled to Germany to continue her musical studies and remained there for six years. Her vivid and perceptive letters home, describing her studies and other musical adventures, were edited for publication by her sister, Melusina Fay Peirce (feminist writer on the reform of domestic architecture and first wife of the philosopher Charles Sanders Peirce). The resulting little book enjoyed great popularity, appearing in twenty-five editions in the United States alone, in several English editions, and in French and German translations.

Women were admitted into European conservatories as performance students in large numbers during the nineteenth century, but many restrictions were placed upon them: instruction was usually segregated by gender, as Amy Fay describes here; the curriculum for women was often a truncated version of that offered to men; and it was not until late in the century that women were admitted as composition students, or that their professional aspirations were taken seriously. Boston composer Mabel Daniels also wrote a memoir, *An American Girl in Munich,* describing her conservatory study a few decades later than Fay's.

FROM *Music-Study in Germany*
(1880)

Berlin, February 8, 1870

• • • • •

The day after Tausig's concert I went, as usual, to hear him give the lesson to his best class of girls. I got there a little before the hour, and the girls were in the dressing-room waiting for the young men to be through with their lesson. They were talking about the concert. "Was it not beautiful?" said little Timanoff, to me; "I did not sleep the whole night after it!"—a touch of sentiment that quite surprised me in that small personage, and made me feel some compunctions, as I had slept soundly myself. "I have practiced five hours to-day already," she added. Just then the young men came out of the class-room and we passed into it. Tausig was standing by the piano. "Begin!" said he, to Timanoff, more shortly even than usual; "I trust you have brought me a study *this* time." He always insists upon a study in addition to the piece. Timanoff replied in the affirmative, and proceeded to open Chopin's *Etudes.* She played the great A minor "Winter Wind" study, and most magnificently, too, starting off with the greatest brilliancy and "go." I was perfectly amazed at such a feat from such a child, and expected that Tausig would exclaim with admiration. Not so that Rhadamanthus. He heard it through without comment or correction, and when Timanoff had finished, simply remarked very composedly, "So! Have you taken the *next* Etude, also?" as if the great A minor were not enough for one meal! It is eight pages long to begin with, and there is no let up to the difficulty all the way through. Afterward, however, he told the young men that he "could not have done it better" himself.

Tausig is so hasty and impatient that to be in his classes must be a fearful ordeal. He will not bear the slightest fault. The last time I went into his class to hear him teach he was dreadful. Fräulein H. began, and she has remarkable talent, and is far beyond me. She would not play *piano* enough to suit him, and finally he stamped his foot at her, snatched her hand from the piano, and said: "*Will* you play *piano* or not, for if not we will go no farther?" The second girl sat down and played a few lines. He made her begin over again several times, and finally came up and took her music away and slapped it down on the piano,—"You have been studying this for weeks and you can't play a note of it; practice it for a month and then you can bring it to me again," he said.

The third was Fräulein Timanoff, who is a little genius, I think. She brought a Sonata by Schubert—the one, I believe, in A—and by the way he behaved Tausig must have a particular feeling about that particular Sonata. Timanoff

TEXT: *Music-Study in Germany, from the Home Correspondence of Amy Fay* (Chicago, 1880), pp. 39–42, 163–68, 210–14.

began running it off in her usual nimble style, having practiced it evidently every minute of the time when she was not asleep, since the last lesson. She had not proceeded far down the first page when he stopped her, and began to fuss over the expression. She began again, but this time with no better luck. A third time, but still he was dissatisfied, though he suffered her to go on a little farther. He kept stopping her every moment in the most tantalizing and exasperating manner. If it had been I, I should have cried, but Timanoff was well broken, and only flushed deeply to the very tips of her small ears. From an apple blossom she changed to a carnation. Tausig grew more and more savage, and made her skip whole pages in his impatience. "Play here!" he would say, in the most imperative tone, pointing to a half or whole page farther on. "This I cannot hear!—Go on farther!—It is too bad to be listened to!" Finally, he struck the music with the back of his hand, and exclaimed, in a despairing way, "*Kind, es liegt eine Seele darin. Weisst du nicht es liegt eine Seele darin?* (Child, there's a soul in the piece. Don't you know there is a *soul* in it?)" To the little Timanoff, who has no soul, and who is not sufficiently experienced to counterfeit one, this speech evidently conveyed no particular idea. She ran on as glibly as ever till Tausig could endure no more, and shut up the music. I was much disappointed, as it was new to me, and I like to hear Timanoff's little fingers tinkle over the keys, "seele" or no "seele." She has a most accurate and dainty way of doing everything, and somehow, in her healthy little brain I hardly wish for *Seele!*

Last of all Fräulein L. played, and she alone suited Tausig. She is a Swede, and is the best scholar he has, but she has such frightfully ugly hands, and holds them so terribly, that when I look at her I cannot enjoy her playing. Tausig always praises her very much, and she is tremendously ambitious.

Tausig has a charming face, full of expression and very sensitive. He is extremely sharp-sighted, and has eyes in the back of his head, I believe. He is far too small and too despotic to be fascinating, however, though he has a sort of captivating way with him when he is in a good humor.

•   •   •   •   •

Berlin, February 10, 1872

A week ago last Monday I went to Dresden with J. L. to visit B. H. . . . B. did everything in her power to amuse us, and she is the soul of amiability. She kept inviting people to meet us, and had several tea-parties, and when we had no company she took us to the theatre or the opera. She invited Marie Wieck (the sister of Clara Schumann) to tea one night. I was very glad to meet her, for she is an exquisite artist herself, and plays in Clara Schumann's style, though her conception is not so remarkable. Her touch is perfect. At B.'s request she tried to play for us, but the action of B.'s piano did not suit her, and she presently got up, saying that she could do nothing on that instrument, but that if we would come to *her*, she would play for us with pleasure.

I was in high glee at that proposal, for I was very anxious to see the famous

Wieck, the trainer of so many generations of musicians. Fräulein Wieck appointed Saturday evening, and we accordingly went. B. had instructed us how to act, for the old man is quite a character, and has to be dealt with after his own fashion. She said we must walk in (having first laid off our things) as if we had been members of the family all our lives, and say, "Good-evening, Papa Wieck,"—(everybody calls him Papa). Then we were to seat ourselves, and if we had some knitting or sewing with us it would be well. At any rate we must have the apparent intention of spending several hours, for nothing provokes him so as to have people come in simply to call. "What!" he will say, "do you expect to know a celebrated man like me in half an hour?" then (very sarcastically), "perhaps you want my autograph!" He hates to give his autograph.

Well, we went through the prescribed programme. We were ushered into a large room, much longer than it was broad. At either end stood a grand piano. Otherwise the room was furnished with the greatest simplicity. My impression is that the floor was a plain yellow painted one, with a rug or two here and there. A few portraits and bas-reliefs hung upon the walls. The pianos were of course fine. Frau Wieck and "Papa" received us graciously. We began by taking tea, but soon the old man became impatient, and said, "Come! the ladies wish to perform (*vortragen*) something before me, and if we don't begin we shan't accomplish anything." He *lives* entirely in music, and has a class of girls whom he instructs every evening for nothing. Five of these young girls were there. He is very deaf, but strange to say, he is as sensitive as ever to every musical sound, and the same is the case with Clara Schumann. Fräulein Wieck then opened the ball. She is about forty, I should think, and a stout, phlegmatic-looking woman. However, she played superbly, and her touch is one of the most delicious possible. After hearing her, one is not surprised that the Wiecks think nobody can teach touch but themselves. She began with a nocturne by Chopin, in F major. I forgot to say that the old Herr sits in his chair with the air of being on a throne, and announces beforehand each piece that is to be played, following it with some comment: *e.g.,* "This nocturne I allowed my daughter Clara to play in Berlin forty years ago, and afterward the principal newspaper in criticising her performance, remarked: 'This young girl seems to have much talent; it is only a pity that she is in the hands of a father whose head seems stuck full of queer new-fangled notions,'—so new was Chopin to the public at that time." That is the way he goes on.

After Fräulein Wieck had finished the nocturne, I asked for something by Bach, which I'm told she plays remarkably. She said that at the moment she had nothing in practice by Bach, but she would play me a *gigue* by a composer of Bach's time,—Haesler, I think she said, but cannot remember, as it was a name entirely unknown to me. It was very brilliant, and she executed it beautifully. Afterward she played the last movement of Beethoven's Sonata in E flat major, but I wasn't particularly struck with her conception of that. Then we had a pause, and she urged me to play. I refused, for as I had been in Dresden a week and had not practiced, I did not wish to sit down and not do myself justice. My hand is so stiff, that as Tausig said of himself (though of him I can hardly believe it), "When I haven't practiced for fourteen days I can't do anything." The old Herr then said, "Now we'll have something else;" and got up and went to the piano, and called the young girls. He made three of them sing, one after the other, and they sang very charmingly indeed. One of them he made improvise a *cadenza,* and a second sang the alto to it without accompaniment. He was very proud of that. He exercises his pupils in all sorts of ways, trains them to sing any given tone, and "to skip up and down the ladder," as they call the scale.

After the master had finished with the singing, Fräulein Wieck played three more pieces, one of which was an exquisite arrangement by Liszt of that song by Schumann, *"Du meine Seele."* She ended with a *gavotte* by Gluck, or as Papa Wieck would say, "This is a gavotte from one of Gluck's operas, arranged by Brahms for the piano. To the superficial observer the second movement will appear very easy, but in *my* opinion it is a very hard task to hit it exactly." I happened to know just how the thing ought to be played, for I had heard it three times from Clara Schumann herself. Fräulein Wieck didn't please me at all in it, for she took the second movement twice as quickly as the first. "Your sister plays the second movement much slower," said I. *"So?"* said she, "I've never heard it from her." She then asked, "So slow?" playing it slower. "Still slower?" said she, beginning a third time, at my continual disapproval. *"Streng im Tempo* (in strict time)," said I, nodding my head oracularly. *"Väterchen."* called she to the old Herr, "Miss Fay says that Clara plays the second movement *so* slow," showing him. I don't know whether this correction made an impression, but he was then *determined* that I should play, and on my continued refusal he finally said that he found it very strange that a young lady who had studied more than two years in Tausig's and Kullak's conservatories shouldn't have *one* piece that she could play before people. This little fling provoked me, so up I jumped, and saying to myself, *"Kopf in die Höhe, Brust heraus—vorwärts!"* (one of the military orders here), I marched to the piano and played the fugue at the end of Beethoven's A flat Sonata, Op. 110. They all sat round the room as still as so many statues while I played, and you cannot imagine how dreadfully nervous I was. I thought fifty times I would have to stop, for, like all fugues, it is such a piece that if you once get out you never can get in again, and Bülow himself got mixed up on the last part of it the other night in his concert. But I got well through, notwithstanding, and the old master was good enough to commend me warmly. He told me I must have studied a great deal, and asked me if I hadn't played a great many *Etuden.* I informed him in polite German "He'd better believe I had!"

●   ●   ●   ●   ●

Weimar, May 21, 1873

Liszt is so *besieged* by people and so tormented with applications, that I fear I should only have been sent away if I had come without the Baroness von S.'s letter of introduction, for he admires her extremely, and I judge that she has much influence with him. He says "people fly in his face by dozens," and seem to think he is "only there to give lessons." He gives *no* paid lessons whatever, as he is much too grand for that, but if one has talent enough, or pleases him, he lets one come to him and play to him. I go to him every other day, but I don't play more than twice a week, as I cannot prepare so much, but I listen to the others. Up to this point there have been only four in the class besides myself, and I am the only new one. From four to six P. M. is the time when he receives his scholars. The first time I went I did not play to him, but listened to the rest. Urspruch and Leitert, the two young men who I met the other night, have studied with Liszt a long time, and both play superbly. Fräulein Schultz and Miss Gaul (of Baltimore), are also most gifted creatures.

As I entered Liszt's salon, Urspruch was performing Schumann's Symphonic Studies—an immense composition, and one that it took at least half an hour to get through. He played so splendidly that my heart sank down into the very depths. I thought I should never get on *there!* Liszt came forward and greeted me in a very friendly manner as I entered. He was in very good humour that day, and made some little witticisms. Urspruch asked him what title he should give to a piece he was composing. *"Per aspera ad astra,"* said Liszt. This was such a good hit that I began to laugh, and he seemed to enjoy my appreciation of his little sarcasm. I did not play that time, as my piano had only just come, and I was not prepared to do so, but I went home and practiced tremendously for several days on Chopin's B minor sonata. It is a great composition, and one of his last works. When I thought I could play it, I went to Liszt, though with a trembling heart. I cannot tell you what it has cost me every time I have ascended his stairs. I can scarcely summon up courage to go there, and generally stand on the steps awhile before I can make up my mind to open the door and go in!

This day it was particularly trying, as it was really my first serious performance before him, and he speaks so very indistinctly that I feared I shouldn't understand his corrections, and that he would get out of patience with me, for he cannot bear to explain. I think he hates the trouble of speaking German, for he mutters his words and does not half finish his sentences. Yesterday when I was there he spoke to me in French all the time, and to the others in German,—one of his funny whims, I suppose.

Well, on this day the artists Leitert and Urspruch, and the young composer Metzdorf, who is always hanging about Liszt, were in the room when I came. They had probably been playing. At first Liszt took no notice of me beyond a greeting, till Metzdorf said to him, "Herr Doctor, Miss Fay has brought a sonata." "Ah, well, let us hear it," said Liszt. Just then he left the room for a minute, and I told the three gentlemen that they ought to go away and let me play to Liszt alone, for I felt nervous about playing before them. They all laughed at me and said they would not budge an inch. When Liszt came back they said to him, "Only think, Herr Doctor, Miss Fay proposes to send us all home." I said I could not play before such great artists. "Oh, that is healthy for you," said Liszt, with a smile, and added, "you have a very choice audience, now." I don't know whether he appreciated how nervous I was, but instead of walking up and down the room as he often does, he sat down by me like any other teacher, and heard me play the first movement. It was frightfully hard, but I had studied it so much that I managed to get through with it pretty successfully. Nothing could exceed Liszt's amiability, or the trouble he gave himself, and instead of frightening me, he inspired me. Never was there such a delightful teacher! and he is the first sympathetic one I've had. You feel so *free* with him, and he develops the very spirit of music in you. He doesn't keep nagging at you all the time, but he leaves you your own conception. Now and then he will make a criticism, or play a passage, and with a few words give you enough to think of all the rest of your life. There is a delicate *point* to everything he says, as subtle as he is himself. He doesn't tell you anything about the technique. That you must work out for yourself. When I had finished the first movement of the sonata, Liszt said "Bravo!" Taking my seat, he made some little criticisms, and then told me to go on and play the rest of it.

Now, I only half knew the other movements, for the first one was so extremely difficult that it cost me all the labour I could give to prepare that. But playing to Liszt reminds me of trying to feed the elephant in the Zoological Garden with lumps of sugar. He disposes of whole movements as if they were nothing, and stretches out gravely for more! One of my fingers fortunately began to bleed, for I had practiced the skin off, and that gave me a good excuse for stopping. Whether he was pleased at this proof of industry, I know not; but after looking at my finger and saying, "Oh!" very compassionately, he sat down and played the whole three last movements himself. That was a great deal, and showed off all his powers. It was the first time I had heard him, and I don't know which was the most extraordinary,—the Scherzo, with its wonderful lightness and swiftness, the Adagio with its depth and pathos, or the last movement, where the whole keyboard seemed to "*donnern und blitzen* (thunder and lighten)." There is such a vividness about everything he plays that it does not seem as if it were mere music you were listening to, but it is as if he had called up a real, living *form,* and you saw it breathing before your face and eyes. It gives *me* almost a ghostly feeling to hear him, and it seems as if the air were peopled with spirits. Oh, he is a perfect wizard! It is as interesting to see him as it is to hear him, for his face changes with every modulation of the piece, and he looks exactly as he is playing. He has one element that is most captivating, and that is, a sort of delicate and fitful mirth that keeps peering out at you here and there! It is most peculiar, and when he plays that way, the most bewitching little expression comes over his face. It seems as if a little spirit of joy were playing hide and go seek with you.

VI

MUSICAL ENCOUNTERS

IV

20 Antonín Dvořák

Jeannette Thurber, founder of the National Conservatory of Music in New York, invited Dvořák to become its director. He agreed, arriving in New York in the fall of 1892 and staying in the United States for nearly three years before returning to Prague.

The celebrated Czech composer was a firm believer in national musics, and he took up residence in the United States at least partly in the hope of helping young American composers find their way to a genuinely "American" sound. A number of his own compositions written during his American sojourn may also have been conceived in this spirit, among them a string quartet and string quintet each called "the American" and his most familiar work, Symphony No. 9, "From the New World." He had undertaken, one New York reporter wrote, "a serious study of the national music of this continent as exemplified in the native melodies of the negro and Indian races" (see footnote 2 below).

Dvořák's impressions of the music of African-Americans and of American Indians, and his understanding of their role in American urban culture, may seem quixotic today, as will his essentialist confusion of a national population with a "race." But there is no question that he took an earnest and energetic interest in the search for a national musical identity which occupied many American composers at the time.

Music in America

(1895)

It is a difficult task at best for a foreigner to give a correct verdict of the affairs of another country. With the United States of America this is more than usually difficult, because they cover such a vast area of land that it would take many years to become properly acquainted with the various localities, separated by great distances, that would have to be considered when rendering a judgment concerning them all. It would ill become me, therefore, to express my views on so general and all-embracing a subject as music in America, were I not pressed to do so, for I have neither travelled extensively, nor have I been here long enough to gain an intimate knowledge of American affairs. I can only judge of it from what I have observed during my limited experience as a musician and teacher in America, and from what those whom I know here tell me about their own country. Many of my impressions therefore are those of a foreigner who has not been here long enough to overcome the feeling of strangeness and bewildered astonishment which must fill all European visitors upon their first arrival.

The two American traits which most impress the foreign observer, I find,

Text: *Harper's New Monthly Magazine* 90 (1895): 429–34.

are the unbounded patriotism and capacity for enthusiasm of most Americans. Unlike the more diffident inhabitants of other countries, who do not "wear their hearts upon their sleeves," the citizens of America are always patriotic, and no occasion seems to be too serious or too slight for them to give expression to this feeling. Thus nothing better pleases the average American, especially the American youth, than to be able to say that this or that building, this or that new patent appliance, is the finest or grandest in the world. This, of course, is due to that other trait—enthusiasm. The enthusiasm of most Americans for all things new is apparently without limit. It is the essence of what is called "push"—American push. Every day I meet with this quality in my pupils. They are unwilling to stop at anything. In the matters relating to their art they are inquisitive to a degree that they want to go to the bottom of all things at once. It is as if a boy wished to dive before he could swim.

At first, when my American pupils were new to me, this trait annoyed me, and I wished them to give more attention to the one matter in hand rather than to everything at once. But now I like it; for I have come to the conclusion that this youthful enthusiasm and eagerness to take up everything is the best promise for music in America. The same opinion, I remember, was expressed by the director of the new conservatory in Berlin, who, from his experience with American students of music, predicted that America within twenty or thirty years would become the first musical country.

Only when the people in general, however, begin to take as lively an interest in music and art as they now take in more material matters will the arts come into their own. Let the enthusiasm of the people once be excited, and patriotic gifts and bequests must surely follow.

It is a matter of surprise to me that all this has not come long ago. When I see how much is done in every other field by public-spirited men in America—how schools, universities, libraries, museums, hospitals, and parks spring up out of the ground and are maintained by generous gifts—I can only marvel that so little has been done for music. After two hundred years of almost unbroken prosperity and expansion, the net results for music are a number of public concert-halls of most recent growth; several musical societies with orchestras of noted excellence, such as the Philharmonic Society in New York, the orchestras of Mr. Thomas and Mr. Seidl, and the superb orchestra supported by a public spirited citizen of Boston; one opera company, which only the upper classes can hear or understand; and a national conservatory which owes its existence to the generous forethought of one indefatigable woman.

It is true that music is the youngest of the arts, and must therefore be expected to be treated as Cinderella, but is it not time that she were lifted from the ashes and given a seat among the equally youthful sister arts in this land of youth, until the coming of the fairy godmother and the prince of the crystal slipper?

Art, of course, must always go a-begging, but why should this country alone, which is so justly famed for the generosity and public spirit of its citizens, close its door to the poor beggar? In the Old World this is not so. Since the days of Palestrina, the three-hundredth anniversary of whose death was celebrated in Rome a few weeks ago, princes and prelates have vied with each other in extending a generous hand to music. Since the days of Pope Gregory the Church has made music one of her own chosen arts. In Germany and Austria princes like Esterhazy, Lobkowitz, and Harrach, who supported Haydn and Beethoven, or the late King of Bavaria, who did so much for Wagner, with many others have helped to create a demand for good music, which has since become universal, while in France all governments, be they monarchies, empires, or republics, have done their best to carry on the noble work that was begun by Louis the Fourteenth. Even the little republic of Switzerland annually sets aside a budget for the furtherance of literature, music, and the arts.

A few months ago only we saw how such a question of art as whether the operas sung in Hungary's capital should be of a national or foreign character could provoke a ministerial crisis. Such is the interest in music and art taken by the governments and people of other countries.

The great American republic alone, in its national government as well as in the several governments of the States, suffers art and music to go without encouragement. Trades and commerce are protected, funds are voted away for the unemployed, schools and colleges are endowed, but music must go unaided, and be content if she can get the support of a few private individuals like Mrs. Jeannette M. Thurber and Mr. H. L. Higginson.

Not long ago a young man came to me and showed me his compositions. His talent seemed so promising that I at once offered him a scholarship in our school; but he sorrowfully confessed that he could not afford to become my pupil, because he had to earn his living by keeping books in Brooklyn. Even if he came on but two afternoons in the week, or on Saturday afternoon only, he said, he would lose his employment, on which he and others had to depend. I urged him to arrange the matter with his employer, but he only received the answer: "If you want to play, you can't keep books. You will have to drop one or the other." He dropped his music.

In any other country the state would have made some provision for such a deserving scholar, so that he could have pursued his natural calling without having to starve. With us in Bohemia the Diet each year votes a special sum of money for just such purposes, and the imperial government in Vienna on occasion furnishes other funds for talented artists. Had it not been for such support I should not have been able to pursue my studies when I was a young man. Owing to the fact that, upon the kind recommendation of such men as Brahms, Hanslick, and Herbeck, the Minister of Public Education in Vienna on five successive years sent me sums ranging from four to six hundred florins, I was able to pursue my work and to get my compositions published, so that at the end of that time I was able to stand on my own feet. This has filled me with lasting gratitude towards my country.

Such an attitude of the state towards deserving artists is not only a kind but a wise one. For it cannot be emphasized too strongly that art, as such, does not "pay," to use an American expression—at least, not in the beginning—and that the art that has to pay its own way is apt to become vitiated and cheap.

It is one of the anomalies of this country that the principle of protection is upheld for all enterprises but art. By protection I do not mean the exclusion of foreign art. That, of course, is absurd. But just as the State here provides for its poor industrial scholars and university students, so should it help the would-be students of music and art. As it is now, the poor musician not only cannot get his necessary instruction, in the first place, but if by any chance he has acquired it, he has small prospects of making his chosen calling support him in the end. Why is this? Simply because the orchestras in which first-class players could find a place in this country can be counted on one hand; while of opera companies where native singers can be heard, and where the English tongue is sung, there are none at all. Another thing which discourages the student of music is the unwillingness of publishers to take anything but light and trashy music. European publishers are bad enough in that respect, but the American publishers are worse. Thus, when one of my pupils last year produced a very creditable work, and a thoroughly American composition at that, he could not get it published in America, but had to send it to Germany, where it was at once accepted. The same is true of my own compositions on American subjects, each of which hitherto has had to be published abroad.

No wonder American composers and musicians grow discouraged, and regard the more promising condition of music in other countries with envy! Such a state of affairs should be a source of mortification to all truly patriotic Americans. Yet it can be easily remedied. What was the situation in England but a short while ago? Then they had to procure all their players from abroad, while their own musicians went to the Continent to study. Now that they have two standard academies of music in London, like those of Berlin, Paris, and other cities, the national feeling for music seems to have been awakened, and the majority of orchestras are composed of native Englishmen, who play as well as the others did before. A single institution can make such a change, just as a single genius can bestow an art upon his country that before was lying in unheeded slumber.

Our musical conservatory in Prague was founded but three generations ago, when a few nobles and patrons of music subscribed five thousand florins, which was then the annual cost of maintaining the school. Yet that little school flour-ished and grew, so that now more than sixfold that amount is annually expended. Only lately a school for organ music has been added to the conserva-tory, so that the organists of our churches can learn to play their instruments at home, without having to go to other cities. Thus a school benefits the com-munity in which it is. The citizens of Prague in return have shown their appreciation of the fact by building the "Rudolfinum" as a magnificent home for all the arts. It is jointly occupied by the conservatory and the Academy of Arts, and besides that contains large and small concert-halls and rooms for picture-galleries. In the proper maintenance of this building the whole community takes an interest. It is supported, as it was founded, by the stockholders of the Bohemian Bank of Deposit, and yearly gifts and bequests are made to the institution by private citizens.

If a school of art can grow so in a country of but six million inhabitants, what much brighter prospects should it not have in a land of seventy millions? The important thing is to make a beginning, and in this the State should set an example.

They tell me that this cannot be done. I ask, why can't it be done? If the old commonwealths of Greece and Italy, and the modern republics of France and Switzerland, have been able to do this, why cannot America follow their example? The money certainly is not lacking. Constantly we see great sums of money spent for the material pleasures of the few, which, if devoted to the purposes of art, might give pleasure to thousands. If schools, art museums, and libraries can be maintained at the public expense, why should not musical conservatories and playhouses? The function of the drama, with or without music, is not only to amuse, but to elevate and instruct while giving pleasure. Is it not in the interest of the State that this should be done in the most approved manner, so as to benefit all of its citizens? Let the owners of private playhouses give their performances for diversion only, let those who may, import singers who sing in foreign tongues, but let there be at least one intelligent power that will see to it that the people can hear and see what is best, and what can be understood by them, no matter how small the demand.

That such a system of performing classic plays and operas pleases the people was shown by the attitude of the populace in Prague. There the people collected money and raised subscriptions for over fifty years to build a national playhouse. In 1880 they at last had a sufficient amount, and the "National Theatre" was accordingly built. It had scarcely been built when it was burned to the ground. But the people were not to be discouraged. Everybody helped, and before a fortnight was over more than a million had been collected, and the house was at once built up again, more magnificent than it was before.

In answer to such arguments I am told that there is no popular demand for good music in America. That is not so. Every concert in New York, Boston, Philadelphia, Chicago, or Washington, and most other cities, no doubt, disproves such a statement. American concert-halls are as well filled as those of Europe, and, as a rule, the listeners—to judge them by their attentive conduct and subsequent expression of pleasure—are not a whit less appreciative. How it would be with opera I cannot judge, since American opera audiences, as the opera is conducted at present, are in no sense representative of the people at large. I have no doubt, however, that if the Americans had a chance to hear grand opera sung in their own language they would enjoy it as well and appreciate it as highly as the opera-goers of Vienna, Paris, or Munich enjoy theirs. The change from Italian and French to English will scarcely have an injurious effect on the present good voices of the singers, while it may have the effect of improving the voices of American singers, bringing out more clearly the beauty and strength of the *timbre,* while giving an intelligent conception of the work that enables singers to use a pure diction, which cannot be obtained in a foreign tongue.

The American voice, so far as I can judge, is a good one. When I first arrived in this country I was startled by the strength and the depth of the voices in the boys who sell papers on the street, and I am still constantly amazed at its penetrating quality.

In a sense, of course, it is true that there is less of a demand for music in America than in certain other countries. Our common folk in Bohemia know this. When they come here they leave their fiddles and other instruments at home, and none of the itinerant musicians with whom our country abounds would ever think of trying their luck over here. Occasionally when I have met one of my countrymen whom I knew to be musical in this city of New York or in the West, and have asked him why he did not become a professional musician, I have usually received the answer, "Oh, music is not wanted in this land." This I can scarcely believe. Music is wanted wherever good people are, as the German poet has sung.[1] It only rests with the leaders of the people to make a right beginning.

When this beginning is made, and when those who have musical talent find it worth their while to stay in America, and to study and exercise their art as the business of their life, the music of America will soon become more national in its character. This, my conviction, I know is not shared by many who can justly claim to know this country better than I do. Because the population of the United States is composed of many different races, in which the Teutonic element predominates, and because, owing to the improved methods of transmission of the present day, the music of all the world is quickly absorbed by this country, they argue that nothing specially original or national can come forth. According to that view, all other countries which are but the results of a conglomeration of peoples and races, as, for instance, Italy, could not have produced a national literature or a national music.

A while ago I suggested that inspiration for truly national music might be derived from the negro melodies or Indian chants.[2] I was led to take this view partly by the fact that the so-called plantation songs are indeed the most striking and appealing melodies that have yet been found on this side of the water, but largely by the observation that this seems to be recognized, though often unconsciously, by most Americans. All races have their distinctively national songs, which they at once recognize as their own, even if they have never heard them before. When a Tsech, a Pole, or a Magyar in this country suddenly hears

---

1. A German saying apparently paraphrased from the poem "Gesänge" (1804) by Georg Seume; the original line reads "Bösewichter haben keine Lieder" ("villains have no songs"). I am grateful to Jocelyne Kolb for locating the source.
2. In an interview in the *New York Herald* (December 15, 1893); reprinted in *I.S.A.M. Newsletter* 14 (November 1987): 4.

one of his folk-songs or dances, no matter if it is for the first time in his life, his eye lights up at once, and his heart within him responds, and claims that music as its own. So it is with those of Teutonic or Celtic blood, or any other men, indeed, whose first lullaby mayhap was a song wrung from the heart of the people.

It is a proper question to ask, what songs, then, belong to the American and appeal more strongly to him than any others? What melody could stop him on the street if he were in a strange land and make the home feeling well up within him, no matter how hardened he might be or how wretchedly the tune were played? Their number, to be sure, seems to be limited. The most potent as well as the most beautiful among them, according to my estimation, are certain of the so-called plantation melodies and slave songs, all of which are distinguished by unusual and subtle harmonies, the like of which I have found in no other songs but those of old Scotland and Ireland. The point has been urged that many of these touching songs, like those of Foster, have not been composed by the negroes themselves, but are the work of white men, while others did not originate on the plantation, but were imported from Africa. It seems to me that this matters but little. One might as well condemn the Hungarian Rhapsody because Liszt could not speak Hungarian. The important thing is that the inspiration for such music should come from the right source, and that the music itself should be a true expression of the people's real feelings. To read the right meaning the composer need not necessarily be of the same blood, though that, of course, makes it easier for him. Schubert was a thorough German, but when he wrote Hungarian music, as in the second movement of the C-Major Symphony, or in some of his piano pieces, like the Hungarian Divertissement, he struck the true Magyar note, to which all Magyar hearts, and with them our own, must forever respond. This is not a *tour de force*, but only an instance of how much can be comprehended by a sympathetic genius. The white composers who wrote the touching negro songs which dimmed Thackeray's spectacles so that he exclaimed, "Behold, a vagabond with a corked face and a banjo sings a little song, strikes a wild note, which sets the whole heart thrilling with happy pity!" had a similarly sympathetic comprehension of the deep pathos of slave life. If, as I have been informed they were, these songs were adopted by the negroes on the plantations, they thus became true negro songs. Whether the original songs which must have inspired the composers came from Africa or originated on the plantations matters as little as whether Shakespeare invented his own plots or borrowed them from others. The thing to rejoice over is that such lovely songs exist and are sung at the present day. I, for one, am delighted by them. Just so it matters little whether the inspiration for the coming folk-songs of America is derived from the negro melodies, the songs of the creoles, the red man's chant, or the plaintive ditties of the homesick German or Norwegian. Undoubtedly the germs for the best of music lie hidden among all the races that are commingled in this great country. The music of the people is like a rare and lovely flower growing amidst encroaching weeds. Thousands pass it, while others trample it under foot, and thus the chances are that it will perish before it is seen by the one discriminating spirit who will prize it above all else. The fact that no one has as yet arisen to make the most of it does not prove that nothing is there.

Not so many years ago Slavic music was not known to the men of other races. A few men like Chopin, Glinka, Moniuszko, Smetana, Rubinstein, and Tschaikowski, with a few others, were able to create a Slavic school of music. Chopin alone caused the music of Poland to be known and prized by all lovers of music. Smetana did the same for us Bohemians. Such national music, I repeat, is not created out of nothing. It is discovered and clothed in new beauty, just as the myths and the legends of a people are brought to light and crystallized in undying verse by the master poets. All that is needed is a delicate ear, a retentive memory, and the power to weld the fragments of former ages together in one harmonious whole. Only the other day I read in a newspaper that Brahms himself admitted that he had taken existing folk-songs for the themes of his new book of songs, and had arranged them for piano music. I have not heard nor seen the songs, and do not know if this be so; but if it were, it would in no wise reflect discredit upon the composer. Liszt in his rhapsodies and Berlioz in his *Faust* did the same thing with existing Hungarian strains, as, for instance, the Racokzy March; and Schumann and Wagner made a similar use of the Marseillaise for their songs of the "Two Grenadiers." Thus, also, Balfe, the Irishman, used one of our most national airs, a Hussite song, in his opera, the *Bohemian Girl,* though how he came by it nobody has as yet explained. So the music of the people, sooner or later, will command attention and creep into the books of composers.

An American reporter once told me that the most valuable talent a journalist could possess was a "nose for news." Just so the musician must prick his ear for music. Nothing must be too low or too insignificant for the musician. When he walks he should listen to every whistling boy, every street singer or blind organ-grinder. I myself am often so fascinated by these people that I can scarcely tear myself away, for every now and then I catch a strain or hear the fragments of a recurring melodic theme that sound like the voice of the people. These things are worth preserving, and no one should be above making a lavish use of all such suggestions. It is a sign of barrenness, indeed, when such characteristic bits of music exist and are not heeded by the learned musicians of the age.

I know that it is still an open question whether the inspiration derived from a few scattering melodies and folk-songs can be sufficient to give a national character to higher forms of music, just as it is an open question whether national music, as such, is preferable. I myself, as I have always declared, believe firmly that the music that is most characteristic of the nation whence it springs is entitled to the highest consideration. The part of Beethoven's Ninth Symphony that appeals most strongly to all is the melody of the last movement, and that is also the most German. Weber's best opera, according to the popular estimate, is *Der Freischütz*. Why? Because it is the most German. His inspiration there clearly came from the thoroughly German scenes and situations of the story, and hence his music assumed that distinctly national character which has endeared it to the German nation as a whole. Yet he himself spent far more pains on his opera *Euryanthe,* and persisted to the end in regarding it as his best work. But the people, we see, claim their own; and, after all, it is for the people that we strive.

An interesting essay could be written on the subject how much the external frame-work of an opera—that is, the words, the characters of the personages, and the general *mise en scène*—contributes towards the inspiration of the composer. If Weber was inspired to produce his masterpiece by so congenial a theme as the story of *Der Freischütz,* Rossini was undoubtedly similarly inspired by the Swiss surroundings of William Tell. Thus one might almost suspect that some of the charming melodies of that opera are more the product and property of Switzerland than of the Italian composer. It is to be noticed that all of Wagner's operas, with the exception of his earliest work, *Rienzi,* are inspired by German subjects. The most German of them all is that of *Die Meistersinger,* that opera of operas, which should be an example to all who distrust the potency of their own national topics.

Of course, as I have indicated before, it is possible for certain composers to project their spirit into that of another race and country. Verdi partially succeeded in striking Oriental chords in his *Aïda,* while Bizet was able to produce so thoroughly Spanish strains and measures as those of *Carmen.* Thus inspiration can be drawn from the depths as well as from the heights, although that is not my conception of the true mission of music. Our mission should be to give pure pleasure, and to uphold the ideals of our race. Our mission as teachers is to show the right way to those who come after us.

My own duty as a teacher, I conceive, is not so much to interpret Beethoven, Wagner, or other masters of the past, but to give what encouragement I can to the young musicians of America. I must give full expression to my firm conviction, and to the hope that just as this nation has already surpassed so many others in marvellous inventions and feats of engineering and commerce, and has made an honorable place for itself in literature in one short century, so it must assert itself in the other arts, and especially in the art of music. Already there are enough public-spirited lovers of music striving for the advancement of this their chosen art to give rise to the hope that the United States of America will soon emulate the older countries in smoothing the thorny path of the artist and musician. When that beginning has been made, when no large city is without its public opera-house and concert hall, and without its school of music and endowed orchestra, where native musicians can be heard and judged, then those who hitherto have had no opportunity to reveal their talent will come forth and compete with one another, till a real genius emerges from their number, who will be as thoroughly representative of his country as Wagner and Weber are of Germany, or Chopin of Poland.

To bring about this result we must trust to the ever-youthful enthusiasm and patriotism of this country. When it is accomplished, and when music has been established as one of the reigning arts of the land, another wreath of fame and glory will be added to the country which earned its name, the "Land of Freedom," by unshackling her slaves at the price of her own blood.[3]

3. The author acknowledges the co-operation of Mr. Edwin Emerson, Jr., in the preparation of this article. [Au.]

21 Frederick Douglass

Frederick Bailey, born into slavery in Maryland in 1817, became a writer and orator of renowned eloquence against all forms of human bondage. He was taught the rudiments of reading by the kindhearted mistress of one household he lived in, and developed the rest of his extraordinary skills on his own. After his escape to New York in 1838, his presence was much in demand at Northern antislavery rallies, where he adopted the surname Douglass in order to avoid recapture until he had raised sufficient money to purchase his freedom.

In addition to extensive travel around the United States, Douglass spent two years on a speaking tour of Great Britain and Ireland, where he lectured on Irish home rule as well as on abolition and met "the liberator," Daniel O'Connell, with whom he found much in common. Douglass served as an advisor to President Lincoln during the Civil War, and after Reconstruction held a variety of government posts until his death in 1895.

Douglass's brief comments about the songs of the slaves, recalled from his own experience, provide a bracing corrective to the more sentimental descriptions by some contemporary white observers.

FROM *My Bondage and My Freedom*
(1885)

Slaves are generally expected to sing as well as to work. A silent slave is not liked by masters or overseers. *"Make a noise," "make a noise,"* and *"bear a hand,"* are the words usually addressed to the slaves when there is silence amongst them. This may account for the almost constant singing heard in the

TEXT: *My Bondage and My Freedom* (New York, 1855), pp. 97–100, 252–53, 278–79. Douglass retold his life story several times; these passages occur in somewhat different form in *Narrative of the Life of Frederick Douglass* (1845) and in *Life and Times of Frederick Douglass* (1893).

southern states. There was, generally, more or less singing among the teamsters, as it was one means of letting the overseer know where they were, and that they were moving on with the work. But, on allowance day, those who visited the great house farm were peculiarly excited and noisy. While on their way, they would make the dense old woods, for miles around, reverberate with their wild notes. These were not always merry because they were wild. On the contrary, they were mostly of a plaintive cast, and told a tale of grief and sorrow. In the most boisterous outbursts of rapturous sentiment, there was ever a tinge of deep melancholy. I have never heard any songs like those anywhere since I left slavery, except when in Ireland. There I heard the same *wailing notes,* and was much affected by them. It was during the famine of 1845–6. In all the songs of the slaves, there was ever some expression in praise of the great house farm; something which would flatter the pride of the owner, and, possibly, draw a favorable glance from him.

> I am going away to the great house farm,
>   O yea! O yea! O yea!
> My old master is a good old master,
>   Oh yea! O yea! O yea!

This they would sing, with other words of their own improvising—jargon to others, but full of meaning to themselves. I have sometimes thought, that the mere hearing of those songs would do more to impress truly spiritual-minded men and women with the soul-crushing and death-dealing character of slavery, than the reading of whole volumes of its mere physical cruelties. They speak to the heart and to the soul of the thoughtful. I cannot better express my sense of them now, than ten years ago, when, in sketching my life, I thus spoke of this feature of my plantation experience:

> I did not, when a slave, understand the deep meanings of those rude, and apparently incoherent songs. I was myself within the circle, so that I neither saw nor heard as those without might see and hear. They told a tale which was then altogether beyond my feeble comprehension; they were tones, loud, long and deep, breathing the prayer and complaint of souls boiling over with the bitterest anguish. Every tone was a testimony against slavery, and a prayer to God for deliverance from chains. The hearing of those wild notes always depressed my spirits, and filled my heart with ineffable sadness. The mere recurrence, even now, afflicts my spirit, and while I am writing these lines, my tears are falling. To those songs I trace my first glimmering conceptions of the dehumanizing character of slavery. I can never get rid of that conception. Those songs still follow me, to deepen my hatred of slavery, and quicken my sympathies for my brethren in bonds. If any one wishes to be impressed with a sense of the soul-killing power of slavery, let him go to Col. Lloyd's plantation, and, on allowance day, place himself in the deep, pine woods, and there let him, in silence, thoughtfully analyze the sounds that shall pass through the chambers of his soul, and if he is not thus impressed, it will only be because 'there is no flesh in his obdurate heart.'

The remark is not unfrequently made, that slaves are the most contented and happy laborers in the world. They dance and sing, and make all manner of joyful noises—so they do; but it is a great mistake to suppose them happy because they sing. The songs of the slave represent the sorrows, rather than the joys, of his heart; and he is relieved by them, only as an aching heart is relieved by its tears. Such is the constitution of the human mind, that, when pressed to extremes, it often avails itself of the most opposite methods. Extremes meet in mind as in matter. When the slaves on board of the "Pearl" were overtaken, arrested, and carried to prison—their hopes for freedom blasted—as they marched in chains they sang, and found (as Emily Edmunson tells us) a melancholy relief in singing. The singing of a man cast away on a desolate island, might be as appropriately considered an evidence of his contentment and happiness, as the singing of a slave. Sorrow and desolation have their songs, as well as joy and peace. Slaves sing more to *make* themselves happy, than to express their happiness.

•　•　•　•　•

The fiddling, dancing and *"jubilee beating,"* was going on in all directions [during the Christmas holidays]. This latter performance is strictly southern. It supplies the place of a violin, or of other musical instruments, and is played so easily, that almost every farm has its "Juba" beater.[1] The performer improvises as he beats, and sings his merry songs, so ordering the words as to have them fall pat with the movement of his hands. Among a mass of nonsense and wild frolic, once in a while a sharp hit is given to the meanness of slaveholders. Take the following, for an example:

> We raise de wheat,
> Dey gib us de corn;
> We bake de bread,
> Dey gib us de cruss;
> We sif de meal,
> Dey gib us de huss;
> We peal de meat,
> Dey gib us de skin,
> And dat's de way
> Dey takes us in.
> We skim de pot,
> Dey gib us the liquor,
> And say dat's good enough for nigger.
> 　Walk over! walk over!
> 　Tom butter and de fat;
> 　Poor nigger you can't get over dat;
> 　　　Walk over!

This is not a bad summary of the palpable injustice and fraud of slavery, giving—as it does—to the lazy and idle, the comforts which God designed should be given solely to the honest laborer. But to the holidays.

1. Juba is the practice of elaborate patterns of hand-clapping and body-slapping as accompaniment to dancing and singing.

Judging from my own observation and experience, I believe these holidays to be among the most effective means, in the hands of slaveholders, of keeping down the spirit of insurrection among the slaves.

· · · · ·

But with all our caution and studied reserve, I am not sure that Mr. Freeland did not suspect that all was not right with us. It *did* seem that he watched us more narrowly, after the plan of escape had been conceived and discussed amongst us. Men seldom see themselves as others see them; and while, to ourselves, everything connected with our contemplated escape appeared concealed, Mr. Freeland may have, with the peculiar prescience of a slaveholder, mastered the huge thought which was disturbing our peace in slavery.

I am the more inclined to think that he suspected us, because, prudent as we were, as I now look back, I can see that we did many silly things, very well calculated to awaken suspicion. We were, at times, remarkably buoyant, singing hymns and making joyous exclamations, almost as triumphant in their tone as if we had reached a land of freedom and safety. A keen observer might have detected in our repeated singing of

> O Canaan, sweet Canaan,
> I am bound for the land of Canaan,

something more than a hope of reaching heaven. We meant to reach the *north*– and the north was our Canaan.

> I thought I heard them say,
> There were lions in the way,
> I don't expect to stay
>   Much longer here.
> Run to Jesus—shun the danger—
> I don't expect to stay
>   Much longer here,

was a favorite air, and had a double meaning. In the lips of some, it meant the expectation of a speedy summons to a world of spirits; but, in the lips of *our* company, it simply meant, a speedy pilgrimage toward a free state, and deliverance from all the evils and dangers of slavery.

22 Richard Wallaschek

Richard Wallaschek (1860–1917) was an Austrian professor of the aesthetics and psychology of music. In the late nineteenth century's flurry of speculation about the origins of music, Wallaschek argued in favor of dance and rhythm as music's sources and against the theory of speech origins put forward by Herbert Spencer. A published controversy between them, incorporating the views of several others as well, appeared in the journal *Mind* between 1890 and 1892.

Considered now as one of the founding generation of comparative musicologists, Wallaschek's work exhibits the scientific orientation characteristic of that school. In *Primitive Music,* written in English during his five-year stay in London, Wallaschek engaged actively with ongoing controversies about the ramifications of evolutionary theory in various spheres of culture.

In common with most of his ethnological contemporaries, Wallaschek regarded living communities of nonliterate peoples as "contemporary ancestors," conflating the passage of historical time with a notional evolutionary scale. In his preface to *Primitive Music,* for instance, he remarks that "it has been my aim to deal with the music of savage races only, while the music of ancient civilisation has merely been glanced at whenever it was necessary to indicate the connecting links between the most primitive and the comparatively advanced culture"—conceptually, that is, his living informants *precede* ancient cultures.

FROM *Primitive Music*

(1893)

HEREDITY AND DEVELOPMENT

•　　•　　•　　•　　•

I know well that the validity of Darwin's law[1] has been denied for the domain of ethics and art (including, of course, music). This opposition has proceeded from men whose epoch-making importance in the field of natural science imposes upon me the duty of the greatest respect, while at the same time it necessitates my weighing my conclusions with the utmost scrupulousness. In the following I confine myself entirely to the domain of music, and I consider myself the more justified in doing this since the historical facts with which ethnology furnishes us could scarcely be taken into consideration sufficiently,

TEXT: *Primitive Music: An Inquiry into the Origin and Development of Music, Songs, Instruments, Dances, and Pantomimes of Savage Races* (London, 1893), chap. 10, pp. 277–89.

1. That is, natural selection.

a connected treatment of the same not existing. Alfred Russell Wallace, in discussing the development of our musical faculties, has made use of the material as furnished by the *English Cyclopædia,* which in my opinion is not quite satisfactory. He says: "Among the lower savages music, as we understand it, hardly exists, though they all delight in rude musical sounds, as of drums, tom-toms, or gongs; and they also sing in monotonous chants. Almost exactly as they advance in general intellect and in the arts of social life, their appreciation of music appears to rise in proportion; and we find among them rude stringed instruments and whistles, till, in Java, we have regular bands of skilled performers, probably the successors of Hindoo musicians of the age before the Mohammedan Conquest. The Egyptians are believed to have been the earliest musicians, and from them the Jews and the Greeks no doubt derived their knowledge of the art, but it seems to be admitted that neither the latter nor the Romans knew anything of harmony or of the essential features of modern music."[2]

I believe that my whole book forms a contradiction to the above statements, and in consequence the conclusions would also have to be changed. In reference to the latter I would like to make one more remark. Wallace says: "The musical ability is undoubtedly, in its lower forms, less uncommon than the artistic or mathematical faculty, but it still differs essentially from the necessary or useful faculties in that it is almost entirely wanting in one-half even of civilised man."[3] To be sure musical activity is *to-day* distributed very unevenly among mankind; but originally it was not the same thing as to-day, in the climax of its development. In fact the whole tribe participates in the musical choral-dance and mimic representation among savages; we have never heard that certain individuals had to be excluded from it through lack of talent. If any one should prove awkward in these dances, some tribes, as we have heard, cut matters short by killing him. Purely musical composition also is much more general than to-day. "Among the Andamans every one composes songs. A man or woman would be thought very little of who could not do so. Even small children compose their own songs."[4] With primitive man music, and painting and sculpture probably as well, are not purely æsthetic occupations in the modern sense, they are most intimately bound up with practical life-preserving and life-continuing activities,[5] and receive only gradually their present more abstract form. And therefore a law like that of "natural selection" has original validity here as well, while it is less easily comprehensible in connection with the music of the present time whose conditions of existence have become too

2. Alfred Russell Wallace, *Darwinism* (London, 1889), pp. 467, 468. [Au.]

3. *Ibid.,* p. 471. [Au.]

4. M. V. Portman, "Andamanese Music," *Journal of the Royal Asiatic Society,* new series 20 (1888), pp. 184, 185. [Au.]

5. I mention this because L. Morgan has said: "Natural selection, which deals with practical life-preserving and life-continuing activities, has little to say to the aesthetic activities, music, painting, sculpture and the like" [C. Lloyd Morgan, *Animal Life and Intelligence* (London, 1890–91), p. 501]. If only music, painting, etc., were aesthetic activities among primitive man! [Au.]

complicated. But after we have recognised the full scope of the law, the spiritual life of man has been brought closer to that of the animals, and in regard to the continuity of both, I would like to add a few more words. Wallace has destroyed the bridge between the spiritual life of man and the animals; a deep cleft separates the two. Darwin attempted to construct the same by trying to trace a number of the psychological traits of man in the animal kingdom; I fear that some of his adherents go too far in this, and that they approach too closely upon anthropomorphism. The hypothetic character of those arguments has been so successfully shown by Prof. Morgan that it is quite sufficient simply to refer to them; but he has also shown that one is not on that account compelled to relinquish the connection between the spiritual life of man and the animals. It is therefore my opinion that it is much easier to show that primitive man still is, in reference to his mental state, an animal. For this view at least we have a more trustworthy collection of empiric facts than for the opinion that the animal is already man, or that there is no connection between the spiritual life of both. To furnish this proof for the whole domain of psychic activity will be one of the tasks of ethnology.

The sense of beauty, in the higher meaning of the term, is an abstract sensation which animals do not possess, just as little as primitive man; how it is nevertheless developed in man in the course of time, is a thing amply illustrated by a mass of reliable observations. For this development the theory of Galton and Weismann[6] seems, in my eyes, to furnish the most satisfactory explanation, especially in the domain of music. To be sure I have not (as I have before mentioned) the impression that music is to be considered an effect of the sense of hearing, and that it is a secondary effect not originally intended by nature; the further development, however, is, in my eyes, only explicable as direct imitation and tradition. Under such conditions it is in no way unlikely (what Weismann also presumed) that we civilised nations, and, for example, the negroes, receive the same degree of musical ability by birth and yet accomplish such different ends. Quite apart from the training of our individuality, they lack examples and the social necessity of coming up to their level. Neither of these can be artificially ingrafted upon their social status, and therefore they are pretty well lost to musical, and probably any other form of, culture.

The average child of civilised parents does not necessarily come into the world with a higher mental equipment than the little savage, as Mr. Nisbet[7] thinks. Nevertheless, it is not obliged to work out everything *de novo* because it comes into *another* world, into a world with a settled tradition. Into this the child gradually grows, and out of it its individuality is formed, while a negro boy will always have the impression that the European world is something

6. Francis Galton, Darwin's cousin and the originator of the science of genetics, and the German evolutionist August Friedrich Weismann both studied mechanisms of heredity, especially the inheritance of talent—though along separate lines and not, as Wallaschek's text suggests, in association.

7. J. F. Nisbet, *Marriage and Heredity* (London, 1889), p. viii. [Au.]

strange to him, not made by his equal. His very colour, if not the general behaviour of his white "friends," will soon convince him of this. All mental progress seems to be traceable in the object rather, while the individuals have remained stationary. More highly gifted individuals are the outcome of sudden favourable combinations, not the climax of a continual line leading up to them.

When primitive music has advanced beyond the first purely rhythmical stage, when an invention of melody takes place which is retained in memory, it has often been observed that these short musical phrases impress just as much to-day as they do among the savages. The advantage we have over primitive man in regard to music is simply that we are able to work up, develop, any given theme, while the former spins out a theme, however short it may be, into a lengthy piece simply through endless repetitions. This art of working up a given theme must be acquired by each individual afresh; the capacity for it is not a whit greater in the present generation than during former times. To be sure it is probable that we learn quicker, but only because we have more numerous and better patterns, and because in our study we save ourselves the trouble of scholastic by-ways, in learning which past generations have, through want of experience, wasted unnecessary time and energy.

On the other hand, those of the savage tribes which are really musical comprehend our music, at least that of a simple character; that means, to the same degree that our peasants do. It is also astonishing how quickly Negro Hottentot and Malay orchestras grasp European dance music and play it immediately, by hearing, in the orchestra.

In the drawings done by savages one can trace exactly the same mistakes and peculiarities as with our children.[8] I do not doubt that this will in time be proved by ethnology more completely than I am able to do within the limits of this abstract. But I might mention that we are able to observe the same in the compositions of children, or more properly in the musical invention of children, even up to the time of boyhood or girlhood, and all this in spite of the fact that the child unconsciously undergoes even in tender youth the influence of modern music.

The origin and development of painting seems also to come under the influence of natural selection. Thus the most important and most original products of Dyaks' painting are the bizarre decorations of their shields. They were bizarre and grotesque in order to frighten the enemy against whom they were held. (The ancient Greek painting of the Gorgo Medusa head originally had the same meaning, *viz.*, to frighten the deity.) The fantastic demons of the Dyaks were the result of a competition in the struggle for life, which sought to constantly increase by new decorations the dread of the defending shields.

8. With perfect justice Hirth has expressly not traced the lack of perspective in the disposition of a child's drawing to atavism, but has designated it as a peculiarity of the spirit of the nursery [Georg Hirth, *Aufgaben der Kunstphysiologie*, 2 vols. (Munich and Leipzig, 1891), vol. 2, p. 583]. Examples of savage drawings in Richard Andree, *Ethnographische Parallelen* 1878, Neue Folge (Leipzig, 1889), p. 56. [Au.]

Other ornaments were originally signs of property, and thus the whole branch of ornamental art owed its origin to the struggle for life.[9]

We also have the best of reasons to suppose that among the "faculties" of the human mind the so-called musical faculty at least has not been heightened in course of time, and that all progress has simply been brought about by objective heredity. Long before this could take place the practice of music was so intimately connected with life-continuing and life-preserving activities that the law of natural selection held good even in the domain of music.

A mere psychological consideration of the case will lead us to a similar result. I venture to say that the old doctrine of separate powers, capabilities (Vermögen, as the German psychologists formerly used to call it) in the human mind has generally been abandoned by modern psychologists. There is no such thing as an independent musical ability, or musical sense, distinctly separable from other faculties. If this is so, it is impossible to say that a special musical faculty is developed under a special law. The human mind is one whole, equally subject to one and the same natural influences. More than that, mind and body are one whole. Where is the physiologist or physicist who could draw a distinct line between a mere physical movement, a reflex action, and an intelligent will? Who can say up to what point the mere corporal faculty extends, and from where the mental one begins? How can we say then that our brain is subject to the natural law of natural selection and our ideas to supernatural or any other influence? How can we venture to apply to this one whole of human being different influences and say, for instance, that one part is developed under natural laws, another under supernatural, again another under direct divine agency? how can we say that the one is a primary effect, the other a secondary one, and that among all there is a special compartment somewhere in the brain carefully locked up and called the musical faculty, which is preserved under the particular care of—we do not know what?

As there is no special musical faculty (the term faculty has always been used like the term soul for the shortness of expression) we must again remember that we said it was not the musical talent alone which made the composer. The artist is the man whose total energy, interest, and labour, whose feelings and ambition are entirely given up to the one artistic object, whatever it may be. If this has happened we speak of a peculiar faculty for this object in a certain man, but this so-called "faculty" is nothing but the resulting tendency of our mind as a whole which turns in a certain direction under certain favourable circumstances. And so the "musical faculty" too is the end of a certain disposition of our mind, towards which all the so-called faculties tend, not a separate starting-point from which they arise. Of course, some organic structures may be more favourable to a certain end, under certain external circumstances, but we shall never be able to find a unique source for any artistic disposition. So it

9. Alois Raimund Hein, "Malerei und Technische Künste der Dayaks," *Annalen des K. K. Natur-historischen Hofmuseums,* Bd. 14, p. 203. [Au.]

may happen that the mental disposition, say of a great politician, would have been much more favourable to artistic development, than that of many actual artists, had he been placed under the most appropriate external conditions. This would not be possible if there were such a thing as a peculiar artistic faculty. It is mental strength in general which characterises the great man of the future, and nobody knows in which direction it will concentrate itself at last. Thus the German poet Victor Scheffel intended to become a painter at first, until one day, quite accidentally, his talent for poetry was discovered by a lady friend and then turned to account by himself. The painter Fritz Uhde felt himself so entirely in the wrong place when he first frequented the painting academy in Dresden that he left it and became an officer. Only later on he took up his former profession again, recognising it, at the same time, as the most appropriate to his talent. Rousseau considered himself a composer only, and wrote his philosophical and educational works, merely occasionally, as an occupation of secondary importance. Had not his opera "Devin du Village" had such an immense success, he would probably have devoted himself entirely to philosophy, and we should not know anything of his compositions. And to what did he owe this success—to favourable circumstances or to the merits of the compositions? Merits? The present generation knows Rousseau as philosopher only, and I dare say there will be many people who never knew that Rousseau composed at all. Goethe once seriously thought of becoming a painter. Zelter, his contemporary, was destined to become a bricklayer like his father, and devoted himself to music comparatively late.

These examples tend to show that general strength and greatness of mind assumes that peculiar shape which in course of time proves itself as the most effective in the outside world and the most appropriate to the circumstances, or as the naturalist would say in plainer language, it assumes the form most *useful* to the individual. This view is not at all in opposition to the fact that great characters assert themselves in spite of their disregarding entirely all the surroundings they have to live in. Thus one may say Richard Wagner would have been more successful in the beginning of his career if he had written in the customary easy-going style of the Italian opera, and with the pomposity of Meyerbeer, in favour with the masses. Precisely so. In the beginning he would have been more successful, but he knew that musical development ought to turn in quite another direction which he pretended to foresee in the future; and with regard to this future of music, which would then prove still more favourable to him than the success of the ordinary musician of his time he wrote what he actually called "Zukunftsmusik." In his earlier days, however, when his operas "Das Liebesverbot" and "Die Feen" had proved failures, he did write in accordance with the taste of the masses, like Meyerbeer, and brought out his "Rienzi." But by this time there happened to be too many competitors in this domain, so he remained unnoticed, and as there was nothing to be hoped from the present he wrote for the future.

Thus it is just the example of Wagner which at first sight seems to tell against the theory of usefulness in art, but which at bottom is eloquent in favour of it. By this theory I do not mean to degrade the action of the artist. The word "use" can be taken in a very ideal sense. He who pretends to despise use is himself too low to conceive a higher meaning of it. If to some friendship is more useful than gain, if the law of usefulness has produced all the beauty in the world, the grandeur of the sky as well as the tender blossoms of the earth, then it will also be effective enough to form the highest artistic ideals the human mind is capable of.

Which artistic direction will be the most useful for a great mind to take is difficult to predict. It depends upon custom, countries, times, even upon the fashion. There have been centuries of poets, of painters, sculptors, architects, while we ourselves seem to live in the century of musicians, I mean of poetical, intelligent musicians of the pattern of Wagner. How such changes in artistic tendency are brought about, how they are felt at once by millions of people on different continents, and why they are responded to, I cannot say. But that they are most effective everybody seems to be aware of.

So much of the past. But how will future events shape themselves? This question has frequently been broached by musicians, especially when they found themselves face to face with a phenomenon so singular and unexpected as Wagner. In their complete surprise and passionate enthusiasm, which can easily be comprehended, they have confessed as their sincere opinion that in him not only music but the whole world in general had reached its climax. From this height all things were expected to decline, and nothing perfectly new could in their opinion be created. This truly Chinese view has, however, hindered the development of music on countless occasions, and has caused such severe struggles as have accompanied the appearance of original geniuses like Berlioz and Wagner. The less are *their* adherents in their turn justified in adopting the same principle, which in the case of the "conservatives" they justly censured. None but the uninitiated could arrive at the above conclusion (and they will probably continue to do so), for any one knowing the prospects of music in the future would already be half a composer; to *theoretically* expound what this future of music may be none, not even the artist, is able to do; the product of his genius, the work of art, alone can and will reveal it. Reasoning in regard to the future of art is futile, but imagination has for a period of five thousand years continued to produce new works of art, and there is no reason why all this should have come to an end in the year 1883. On the contrary, this assumption seems to my mind both narrow-minded and unfounded. Unfounded because there is no absolute standard of beauty, for we, with our purely subjective and individual conception of art, should never make the preposterous assertion that in this way and no other can art attain to absolute perfection. A work of art is made *for* us and is consequently subject to all changes *in* and *through* us.

An experience of my own has always been to me an appropriate example of how opinion may change in course of time. My teacher of counterpoint once took up Bach's mass in B minor and said: "In this work is comprehended all musical wisdom, beyond it we can never go." From the point of view of musical labour and polish, or of the art exercised in execution, he was no doubt right. But there is still another point of view, that of colouring and emotional element, and this has found grander and more eloquent expression in Wagner than in any other composer. Incidentally I may mention that this constitutes, in my opinion, Wagner's supreme mastership. Nobody can say which point of view coming generations will take, for we are not the coming generation, and only in the divinely inspired artist will it be anticipated.

The above negative decision in regard to the future of art is not, however, free from a certain narrowness of view which has excluded the consideration of the long evolution of music, and especially of dramatic music. What a length of time has not elapsed since the first attempt to represent the events of chase and war before the assembled company in order to induce it to participate in common action. How long a time did not elapse before these primitive dances and animal pantomimes could have become customary, and before their old stereotyped form could at last lead to innovations and improvements. Let us not forget that those dances occurred among people who in every other respect have not advanced beyond the civilisation of the stone period. In comparison with them a dramatic festival as advanced and accomplished as the corrobberree or the kuri-dance in Australia represents an epoch in literature, an artistic advancement of centuries. And how simple, how childish this drama appears when compared with the ancient Indian drama, of which we are told that only in later stages was the customary song replaced by spoken words. The tropic glow, the fiery passion of a Sakuntala designate a height of perfection which again is separated by centuries from the epoch of the corrobberree. And still, what is this when compared with the drama of Pericles' time, or of the Roman theatre, both of which have so many characteristics in common with modern dramatic art. But this is the period with which in so many cases our historical investigations used to commence, while for the times preceding we had merely a geological interest. What changes had not occurred in the drama up to the Roman period, and what changes were still to come. Lost in the mental darkness of the middle ages, it nevertheless at last found the saving path from the grimacing, immoral derivations of the old mysteries to the bright splendour of the artistic stage, from mysterious choirs and disreputable cloister-alleys to the open and unreserved tribunal of the people, to those boards that represent the world, a free play, inspired as once before by love of mankind and taken from its varying fates. Now the first oratorios appeared, now the first operas were produced, small in the beginning and diffident, but soon centres of interest for the entire spiritual life of society. On their account parties were formed, on their account the whole of Paris was once roused to passionate enthusiasm and fierce hatred; indeed, in the days of Gluck and Piccini even politics were forgotten for a time, so entirely absorbed were the parties in the musical questions of the day.

But these miracles know no limits. The stage is animated with new characters; the figure of stone appears in the gloom of night; in dungeons deep a prisoner awaits the blessed hour of liberty; elves flit through the air; the spirit of the earth leaves with aching heart the deceitful love-phantom of human life; the Italian carnival crosses the stage in wanton revelry; till at last the daughters of the Rhine rise from the depths of the holy river, Sigfried's horn resounds, and Walhall, the resplendent seat of the gods, shines in sublime grandeur.

This is for the present the last stage in the long line of evolution, more varied and more eloquent in the history of the musical drama than in any other domain of human accomplishments. A review of this domain of our mental activity betrays as much vital creative power as it reveals the prospect of new and glorious blossoms, and an insatiable desire on our part to enjoy them in their full splendour and their eternal youth.

Such at least is the conclusion to which the theoretical observer may come; to everything else the creative artist will return answer.

INDEX

Note: Numbers in boldface refer to pages where definitions for a term are found, or to the source reading passages themselves.